Immigration and Women

# Immigration and Women

*Understanding the American Experience*

Susan C. Pearce,
Elizabeth J. Clifford,
and Reena Tandon

NEW YORK UNIVERSITY PRESS
*New York and London*

NEW YORK UNIVERSITY PRESS
New York and London
www.nyupress.org

References to Internet websites (URLs) were accurate at the time of writing. Neither the authors nor New York University Press is responsible for URLs that may have expired or changed since the manuscript was prepared.

Library of Congress Cataloging-in-Publication Data

Pearce, Susan C.
Immigration and women : understanding the American experience /
Susan C. Pearce, Elizabeth J. Clifford, and Reena Tandon.
p. cm.
Includes bibliographical references and index.
ISBN 978-0-8147-6738-2 (cl : alk. paper) — ISBN 978-0-8147-6739-9
(pb : alk. paper) — ISBN 978-0-8147-6826-6 (ebook)
1. Women immigrants—United States. 2. United States—Emigration
and immigration. 3. Immigrants—Government policy—United States.
I. Clifford, Elizabeth J. II. Tandon, Reena. III. Title.
JV6602.P43     2011
305.48'969120973—dc22          2010048352

New York University Press books are printed on acid-free paper, and their binding materials are chosen for strength and durability. We strive to use environmentally responsible suppliers and materials to the greatest extent possible in publishing our books.

Manufactured in the United States of America

c   10 9 8 7 6 5 4 3 2 1
p   10 9 8 7 6 5 4 3 2 1

*This book is dedicated to
the immigrant women in our lives:
past, present, and future.*

# Contents

PART IV: WHERE THEY ARE GOING

# Acknowledgments

The authors would first and foremost like to thank the many women who were gracious and generous enough to share their stories with us; without these "immigrating women," there would have been no *Immigration and Women*. While some are named in this book, others chose anonymity, and we use pseudonyms to refer to them. We thank all equally. Second, we gratefully appreciate Ilene Kalish, Aiden Amos, and Despina Papazoglou Gimbel of New York University Press, as well as Salwa Jabado, formerly of the Press, for all of their assistance, advice, and encouragement, as well as their professional skills in moving this book to press.

Susan C. Pearce would like to thank the Department of Sociology at East Carolina University for its support and advice in completing this project, with particular appreciation to department chair Leon Wilson and to former chair Lee Maril, now director of the ECU Center for Diversity and Inequality Research, which is an important home for this research. She would like to thank the members of the ECU Women's Studies Program and Melinda Kane for feedback on draft chapters and Chris Baker for his enthusiastic assistance in the many details of editorial work. Susan gratefully acknowledges the financial support of the Center for Women's Studies of West Virginia University, directed by Barbara Howe, and of the WVU Eberly College of Arts and Sciences. The Division of Sociology, Anthropology, and Criminal Justice at WVU, chaired by Melissa Latimer, was an important home for the book's inception and initial research. Susan is also indebted to the support of Natalie Sokoloff, James Friedberg, Laura Douglas, Pat Hatch, and Val Vojdik. She would like to thank the many individuals who helped open doors to interview contacts, including Don Mitchell, Alex Stepick, and Rachel Owens, among others, who made the research process so fruitful and enjoyable. She thanks her family for support, inspiration, and distractions. Finally, huge kudos to her coauthors, Beth and Reena, for sharing this project and for their never-ending energy across its many stages.

Elizabeth J. Clifford wishes to thank especially her coauthors, Susan and Reena, for their vision, support, and hard work on this project. She would also like to thank her colleagues in the Department of Sociology, Anthropology, and Criminal Justice at Towson University, as well as those in other departments and divisions of the university, who share her interest, passion, and commitment to issues of immigration. Her husband and parents also deserve particular mention, for their encouragement, support, and wisdom to know when, and when not, to ask how the book was going. Lastly, her children, Quincy and Ella, made this work worthwhile and at the same time provided frequent needed, and enjoyable, distractions from it. She hopes someday they will read it. She would also like to thank Towson University for granting a semester of sabbatical leave, which helped facilitate the research and writing of this book.

Reena Tandon would like to thank all those who have been a part of her immigrating life through the inception and completion of this book: first to the coauthors, Susan Pearce and Elizabeth Clifford, companions in writing, who kept it going for her through the transitions. She would like to thank Constance Nathanson for the advice and discussions that helped extend her research interests in the U.S. context and Kenneth Hill, former director of the Hopkins Population Center, for his support that helped her research find ground in new soil. She owes gratitude to Priscilla Gonzales, Xiomara Corpeno, Luna Ranjit, and Nahar Alam for their support with organizing interviews and translations. And those whom Reena cannot thank enough are her family, her husband, and friends and colleagues across the globe, who are sources of sustenance—emotional and intellectual—especially her mother, herself an immigrant, who holds the fluid worlds together for her. For her daughter Ananya—whose hand she was holding when this project started and, as the book was ending, realized that it was her daughter who held her hand . . . and whose immigrating life will continue beyond her own—she has no words.

An earlier version of chapter 2 was published by the Immigration Policy Center of the American Immigration Council in 2006, with the title "Immigrant Women in the United States: A Statistical Snapshot." Some statistics have been updated, along with other revisions. Chapter 6 grew out of the report "Today's Immigrant Woman Entrepreneur," published by the Immigration Policy Center in 2005, and the current chapter includes expanded use of the qualitative interviews conducted for that more statistical summary. An early version of chapter 6, with the title "Mighty Oaks among Us: The Quiet Revolution of Immigrant Women's Entrepreneurship in the United States," was presented at the annual meeting of the American Sociological Association, Boston, Massachusetts, August 11–14, 2008, and Susan is grateful for the feedback of Vasilikie Demos on that version.

# "We Can't Go Back"

*Immigrant Women, Intersections, and Agency*

> Women are migrating and will continue to do so. Their needs
> are urgent and deserve priority attention. Only then will the
> benefits of international migration be maximized and the
> risks minimized.
>
> —United Nations Population Fund, 2006[1]

In 1836, a young Polish woman named Ernestine Susmond Potowski
Rose made her way across the Atlantic to her chosen destination, the United
States. Her exit from Poland was prompted by her adamant refusal to agree
to an arranged marriage. Ernestine had filed a lawsuit against her father, a
Jewish rabbi, over control of her inheritance; she arrived, consequently,
after sojourning in other European countries, marrying an Englishman, and
espousing an avowed rejection of religious beliefs regarding women's inferi-
ority. An active and controversial leader and eloquent public speaker for the
movements to abolish slavery and forward women's rights, Ernestine Rose
went on to earn the nickname of adulation "Queen of the Platform."[2]

In 1986, a full 150 years later, the young attorney Sheela Murthy left her
native India to enter law school at Harvard University, where she earned her
LLM (master of law) degree the following year. Sheela's migration—across
a different ocean from that traversed by Ernestine—was motivated in large
part by an activist desire to improve the lives of women through the law. By
doing so, Sheela was echoing Ernestine's ambition and underscoring the fact
that the revolution that the Queen of the Platform and her cohort under-
took had remained unfinished. Sheela's decision to migrate to the United
States and study law meant that she broke out of the mold of a traditional
adult path for women in her society, as had Ernestine. Today, Sheela runs
the successful Murthy Law, an immigration law firm in Baltimore, Maryland, that she founded, which provides legal assistance to both women and

America – freedom, progressive rhetoric

men nationally. Twenty years after Sheela set foot in the United States, her firm was acknowledged as one of the world's leading U.S. immigration law firms by international law-firm rating agency Chambers Global. Across 2007, 2008, and 2009, *Super Lawyers International* named Sheela Murthy a "Maryland Super Lawyer."

The Queen of the Platform and the Maryland Super Lawyer represent two eras in U.S. immigration history and two different world regions. And they illustrate a phenomenon that is not consciously recognized in the American immigration stories that we tell ourselves about ourselves or in the shared social memory of our founding myths: the presence of foreign-born women as leaders and contributors to the cultures and structures of the United States. This relative silence on the active roles of immigrant women carries over into the scholarly arena. Denise Segura and Patricia Zavella recently characterized this absence in the following way: "[Foreign-born] women's economic contributions, creative adaption strategies, cultural expressions, and everyday contestations remain largely unrecognized in scholarship."[3] The United Nations Population Fund has also charged that "policymakers continue to disregard both [migrating women's] contributions and their vulnerability."[4] We concur with these diagnoses and offer this book in an attempt to help correct the imbalance in scholarship and policymaking.

In the first decade of the twenty-first century, the image of the typical immigrant in the American popular cultural imagination is a monolithic one: it is that of a working-class Mexican or Central American man. This stereotype continues despite statistical evidence that approximately 50 percent of all global migrants are women[5] and that today women and girls constitute the majority of legal immigrants to the United States.[6] The stereotypical public image also misses the wide diversity in national origins that constitutes the current American immigration landscape: foreign-born women, men, girls, and boys represent more than 140 countries.[7] Globally, women are migrating more than ever in history: they comprise 49.6 percent of all migrants worldwide.[8] Until recently, however, women have been ignored or marginalized in immigration and refugee policy. Due to this prolific presence yet perceptual absence, the United Nations Population Fund has begun to label the phenomenon of globally migrating women as "a mighty but silent river."[9]

This book is an overview of the social, cultural, and employment terrains inhabited by adult foreign-born women in the United States in the early twenty-first century, with attention to the stories that these women narrate about their lives. The book's authors came to this project from our own critical awareness of this perceptual absence: immigrant women in American

Figure 1.1. Sheela Murthy. (Copyright Murthy Law Firm)

society are relatively invisible as a recognizable group and have yet to form a collective political or cultural voice. We emphasize the term *relatively*, because we do recognize, quite insistently, that immigrant women are an increasing, significant presence in the daily lifeworlds of Americans across all regions of the United States; these individual relationships between the native-born and immigrant women are visible to those who participate in them, despite the less visible construction of these women as an aggregate group in our cultural myths. That presence in the authors' own lifeworlds—and the fact that one author *is* an immigrant woman—are the key motivations behind our interest in this subject. In the words of anthropologist Clifford Geertz, this subject arose out of our "local knowledge"[10]—as well as research knowledge—and our curiosity to deepen and expand that knowledge; in social-science lingo, it was inductively as well as deductively inspired.

This book's authors coincidentally represent four of the major waves of American immigration: Susan Pearce primarily traces her ancestry to northern Europeans who arrived prior to and immediately after the American Revolutionary War. Elizabeth Clifford's Irish ancestors were among the nineteenth-century immigrants escaping the renowned potato famine, and the Polish side of her family arrived during the Ellis Island era of the Great Immigration at the turn of the twentieth century. Reena Tandon, from India, is a member of the post-1965 wave of immigration that is predominantly peopled by those from non-European countries. And like so many contemporary immigrants, Reena Tandon's sojourn has been multiply transnational: her first venture from India was as an educational migrant to Australia. She then moved to the United States for her postdoctoral research and has now migrated to Canada. Grounded in these personal and family immigration histories, we set out to try to understand the multiple meanings of immigration for women today.

### Women, Migration, and Research

The female face of migration today is not only an American phenomenon but one manifestation of an international phenomenon. The United Nations has recently announced that at the global level, "[t]he demand for women migrants is at an all-time high and growing."[11] The researcher Rhacel Salazar Parreñas recently observed that "[i]ndeed, men who seek low-wage jobs in construction or heavy manufacturing no longer lead the flow of workers from poorer to richer nations in the new global economy."[12] It is the charge of some scholars that migration scholarship has not yet given adequate attention to this "feminization of migration."[13] Such critics also insist that migration scholarship has yet to examine the manner in which nearly every aspect of the immigration experience is somehow gendered, for both women and men.[14]

It has been more than twenty years since Mirjana Morokvašic announced, in her introduction to a special issue of *International Migration Review*, that "Birds of Passage Are Also Women."[15] Despite a growing number of titles that address the question of gender, however, scholarly books, articles, and conferences about migration continue to appear each year with little or no mention of women or gender.[16] The United Nations Department of Economic and Social Affairs has critiqued researchers and policymakers for this absence.[17] Yet migration cannot be fully understood apart from a sociological understanding of its gendered qualities. A vivid illustration of the gendered nature of migration processes is found in a study by sociologist Vasilikie Demos. Stimulated by the stories of her Greek immigrant grandmothers, Demos's research on early-nineteenth-century Greek migration to the United States and Australia demonstrates that the Greek tradition of the dowry to accompany a woman's marriage was a powerful motivator of both male and female immigration. In addition to young women who might migrate to earn their dowry, Greek men quite often migrated alone to underwrite a daughter's or sister's dowry and sent remittances from their earnings back home.[18] Today's Greek society is less likely to manifest such motivations; nevertheless, this example illustrates that the intersection between gender and migration has a long history.

As Pierrette Hondagneu-Sotelo and the contributors to her edited volume *Gender in U.S. Immigration* describe it, gender shapes the processes of migration in critical, central ways. In other words, taking a gender lens in research on immigration is not only an attempt to understand immigrant *women*. It is an attempt to understand *immigration*. This involves an interpretive shift in research, moving beyond conceiving of gender as a "variable," which was certainly an important initial step for pioneering women's and gender studies literature, toward viewing gender as a basic ground of experience. Scholarly views of gender have progressed in this direction in recent years. As Beth Hess and Myra Marx Ferree have observed, sociological research has moved from early approaches that examined sex differences as characteristics somehow "owned" by an individual to a recognition of the core relational or social meanings of gender and how gender is an organizing principle in all arenas of social life.[19]

It is important to emphasize, as has the growing field of masculinity studies,[20] that women are not the only people who are gendered. Men's behaviors, attitudes, and choices are also profoundly shaped through gender socialization, although it was the feminist and women's studies literature that pioneered research investigations into the gendering processes of relationships and societies. Nevertheless, the continued imbalance of privilege and rights based on gender and the subconscious association of the term *immigrant* with *male* provide the impetus behind our decision to offer a book that concentrates on the experiences of women.

Among scholars who study immigration and gender, it is a familiar truism to state that immigrant women are a multidimensional group, defying any stable definition of the word *woman*. Therefore, the gender "ground" is a shifting one. In a similar vein, another recognized truism is that these women are agents in their destinies, within and against the structural tempests that they navigate. Yet the familiarity of such truisms does not render them unworthy of discussion and demonstration. We bring these multidimensional features into stark relief in this study because they are under-emphasized and underrecognized; such an underemphasis risks lending support to a "natural attitude"[21] that the immigrant is male, of a particular ethnicity and class, and the family's lead pioneer. A case in point that illustrates the agency of women as this pioneer—even in families migrating together—is the memory of *Svetlana*,[22] whose story is included in this book. She and her husband escaped the Soviet Union surreptitiously, but after arriving in England en route to the United States, her husband got cold feet and wanted to return home. She flatly told him, "No, you have to stay. We can't go back." And . . . they made the originally intended journey to the United States.

There is a near absence of immigrant women in the public cultural image—the shared social imaginary—as a unified cohort in the United States. This claim can be approached descriptively by recalling 2008 and 2010 election-year debates about immigrants as contributors to criminal and economic instability, accompanied by local-level protests over day laborers gathering in parking lots seeking work.[23] When nativist-oriented discussions mention women, it is often in the context of fertility: either the women are *too* fertile, or they are using childbirth to get a foot in the (U.S.) door. This stereotype of the foreign-born woman bearing an "anchor baby" to gain residency and public benefits may be the most recent incarnation of the "welfare mother" myth. And like the "welfare mother" myth of the nonwhite poor woman with uncontrolled fertility who milks the public coffers for her enrichment, nativist outrage over immigrant women has racial overtones. The fear is the loss of a perceived national identity rooted in racial whiteness as more nonwhites migrate and populate the country, upsetting the historical racial balance.[24] Patricia Hill Collins has observed that the stereotype of the black welfare-dependent woman is a "controlling image" that emerged as black women began to demand access to political and economic power.[25] We have yet to document whether this process is also the case for immigrant women, but there is certainly a consistency in public culture between the two myths (of black and immigrant women), and public moral panics regarding the overfertile immigrant can be traced back to earlier centuries.

There is more to our statement that the presence of a community of immigrant women is still relatively invisible and silent in the discourses of the public sphere than a social-scientific observation. There are political implications to this claim. Invisibility and silence translate into a relative unavailability of social and political power—a reality that the late writer Tillie Olsen, daughter of immigrants, explored in her book *Silences*. In that book, Olsen articulated the challenges that individuals who are outside of social privilege have when they attempt to contribute to literary fields as writers: time and space are luxuries, their voices are considered politically controversial, and their words may be devalued by their audiences.

In the twenty-first century, international migration has become a critical player in the global economy at a scale far beyond that of the nineteenth-century Greek dowry remittances. Global migration generates twenty trillion U.S. dollars each year, adding ten billion dollars to the U.S. economy alone. Even though migrants send much of the money that they generate to their home countries, helping boost those economies, most of those dollars are spent in the receiving country.[26]

## Imagining This Community

Saskia Sassen has recently written, "Through their work in both global cities and survival circuits, women, so often discounted as valueless economic actors, are crucial to building new economies and expanding existing ones."[27] It is our hope that the research presented here, based in interviews with immigrant women across national origins, will contribute to the acknowledgment of this dynamic, adding to the construction of an "imagined community" of immigrant women. Benedict Anderson proposed in his book *Imagined Communities* that the modern nation is an imagined community since its members do not all know each other but symbolically create a shared image of themselves as a unified group. In a similar sense, we could ask whether more scholarly attention to the female face of immigration might help sketch the outlines of a silhouette of an imagined community.

Our second task after proposing a gender perspective, or lens, for studies of migration is to propose a "nativity" lens for studies of gender and women. This task dovetails with the recent direction in gender and women's studies termed "intersectionality," a theoretical handle that legal scholar Kimberlé Crenshaw pioneered and Patricia Hill Collins and many others have elaborated.[28] According to intersectionality theory, one's gender will inevitably constrain or enable one's life options—but this process does not occur in a vacuum, separate from other statuses such as race or ethnicity and their social constructions. If you are a white woman, for example, you might encounter a particular form of sexism that is distinct from that experienced by a woman of color. In this book, we propose that nativity—whether a woman was born in the United States or elsewhere—is a key social location that intersects with and influences the experiences that one has as a woman or a man. This is a point that is often missing or underemphasized in analyses of intersections between gender, race and ethnicity, and social class. Edna Erez, Madelaine Adelman, and Carol Gregory have recently charged that many scholars tend to write about the social location of immigration as if it were another racial category. They suggest that "[r]ather than consider immigration as a variable or static category within race, we consider immigration as part of the multiple grounds of identity."[29]

In the past decade, theorists have worked to advance the critical theoretical approach of intersectionality, while proposing alternative metaphors, such as "interlocking systems" and "matrix of domination," both proposed by Patricia Hill Collins.[30] The advantage of these alternative metaphors, according to Collins, is that they do not locate the social dynamics of gender and cultural diversity in the individual personal identity of the (working-class, Latino, or African American) woman, for example; rather, this interaction happens between the *systems* of social class, gender divisions, and racial and ethnic status hierarchies. In other words, it is not a person's essence or inherited group membership(s) that combines to dictate one's life choices but the ways in which societies define the meanings of those group memberships and allot them varying, unequal amounts of power. And, as Wendy Hulko has illustrated, the dynamics of interlocking systems vary, depending on the time and location of each individual's experience.[31]

## Gender, Nativity, and Agency

In this book, we give central attention to the theme of human agency among immigrant women: how these women act independently within, despite, and against the structures of society. Scholars such as French sociologist Alaine Tourraine have called for a "return of the actor" within social sciences, in order to integrate the important role that human action takes in societies, as individuals negotiate, change, and reproduce larger social structures.[32] Theories of intersectionality and interlocking systems recognize that individuals often resist structural constraints, exercising their agency. Yet there continues to be a tendency in such theory and research to emphasize the structural partner over the agency partner in the structure-agency dance. This is understandable, given the power of such structures as economic globalization and bureaucracies, with their self-perpetuating qualities, as emphasized by Max Weber.[33] The 2009 global financial crisis, for example, took the form of an interinstitutional meltdown, appearing at times to be impervious to intervention or even accurate analysis. Among key tenets across the authors' fields of sociology and social work, in fact, is the insistence that social processes are *extra*individual: they precede and follow each person's lifespan and are largely outside the control of any individual.

Historically, however, social scientists have developed our analysis of structures more fully than our analysis of individual agency; we also have not adequately explored the dynamics of the structure-agency dance. This is in the process of changing. In fact, the International Sociological Association has recently announced that "[d]eterminism is dead in the social sciences."[34] In this book, we listen to the stories of immigrant women and attempt to understand the nuances of how human agency operates in interaction with these overwhelming structures. If anything characterizes immigrants, in fact, it is *movement*—an act of agency that requires complex decision-making, organization, and reflection in the face of uncertainties. Segura and Zavella refer to such movement as "subjective transnationalism."[35] The stories presented here demonstrate how action extends beyond geographical movement to more personal, political, and cultural movements. Thus, we should keep in mind that agency is both individual and collective.

Our research expands the conception of agency in various ways. Often, researchers emphasize one dimension of agency: the act of resistance to counter the constraints of the structures. And we have numerous examples of this dimension in this book. Agency has many other dimensions, how-ever, including creativity, relocation, reinvention of the self, leadership, and responsibility for relationships. The theme of multidimensionality can be heard in the following observation by Barbara Ehrenreich and Arlie Russell Hochschild, introducing their anthology *Global Woman*: "[T]he world's most invisible women . . . are strivers as well as victims, wives and mothers as well as workers."[36]

Mustafa Emirbayer and Anne Mische demonstrate in their theoretical treatise on agency[37] that acts of agency are multidimensional, particularly in a temporal sense; individual actions, for example, can be variously oriented toward the present, past, or future. Immigration is an act of agency that encompasses such temporal dimensions, and in quite different ways than for the native-born, since the relationship to the past involves a specific rupture in time, and that rupture carries a host of meanings for the immigrant. In our study, by listening to and helping to amplify the voices of women whom we interviewed, we explore these temporal and other dimensions, such as the spatial dimension. That rupture in time, for example, is also a spatial rupture; the past is geographically distant at the same time that it is temporally distant.

Along with theorists Anthony Giddens[38] and Jürgen Habermas,[39] we view the work of individual agents as part and parcel to the process of both reproducing and changing societal and global structures. In this book, we are creating a conversation between theories of intersections and theories of agency, without losing sight of the social structures that place boundaries around agency, shape its contours, and even propel agency. As Karl Marx wrote, "Men make their own history, but they do not make it just as they please; they do not make it under self-selected circumstances, but under circumstances existing already, given and transmitted from the past."[40] More recently, French theorist Pierre Bourdieu has offered a theoretical handle for the dynamic, fluid relationship between the actions of individuals and the social relationships ("fields") in which they act. Bourdieu proposes the concept of "*habitus*," or a "socialized subjectivity," which is made up of behavior, values, and orientations that are inherited from socialized patterns in a culture, but which are always subject to change as individuals innovate through their everyday practices.[41] In the research contained in this book, we listened to stories of how immigrant women expressed such subjectivity by remaining open to this fluidity of the individual's relationship to her social fields.

## Process of Our Research

> Please refer to me as "Victoria" in your study, because I have
> been victorious.
>
> —interview respondent's choice of her own pseudonym

We carried out this research using a mixture of methods: in-depth interviews
and an analysis of existing data from the U.S. Census. Most of the book consists of our reports of the qualitative interviews, since our research goal was
to amplify the women's voices. We conducted eighty-nine interviews with
women who reside in the following locations: Atlanta, Georgia; Baltimore,
Maryland; Chicago, Illinois; Los Angeles and Orange County, California;
Houston, Texas; Miami, Florida; Morgantown, West Virginia; New York,
New York; Pittsburgh, Pennsylvania; and Washington, DC.[42] We use a mix of
pseudonyms and actual names in the book, depending on each individual's
expressed preference. We have indicated pseudonyms by the use of *italics*.

We analyzed the interviews using an interpretive, grounded-theory
approach. What is meant by grounded theory? It is a method of interpret-
ing research findings, proposed by sociologists Barney Glaser and Anselm
Strauss in the 1960s, which allows theoretical categories to emerge out of the
empirical research.[43] This is in contrast to more deductively inspired studies
in which researchers mine the findings for evidence to support or refute a
specific, perhaps narrowly defined, theory. Our approach is close to the one
that Kathy Charmaz has proposed, which she dubs "constructivist grounded
theory,"[44] a more fluid, open, less mechanistic grounded-theory analytic process than the original Glaser and Strauss method. In this approach, the full
human story behind the voices can be heard and used in the analysis, in a
style that John Van Maanen terms "impressionist tales" and Patricia Clough,
following Howard Becker, calls "emotional realism."[45]

Our response to the invisibility and silences that we have mentioned is to
emphasize voices in the presentation of the research. Our goal of amplifying
women's voices resonates with methodological questions that feminist theory
has raised, regarding the risk of scholarship to objectify women, removing their
agency as subjects. We also seek to excavate the "situational knowledge" that
women possess—an insistence of Dorothy E. Smith that research pay attention
to the "everyday/everynight world"[46] that grounds women's experiences differently from men's. At the same time, our research method runs up against challenges posed by feminist theory as well, particularly regarding epistemology,

or the science of knowledge. The philosopher Gayatri Chakravorty Spivak, for example, asked the question, "Can the subaltern speak?" in her essay with that same title. Spivak suggested that populations that have been subordinated by colonialism or social class hierarchies cannot be given full voice by the well-intended intellectual. By creating a platform where marginalized individuals can express their points of view, the risk is that the scholar will homogenize the group as if it shares a single culture, resulting in both a misrepresentation and a contribution to continuing the silence. We want to hold Spivak's question before us as a reminder to refrain from attempting to speak "for," or to assume community and commonality where none exists. We do not intend to speak "for" but to help amplify voices and to illustrate their heterogeneity. In doing so, this book can be a modest platform for immigrant women's agency.

In this sense, we are incorporating Spivak's critical, skeptical position—a characteristic of postmodern theorists more generally—about the research-er's ability to see, hear, and represent the meanings that the marginalized experience. Ironically, this skepticism potentially serves the goal of offer-ing a fuller and more comprehensive portrait of immigrant women. Adrian Holliday has explained how this works: "[B]ecause she reflectively seeks to acknowledge in which way she is the arch designer of the data collection, and how she disturbs the surface of the culture she is investigating, the postmod-ern researcher is in a position to dig deeper and reveal the hidden and the counter."[47] We approached our listening tasks in this spirit, and we hope that we have touched at least some of the "hidden and the counter."

## The Women

The women who were interviewed for this book immigrated as adults—ages eighteen and above.[48] Women who came to the United States as children have distinct experiences from those who came as adults, particularly since they have been partially socialized through the American educational system. We learned, however, that although there are both sociological and demographic differences between the first generation and the 1.5 generation—as the for-eign-born who arrived in the United States as children are categorized—we met a number of women of this 1.5 generation who proudly self-identify as immigrant women. Among those is Sonia Pressman Fuentes, who immi-grated with her family as a child and grew up to become a successful lawyer and activist, cofounding the National Organization for Women with several other activists in the 1960s, and who continues to write and speak on behalf of women's and immigrant rights.[49]

Definitions of *immigrant* may vary depending on whether one follows legal definitions, categories used by the U.S. government and demographers, or group-membership descriptions of social scientists. For example, after a foreign-born person naturalizes and becomes a citizen, he or she is no longer subject to the laws of the Immigration and Nationality Act. He or she, therefore, is no longer bureaucratically considered to be an immigrant. And the U.S. Census Bureau counts all foreign-born individuals who are residing in the country, regardless of whether they are in a temporary or more permanent immigration status, using the term "foreign-born." In this book, we use the term *immigrant* to include those on immigrant and "nonimmigrant" visas as well as those who have naturalized. Thus, our sample is broader than one that an immigration attorney might select and narrower than some demographers might select, since we are focusing on the first generation.

We concur with theorists who propose that research needs to be more attentive to the interpretive work of the individuals who are the subjects in our studies. Max Weber wrote that sociologists need to approach the study of society from the point of view of the actor—or the subjective, intended meanings as articulated by the individual whose behavior we are attempting to understand.[50] As Isaac Reed[51] and others have argued, individuals have the same cognitive abilities as social scientists to reflect intelligently on the meanings and motivations of their activities and the social structures in which they act. In other words, people know why they are in the United States and why they have encountered success, exploitation, discrimination, or acceptance. They have observed the twin towers collapsing on 9/11 or the North Atlantic Free Trade Agreement (NAFTA) policies in action; or they have learned the secrets of success in business. We have a wealth of interpretive information that the women interviewed here offered as they reflected on the experience; we hope that the interview process provided a platform for them to do further reflection.

Although we have limited this study to women, inevitably, we also met a number of men, including husbands, fathers, sons, and others, whose stories also helped flesh out the research. We remember the image of the male college student standing proudly with his arm around his mother as they both waved goodbye from their front porch following the interview with his mother, an entrepreneur from Mexico. We learned of this student's passionate activism on behalf of the DREAM Act to allow children of undocumented immigrants equal access to higher education and his commitment to its passage to benefit his financially struggling female friends. The Vietnamese dentist who is married to radio producer Susie Thang enthusiastically offered information about the couple's joint contributions to the musical arts in Houston. There was also the brother of *Khursheeda,* who taught her to ride the subway and helped her find work, and the husband of *Sarla,* who took care of their children once she took a live-in domestic job. And a host of men in their roles as immigration rights activists, scholars, or business consultants assisted us in locating women to interview, many glowing with admiration for the individuals whom they recommended. The public image of the immigrant man, in fact, is also in dire need of revision. In contrast to public perceptions of day laborers as unattached transients, a national study found that immigrant men are strongly connected to their families and are active in religious and other avenues of civic life.[52]

## *Plan of the Book*

We have arranged the chapters of this book thematically. Most chapters, with the exception of chapter 2, consist primarily of presentations and interpretations of the interviews, using a storytelling style to help the reader get to know the women's personalities and hear their voices.

In part 1, consisting of chapter 2, we explore the question of who immigrant women are and were, combining historical and present-day overviews of the phenomenon of immigrating women. We offer a historical portrait of immigrating women and the gendered history of immigration policy, followed by a demographic portrait of immigrating women to the United States in the early twenty-first century.

In part 2, we delve into the means through which today's immigrant women arrive. First, in chapter 3, we take up regular means, such as through family-reunification visas, employment visas, and the refugee and asylum program. We analyze women's experiences as both agents and recipients of these programs, as well as barriers that visa policies often pose. In chapter 4, we review the irregular, or extralegal, means through which women also enter. A growing proportion of the country's undocumented population is female, for example. And the United States is a destination country for the criminal trade in human beings through sex and other labor trafficking.

Our task in part 3, consisting of chapters 5 through 8, is to explore what the immigrating women do. In chapter 5, we become acquainted with the many women who are largely invisible as a group, because their labor as domestic workers is behind closed doors of private households. We hear women's descriptions of their employment, expectations, and treatment and learn about this sector's potential for abuse and exploitation. Chapter 6 offers a look at the "other" side of immigrant entrepreneurship that is rarely noticed: the female side. Leaving behind their grandmothers' patterns of sharing work in their husbands' shops, these women are striking out on their own and sometimes hiring their husbands as employees. Chapter 7 describes the women whom Donna Gabaccia calls "gender pioneers":[53] the women who have immigrated and gone on to forge new paths in gender-atypical occupations. These engineers, construction workers, and others came to their professions through varying pathways. They detail their professional paths, how their peers regard them, and what motivates their continued progress. Chapter 8 presents the cultural contributions of immigrant women, particularly in the realm of the arts. We analyze interviews with visual artists, writers, dancers, actors, filmmakers, and musicians and interrogate many of their artworks as venues of reflection on and vision of the gendered immigrant experience.

Our last two chapters make up part 4, in which we look at what immigrating women are doing to shape their, and our, future as a community and a country. Chapter 9 singles out the work of several immigrant women activists in the realms of politics, society, and culture. Through thick descriptions of their activities to bring about structural change, we learn more about the resistant side of agency. This chapter also provides a depiction, in these women's own words, of the broader challenges that women and immigrants face, as well as proposed solutions.

In chapter 10, we bring the full portrait together and offer further interpretations of the gender-nativity intersection (and others), as well as the meanings of human agency for those intersections. We reflect on these interpretations in their historically contingent settings. And, in the spirit of public sociology, we summarize proposed policy recommendations.

# I

# Who They Are

# 2

## "Your Story Drops on You"

*Who Are These Women?*

It is 1774, in Great Britain. A woman named Ann Lee has finally convinced her brothers and husband to migrate with her to the American colonies. Although illiterate, Ann is nonetheless familiar with the legal philosophy of English judge William Blackstone, who insisted that "[t]he very being or legal existence of the woman is suspended during marriage, or at least incorporated and consolidated into that of the husband."[1] Ann has adamantly expressed her impatience with Blackstone's philosophy; additionally, in the midst of disappointments in her personal life and with her surrounding culture, she has become attracted to the emotionally expressive new Christian Protestant sect Shaking Quakers. Her rise as a charismatic orator of this group has earned her the anger of English authorities and street mobs who have subjected her to physical punishments. Ann escapes across the Atlantic and devotes her life to leading the American (renamed) Shaker movement, which eventually attracts some six thousand members. Although the practice of celibacy took its toll on the Shaker movement, which has all but vanished today, this group's unique, simple approach to architecture, furniture style, and music continues to exert its influence in American culture.[2]

It is more than one century later: the year 1872, in rural China. A teenage girl has been sold by her financially desperate parents and forcefully smuggled to the frontier settlements of the northwest United States. Arriving with no knowledge of the English language or the culture of her new home, this individual, who later becomes known as Polly Bemis, unwittingly becomes caught up in a chain of women sold to Chinese men who had immigrated earlier, for marriage or as servants. Living in a generation when Chinese women's feet are routinely bound to assure their submissiveness, Polly is expected to spend her days in servile devotion to her master's needs. As Polly acculturates to the harsh living environment of the mountains of Idaho, she eventually breaks out of her situation, marries an American man, and goes on to become one of the leading pioneer women in the Northwest, living to an old age. A legend is built around Polly: among other activities, she ran a boarding house, was renowned for her hard work managing the ranch with her husband, and earned a respectful reputation in the region for her strong character and wit.[3]

These two historical vignettes, each exhibiting its own particularity, offer the beginning sketch of an outline of a more general demographic portrait of women immigrating to the United States. Even relatively early in U.S. history, as is evident in these stories, there was diversity—in national origins, in regional settlement patterns (east and west coasts), and in the contexts of exit (one voluntary and the other forced). Both of these women were able to prevail against strong odds—particularly in eras when their rights as women were few—and to have a lasting impact on their new homeland. Despite their legacies, however, Ann Lee and Polly Bemis are far from common household names in the twenty-first century.

This chapter positions the story of migrating women within the dynamic historical narratives that define their migration constraints and opportunities. Included in those narratives is the evolving nature of U.S. immigration policy as it has been shaped by issues of gender. Following an outline of these historical contexts of migration, we review recent statistics on the demographic characteristics of the foreign-born women living in the United States today.

## Migration, Gender, and History

An interpretation of the meanings of immigrant experiences must be a historicized one. The historical context of any era has a major impact on the meanings and parameters of women's and men's immigrant experiences. Alejandro Portes and Rubén G. Rumbaut emphasize the impact of particular "contexts of exit" and "contexts of reception" on the adaptation process for immigrants. Early on in immigrants' migration experience, Portes and Rumbaut explain, the conditions under which people left their home countries strongly influence their settlement in their new host country; but as time passes, it is the context of reception that plays a more lasting role on the experience. The authors suggest that there are three aspects to these contexts: government policies to promote or restrict immigration, features of labor markets, and the presence and characteristics of the ethnic community into which the new immigrant enters—or does not enter, if a group of coethnics does not live in the same vicinity.[4] Jeffrey G. Reitz has advanced this same argument and adds a fourth category, "the changing nature of international boundaries, part of the process of globalization."[5] Reitz also suggests that culture is often a part of this mix of the four intersecting conditions. We insert another condition, which is that immigrants' experiences also depend on the state of gender expectations, relations, and rights—a component of culture yet at the same time a condition that is relatively autonomous, as a "ground" for social relationships and institutional arrangements.

On the other hand, we emphasize just as strongly that there are many patterns of women's immigration experience that parallel those of men, although they may not appear as immediately evident. Both women and men, for example, find themselves needing to escape imminent threats of religious, ethnic, or political persecution; desire greater opportunity for themselves and their families; are displaced by natural disasters; and are driven from their homes due to war or economic shifts. People's movements across borders are rooted in historical "big structures" and "large processes," terms from Charles Tilly's descriptions of the overarching, grand social movements of history.[6] Argentinean American artist Natasha Duwin, portrayed in this book, for example, fled hyperinflation in her home country. Reflecting on her life, she proffered an explanation that depicts how the forces of history can affect the individual migrant: "There is a Spanish phrase that says, 'Your story drops on you.'"

## Historical Contexts of Exit

A shorthand version of the large processes that span 250 years of immigration to the United States include the Industrial Revolution, which disrupted European traditional labor patterns and transformed and expanded cities; European colonialism, which altered national borders, restructured local economies, and deracinated power structures; the two world wars of the twentieth century; the fall of empires in various parts of the world; the mid-twentieth-century east-west Cold War, which created political refugees from a range of world regions; and the Cold War's demise, resulting in economic dislocations, greater mobility for many people from the former communist states, and a growing market for opportunists who exploit the desperate. Africa's decolonization and postcolonial consolidations have resulted in population movements of various types. Another postcolonial region, Latin America, experienced a wave of twentieth-century authoritarian regimes, mobilizations against those regimes, civil wars that included some major U.S. interventions, and rocky transitions from authoritarianism—and, paralleling eastern-central Europe and Central Asia, currency crises and hyperinflation often accompanied the transition. Across and within these global events have been major ethnic/racial/religious conflicts, resulting in pogroms and other forced relocations, genocides, border changes, and coups d'état.

Domestic and international wars are among the oldest explanations for cross-border migration as well as internal displacement; in recent decades, however, those conflicts have been displacing growing numbers of women and children. For instance, in the 1970s, the Vietnam War uprooted many women from Vietnam and Cambodia, large numbers of whom were able to gain refugee admission to the United States. Civil wars and genocides in the Balkan (former Yugoslavian) states and in such African countries as Rwanda, Somalia, Sudan, Zimbabwe, and Liberia during the 1990s and into the twenty-first century resulted in substantial numbers of women forced to flee. With these women housed in refugee camps in third countries such as Kenya while awaiting a decision on their refugee applications, it can take years before the successful ones are allowed to move to a more stable environment. The Iraq War that began in 2003 and a parallel war in Afghanistan have added to the destabilization of women and children and to the increase in refugee flows.

A key context of exit is that of (evolving) nation-state policy. In recent years, for example, several countries banned their women from emigrating out of concerns of losing population and members of their own labor force. Although such a practice would seem to counter immigration flows, these bans did not succeed in preventing labor emigration by women. On the contrary, women migrated irregularly, including getting caught up in the underworld of human trafficking. Upon learning about these practices, several countries reversed course and lifted their ban, as did Nepal in 2003 and Bangladesh in 2004.[7] Other countries, such as Sri Lanka and the Philippines, actively encourage women to emigrate and send remittances back home, and these countries have become dependent on such remittances.[8] Ironically, many of these women become caretakers of their employers' children in their new home country but must leave their own children behind under the care of others for years at a time.[9]

Although armed conflict and other emergent crises inevitably displace broad numbers of a country's populace, poverty and lack of opportunity are more regular "feeders" of migration. Women and girls continue to constitute the largest proportion of the world's poor. Despite some significant gains in poverty reduction due to governmental and nongovernmental agencies' interventions, gender inequalities continue to prevent women from rising out of poverty. The average gap between men's and women's wages across the globe is 17 percent, with some countries reporting a gap as large as 51 percent.[10] Among the reasons for this disparity are the tendencies of women to be underpaid or unpaid, to work in more informal jobs, to be denied access to education, and to outlive breadwinner husbands. The cost of travel is going to deter the poorest women from migrating, particularly when it means crossing oceans; those who are able to leave their home will have some means of doing so, even if those means have come from pooled family resources.

The globalization process in its various forms—characterized by Arjun Appadurai as consisting of the five dimensions of ethnoscapes, mediascapes, technoscapes, financescapes, and ideoscapes[11]—has enhanced both the need and the opportunity of migrating. Today, 191 million people live in a country other than the one in which they were born.[12] Broader and easier transportation opportunities are clearly a major contributor to this trend—and are in turn developed by the trend. Such changes also result in immigrants' growing tendency to live binationally and, if they have both the financial means and legal status, to travel home regularly.[13] Regarding "financescapes," the rapid growth toward a global economy includes a central player: the "global factory," a continuously moving target, with manufacturers chasing the ever-changing lowest wage settings for their enterprises. Within such enterprises, women are securing low-paying positions but are just as likely to lose these jobs due to factory mobility and the lax state of regulation in areas such as Free Enterprise Zones. The global recession and sudden collapse of global markets in 2008 and 2009 were compounding this process further. Immigrant women in domestic work, for example, whether documented or undocumented, earn among the lowest pay on the wage scale but are at high risk of quick dismissal as their employers lose jobs or homes.[14] These situations exemplify what the United Nations terms "vulnerable employment," which is the category of jobs that women are more likely to hold than men.[15]

### Where We Have Been: The Women-and-Immigration-Policy Context of Reception

As these contexts of exit help determine the who, how, where, and why of migrant women's agency, there are particular structural and cultural contexts into which immigrant women enter when they migrate to the United States, further contributing to the shaping of their experiences. In this section, we review the relationship between immigration policy and women across history. Martha Gardner explains in her history of gender and immigration policy,

In the late nineteenth and twentieth centuries, fluctuations in laws governing the arrival and citizenship of immigrant women were symptomatic of the major changes that punctuated this period—the growing concern about the nuclear family, the increased participation of women in wage labor, the shift from an industrial to a service economy, the increase in migration to the United States of nonwhite, non-European peoples, and the growth of the United States as a global power. The perception of immigrant women and their citizen daughters either as assets or as threats to assimilation and nation building is linked to these important shifts in social, economic, and international power relationships.[16]

Since the earliest years of U.S. state formation, gender ideologies have contributed to the scripting of immigration policy. Full citizenship, of course, which would entail suffrage, as well as property, political, and other rights, was not available to any women—whether native- or foreign-born—until the twentieth century. Nevertheless, women could be granted the title of U.S. citizen without this full set of rights. As a group of colonies, the proto–United States had inherited elements of the common-law tradition of England, under which a married woman's legal status was derived from that of her husband. This was known as the law of coverture, the philosophy of which was summarized in the words of jurist William Blackstone, who is quoted in the opening to this chapter. As a more formal immigration policy developed in the United States, it reflected this inherited philosophy—and this extended to laws governing women's citizenship. There were contrasting outcomes of such laws and traditions for the migrating woman. On the one hand, a white woman (under certain conditions) could receive citizenship immediately upon migrating if she was joining her husband who had preceded her and naturalized. On the other hand, married women did not possess immigration status independently from their husbands, a system that granted immigrant men a great deal of control over their wives and children. Based on an 1855 law, a woman's derivative citizenship was granted if she herself was eligible to be naturalized on her own; the courts used this law to reject citizenship to nonwhite women, since the courts were using racial eligibility criteria stated in the naturalization law.[17]

Examples of how these laws played out in reality included the practice that, between 1907 and 1922, a female (native-born) U.S. citizen could lose her citizenship if she married an immigrant man. Although she could receive her citizenship back if her husband naturalized, there were several categories of Asian men who were restricted from naturalizing, preventing women who married a man from one of these countries from regaining her citizenship.[18] In the year 1920, a case was reported in Kentucky of an American woman whose German husband had died while she was pregnant with their child; when the baby was born, it was taken and sent to live with her husband's relatives in Germany.[19] Thus, even custody of a woman's naturally born (and U.S.-citizen) child was not secure. In addition, women who were U.S. citizens or lawful permanent residents could not file a petition for their foreign-born husbands to immigrate, although U.S.-citizen men could do so for foreign-born wives.[20] The flip side of the exclusionary history of coverture laws was that some immigrating women were able to use this derivative citizenship to immigrate when they could not have done so alone. For example, certain Asian men—merchants and farmers—were exempt from Chinese exclusion laws, and women who married these men were allowed to naturalize.[21]

Women's legal status began to change when American women won the right to vote in 1920 as a result of a seventy-two-year-long social movement, and even then, it changed only gradually. And partly as a result of women's organizing to contest the loss of citizenship through marriage, Congress passed the 1922 Cable Act, or the Married Women Act, which ended the practice of U.S.-citizen (white or black) women's losing citizenship, although immigrant women who were excluded from citizenship based on their race could not regain citizenship.[22] The Cable Act also excluded women who were married to men who could not naturalize because of their race. In 1931, Congress dropped this provision of the act.[23] Generally speaking, immigration policy has sometimes taken two steps forward and one step back, or two steps back and one step forward, when it comes to women. The timeline in Appendix C highlights the legislation throughout American history that has affected women particularly. Key obstructions for women range from the 1875 Page Law, which prevented Asian women from immigrating on the assumption that they would only be coming for "lewd and immoral purposes," to the 1996 Illegal Immigration Reform and Immigrant Responsibility Act, which limited previously available public benefits for immigrants. The latter law affected both documented and undocumented immigrants and narrowed the pool of noncitizens who were eligible to receive public benefits such as Food Stamps (now termed "Supplemental Nutrition Assistance Program"), Supplemental Security Income, and Temporary Assistance to Needy Families (TANF), requiring a five-year waiting period for some categories of foreign-born residents.[24]

Examples from the two-steps-forward column include the 1952 Immigration and Nationality Act, which immigration rights advocates helped push forward, resulting in laws written in gender-neutral language and consequently ending the decades-old practice of separate laws and rights for men and women. (This act remains the heart of U.S. immigration law.) And in 1994, the Violence against Women Act provided immigration relief for spouses in violent marriages; under this law, a woman has the right to file her own petition to be a lawful permanent resident without any assistance from her spouse.

Like the policy history, immigration history is a story of change. The policy restrictions and allowances are examples of the social structures that constrain and enable the entry of immigrating women—illustrations of the influence of the context of reception on immigrants' lives. And the changes in policy reflect the active work of individuals on both the immigration "restrictionist" and immigration "rights" sides of the fence—although their work may result in unintended consequences. Historian Roger Daniels has documented the convoluted twists, turns, compromises, and deal-making that have characterized every phase of immigration policymaking at the executive and legislative levels. To illustrate the complexity and ongoing fluctuation of these laws, Daniels notes that between 1986 and 1998, Congress passed twenty-one significant pieces of immigration legislation.[25]

## Where We Are Now: The Contexts of Reception Today

Currently, this is a time of increasing national, cultural, and linguistic diversity for the United States. In 2008, 1,107,126 immigrants entered the United States through formal, official channels (including those already living in the United States who adjusted their immigration status), and approximately 500,000 entered through unofficial channels. As of the year 2000, the number of residents or citizens with Latino heritage had surpassed the number of African Americans in the United States.[26] In 2006, 21 percent of all children living in the United States had at least one foreign-born parent; the majority of those children were native-born.[27]

With the tragic events of September 11, 2001, in recent memory, however, that diversity is being met with caution and backlash from some sectors of society, which is reflected at the national policy level. A host of restrictive laws, including the PATRIOT Act, have been enacted to secure borders, arrest "suspicious" foreign-born individuals, and put new surveillance measures in place. In addition to effects of the post-9/11 xenophobia on immigrants, the 9/11 attacks themselves victimized the foreign-born. Approximately 500 of the 2,752 who lost their lives in the World Trade Center attacks were foreign-born, representing more than ninety-one countries; thousands of the estimated forty thousand individuals who helped clean up Ground Zero after the attacks were immigrants, unknown numbers of whom contracted serious illnesses from the toxins at the site.[28]

The historical context for gender norms in the United States in 2010 is one in which women are more fully integrated into public spheres such as politics, the economy, and the media than ever before. The House of Representatives had its first female Speaker of the House, a female presidential candidate ran a strong campaign in the Democratic Party primaries of 2008, and this candidate became the third female secretary of state. Former bastions of male employment have opened to women; for example, in 2010, there were a reported forty-two thousand women in religious clergy positions. Despite such gains, however, many aspects of public and private experiences for women had not dramatically changed by 2010. Only 17 percent of the members of the 111th Congress beginning its work in January 2009, for example, were women.[29] The megastore Wal-Mart was in the midst of the largest women's employee class-action lawsuit in history; and an estimated 1.3 million women experienced physical abuse by their intimate partners each year.[30]

## A Demographic Portrait

With this background on global contexts of exit and domestic contexts of reception in mind, we turn to a description of the population of immigrant women who live in the United States today. The following demographic portrait of foreign-born women is based primarily on statistics from the U.S. government; most of this information is from the U.S. Census Bureau, with additional data from the U.S. Citizenship and Immigration Services of the Department of Homeland Security (formerly the Immigration and Naturalization Service, or INS). While these government data are clearly useful for observing national patterns, we emphasize that they also come with admitted imperfections. The Census Bureau, for example, recognizes that immigrants are particularly difficult to count fully, and its data may underrepresent the foreign-born by as much as 10 percent. To give another example of the gaps in data, we now know that across an entire year in 1997, the INS misplaced or lost the millions of I-94 cards that foreign visitors complete upon entrance to the United States at airports.[31] Due to these and other factors, such as changes in immigration categories, Roger Daniels has observed that "all immigration and census data are somewhat suspect,"[32] and contradictions between various sets of data—even within government reports—are common.

For a portrait of national patterns, however, the government data are among the best we have at the moment. Further, these data warrant much more mining from a gender perspective than has been commonly attempted. We compare data from the decennial censuses since 1850 and update the information with the 2008 American Community Survey. Finally, we look at gender patterns in the statistics of newly immigrating lawful permanent residents (LPRs). Comparisons across these distinct sets of data, however, must be made very cautiously—if it all.

## Patterns across History

We can trace the broad outlines of the historical patterns in women's immigration by examining U.S. decennial census data across the past century and a half. Although the annual census dates back to 1790, individuals were not asked about their nativity in the census questionnaire until 1850; therefore, we only have data on the foreign-born since that date. Additionally, the definition of "foreign-born" for the purpose of the census has changed; only since 1890 have the foreign-born with at least one U.S.-citizen parent been categorized as native-born. Prior to that date, such individuals were counted as foreign-born.[33] This means that the numbers of foreign-born in the 1850–80 years are not fully comparable with the subsequent decades of census data. Additionally, the 1850 and 1860 censuses counted only the "free" population, so they represent only a portion of the people of African descent, whether born in the States or elsewhere. Our census results also reflect the dynamics of the gender-nativity intersection, because through the 1910 census, the questionnaire only asked the citizenship status of men over the age of twenty-one. The historical trends that we report in this section are of all adult immigrant women, including those who migrated as children and those who came as adults.

In the earliest eras for which we have data, more men immigrated than women, often leaving a family in their home country. In 1870, for example, there were 120 foreign-born adult men for every 100 foreign-born adult women. As the decades passed, we see similar ratios reported, and they rose to a peak of 132 males to 100 females in the year 1910, near the height of the Ellis Island–era Great Immigration. Since that time, the ratio gap narrowed more each decade until women actually outnumbered men in the 1960 census, which reported 95 foreign-born men for every 100 women. By 1970, it had dipped further, to 86 men for every 100 women. This gender imbalance decreased in the ensuing decades, and the year 2000 is the first time that the ratio of foreign-born males to females is just about 1 to 1, with women still constituting a slight majority.

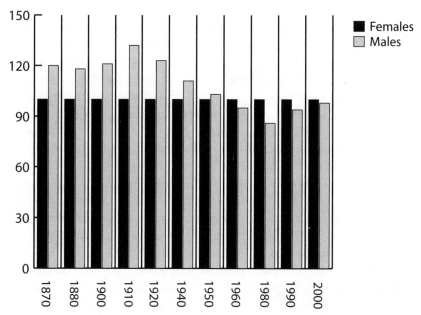

FIGURE 2.1. *Ratio of foreign-born adult men to women,*
*United States, 1870 to 2000 (number of males per 100 females).*

*Source:* Gibson and Jung, "Historical Census Statistics on the Foreign-Born Population of the United States: 1850–2000"; U.S. Census Bureau, U.S. Decennial Census 2000, "Table 7: Age and Sex of the Foreign-Born Population, 1870 to 2000, Ages 18 and Older" (data for ages eighteen and older not available for 1930 and 1970). *Note:* Most of the 1890 census records were destroyed in a fire. We are using secondary data which includes 1890 but does not explain the data's origin, so we omitted that year. The remaining figures in this chapter select for women who migrated as adults; this delineation was not available for all years in the historical census data, so the numbers here reflect all adult foreign-born, regardless of age of immigration.

Regarding the regular, official means of entry, the proportion of women immigrants who enter the United States or adjust their status to become lawful permanent residents has been increasing steadily across the years. In the mid-1980s, roughly equal numbers of women and men became LPRs. By the year 2008, 471,844 adult women and 374,684 adult men immigrated as LPRs.[34] This means that 56 percent of the new LPRs were women.

Why these fluctuations in gender ratios across the years? First, we should keep in mind that there was probably undercounting of immigrant women through the 1910 census, as mentioned earlier. Second, the earliest immigrants arrived in an era when expectations for women were more strictly defined than they are in the present day. Women's responsibility for running a household, caring for children, and supporting the needs of a breadwinner husband would have been the norm for the vast majority—across social classes—and regardless of whether they also held a wage-sector job. In line with such dominant definitions of the "normal" family, and gendered ideologies such as the "cult of domesticity" during the Victorian era, the new country's developing immigration policy also gendered the immigration process for women. Historically, therefore, the immigration pattern to the United States since laws began to regulate these matters would have been predominantly male. This balance did not begin to shift until the 1930s, with the legislative changes that allowed "war brides" to join their American soldier husbands in the United States.[35]

This is also a story of the successes of the women's and civil rights movements. Along with Polish immigrant Ernestine Rose and an army of native- and foreign-born suffragists, the first wave of the American women's movement set the wheels in motion that resulted in the eventual mid-twentieth-century reforms in immigration policy to erase the gender restrictions in the law. As women's attitudes about family roles have shifted over the decades, the pattern of *agency* in decisions to emigrate from the home country also shifted. Among Italians, for example, men traditionally emigrated, leaving entire villages in home countries without their "menfolk." Approximately 80 percent of Italian immigrants to the United States in the early twentieth century were men. Since the 1960s, married Italian women have been more likely to immigrate with their husbands; they are not satisfied to be left behind.[36]

African Americans have had a major influence on the progress of immigration policy. The vignette of the Chinese immigrant Polly Bemis ("China Polly") illustrates a history of women brought to this country against their will. This was also the fate of countless millions of women forcefully brought from Africa to the Americas across more than 250 years. Although a comparison of African American and immigrant histories reveals stark contrasts in opportunity and access to societal "goods" between the groups, women from these backgrounds have also shared political struggles. Mississippian Ida B. Wells Barnett and New Yorker Sojourner Truth were notable examples of African-descended women who resisted the legacy of slavery and took up leadership roles to transform the political and social terrain for immigrant and native-born women and people of color, benefiting immigrant women. Decades later, activists in the civil rights movement influenced immigration policy further. Passed in the midst of the civil rights movement, for example, the Hart-Celler Act (Immigration and Nationality Act) of 1965 abolished the national quota system that had characterized immigration policy since 1921—one that had strongly favored north-ern and western Europeans. The act resulted in dramatic shifts in the national origins and skin colors of immigrating populations, to reflect the broader diversity of the globe. Commenting on these efforts, researcher Salih Omar Eissa has recently observed, "From Jim Crow to the Civil Rights Movement to desegregation, African Americans have been instrumental in transforming the sociopolitical climate in the United States, creating an environment far more accepting of new immigrants."[37]

This shift away from European dominance in national origins is visible in the demographic data on immigrating women. In 1940, for example, Italy was the top country of origin for adult immigrant women in the United States. But Italy had dropped to seventh place by 1990 and sixteenth by 2000. Another Euro-pean country, England, was among the top-ten countries of origin throughout most of the twentieth century but had dropped to fourteenth by 2000. As these "older" immigrant-sending countries declined on the list, they were replaced by others from the regions of the world that were labeled after the 1960s as sending regions of "new" immigration. China, for example, has long been a sending country, dating at least to the California gold rush, but did not send the numbers that Europe was sending in the nineteenth century, due in part to restrictionist U.S. laws regarding Chinese immigrants. Today, this situation has changed. China first appeared on the top-ten list for immigrant women in 1980, and El Salvador and the Dominican Republic joined the top ten in 2000.[38]

How did the Hart-Celler Act affect the feminization of immigration to the United States? In addition to opening doors to all world regions and enhanc-ing immigrant diversity, the act placed the goal of family reunification at the heart of U.S. immigration policy, where it remains to this day. The visas cre-ated by these new laws allow wives, mothers, daughters, and other female relatives to join men who immigrated before them to the United States, just as they allow husbands, brothers, and sons to join women who preceded them. Together with a change in the ethnic profile of new immigrants, there-fore, the Hart-Celler Act also effected a change in the gender profile. In addi-tion to the family-reunification visas, this act also created what are called "employment-preference" categories, which offer legal employment visas to foreign-born individuals who are qualified to fill those positions. As a result, more than thirteen thousand South Korean medical professionals have immigrated to the United States since 1965; most of them were female nurses. In fact, the United States has a history of recruiting immigrants to fill nursing shortages; immediately after World War II, for example, the U.S. government began recruiting nurses from the Philippines under the Exchange and Visitors Program (EVP).[39] In the 1960s, 80 percent of the program's participants were from the Philippines, and most of those were nurses. Many of these nurses were able to remain or return to the States later, as they preferred both the salaries and working conditions to those in their home country.[40]

## Immigrant Women Today

In 2008, the U.S. Census Bureau conducted one of a series of annual surveys of a sample of the U.S. population, which it initiated in 2001, called the American Community Survey. Each year, the bureau has expanded the sample and the number of U.S. locations where it administers the survey, and the 2008 sample (the latest data as of this writing) included the largest group of participants to date. On the basis of the estimates available from this survey, we are able to view a broad portrait of the foreign-born populations—with a caveat that these numbers represent estimates extrapolated and calculated from these samples. In order to view the portrait that represents the women interviewed for this book, we have selected only those women who immigrated to the United States as adults. Therefore, the following descriptions are of individuals who were born abroad (but not born to U.S.-citizen parents) and who migrated to the United States at age eighteen and older. We include both noncitizens and naturalized citizens in the analysis here. What do we know about the foreign-born women in the United States? What characteristics do they share, what trends can we observe, and how internally diverse are they as a group?[41] We use the terms *foreign-born* and *immigrant* interchangeably here.

### Gender and Geography

First, the data indicate that more foreign-born women reside in the United States than foreign-born men. Among the foreign-born adults ages eighteen and older who immigrated as adults to the United States, women make up just over 51 percent of the total. Residing in the United States today are 13,000,583 foreign-born women, in contrast to 12,466,707 foreign-born men. Many of the foreign-born women in U.S. society are newcomers. In fact, 38 percent of all foreign-born women residing in the United States in 2008 had been in the country for ten years or less.[42] Another 28 percent had been here between eleven and twenty years.

Immigrant women represent 148 different countries of origin; this does not necessarily mean that the women migrated directly from those countries, as many may have lived or even grown up elsewhere prior to their migration to the United States. Mexican-born women are the most numerous group

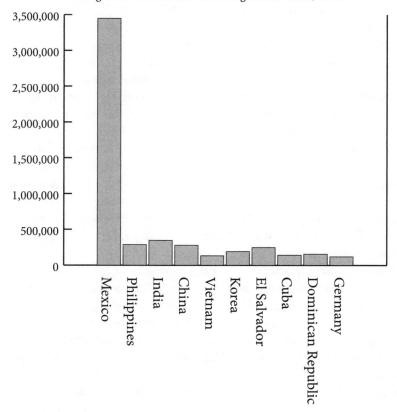

FIGURE 2.2. *Top-ten countries of origin: foreign-born women residing in the United States who immigrated as adults, 2008.*

*Source*: Ruggles et al., "Integrated Public Use Microdata Series: Version 4.0."

and make up 24 percent of the total (or 3,075,732), and the least numerous group originated in Guinea (1,921). Figure 2.2 illustrates the top-ten countries of birth of immigrant women. With the exception of one European country (Germany), it is Latin America and Asia that are the predominant "sending" regions of the world.

If we continue down the list of the top-twenty countries of birth, more diversity of world regions appears, as this list includes Canada, Caribbean islands (Jamaica and Haiti), the eastern areas of Europe (Poland and Russia/former USSR), and Japan, as well as Central and South America (Guatemala, Peru, and Honduras). Although lower numbers of immigrants to the United States were born in Africa than on other world continents, the most populous country in Africa—Nigeria—is the top-sending African country for adult female immigrants: 69,402 of immigrant women were born in Nigeria. Second to Nigeria is Ethiopia, the birthplace of 47,589 women immigrants.

The ratio of women to men within nation-specific immigrant communities varies widely, resulting in gender imbalances in a number of cases. In 2008, for example, both Mexico and India were the countries of origin for more men than women: 120 Indian men for every 100 women, and 124 Mexican men for every 100 women. Quite a few of the top-sending countries, however, sent more women than men. These include the Philippines (162 women per 100 men) and Korea, which was the country of birth for 144 women for every 100 Korean men. And there are twice as many German women as German men (230 women per 100 men); similarly, there are 219 Japanese women for every 100 Japanese men. Although the country of Estonia is the birthplace of a relatively low number of immigrant women—a total of 4,410 in 2008—Estonians represent the highest female-to-male ratio among all countries of origin, with 244 women per 100 men.

These gender differences within national origins reflect, in part, the gendered nature of immigration policy, as indicated earlier; not only might certain visas target specialties that are gendered, such as engineers and technicians, but the immigrants with such specialties are recruited in specific national clusters, such as that of India. Due to the recruitment of nurses and household workers from the Philippines, for example, the high ratio of women to men from that country is not surprising. Other policy influences include the War Brides Act, mentioned earlier; some of the countries sending higher numbers of women are those where American military men were fighting in World War II, the Korean War, and the Vietnam War.

Another country with higher numbers of women immigrating is Jamaica, a trend that has been visible beginning with the passage of the 1965 Immigration Act. In 1967, 76 percent of Jamaican immigrants arriving in the country were women. Although this percentage has declined over the years, with women constituting 52 to 54 percent of Jamaican immigrants in the 1980s and 1990s,[43] in 2008, there were 137 foreign-born women from Jamaica in the United States for every 100 Jamaican men. Sociologist Nancy Foner has observed that the long history of Jamaican female immigration reflects the strong desire among Jamaican women for financial independence. Women in Jamaica have been in the workforce since the days of slavery and continued working in paid occupations after emancipation in the 1830s. Additionally, Caribbean women in general are breaking traditional immigration patterns in other ways, often being the leaders of their families' "chain" migration.[44]

Perhaps ironically, one result of tighter border controls between the United States and Mexico since the early 1990s was that the number of female immigrants from Mexico actually increased. Throughout most of the twentieth century, there has been regular circular migration of Mexican men to the United States for seasonal work; in fact, they were periodically recruited through government initiatives such as the Bracero program to attract agricultural labor. With heightened border enforcement and visa-processing delays, especially after 9/11, circular migration became more difficult. Therefore, more wives and children are joining the men in their families in the United States.[45] Although the numbers continue to indicate that more Mexican men than women are living in the United States, this ratio has decreased over the years.

We have presented the national origins of immigrant women here, but it is important not to conflate one's national origins with one's ancestry, ethnic identification, or the category that many people continue to describe as "race." A more detailed disaggregation of the census data through the lens of these other categories would yield a highly more complex picture: Nicaraguans of Native American ancestry versus those of predominantly European background, Canadians of Pakistani origin, and UK citizens who are of African descent, to name but a few. In fact, such analysis could enrich our picture of immigrant diversity even further.[46]

*Settlement Patterns*

California is currently in the lead as the choice of residence for immigrant women (and men). The 3,334,911 immigrant women who reside in California represent 26 percent of all immigrant women across the country. This state hosts more than twice the number of those in the second-most-popular host state, which is New York; the 1,555,352 immigrant women in New York State represents 12 percent of the nation's immigrant women. Los Angeles (and the surrounding vicinity) leads the country with the largest number of immigrant women and men.

Among the leading states where immigrant women settle, however, virtually every geographic region of the United States is represented. Not unexpectedly, these states include emerging gateways such as Virginia and Georgia. Florida and Texas, respectively, trail New York in numbers of immigrant women that they host: each of these two states has just over 300,000 fewer than New York (1,254,809 in Florida and 1,221,797 in Texas). Although the trends for immigrant men largely mirror these same state-settlement patterns, there are a few distinctions between women and men. For men, Florida actually trails Texas, reversing these states so that Texas is in third place and Florida is in fourth place. More notably, Georgia is sixth on the list for men, in contrast to tenth for women. Among the remaining fifty states, settlement patterns of women and men are fairly comparable, with small ordering differences such as those that we noticed in the top-ten states. The largest gender disparity is in Hawaii, which hosts 93,703 immigrant women but only 61,270 men.

### Age and Education

In 2008, immigrant women across nationalities represented a wide age range, with the majority under age fifty; 10 percent were younger than age thirty, indicating that quite a number are moving to the United States as young adults. An additional 23 percent were in their thirties, and 23 percent were in their forties. Although fewer women were concentrated in the age ranges of fifty to fifty-nine (18 percent) and sixty to sixty-nine (13 percent), it is notable that a full 19 percent of all immigrant women were retirement age (age sixty-five and over, with several thousand women in their nineties). Compared to their predecessors, today's immigrant women to the United States are more likely to be educated, single, and employed. As we look at the numbers, however, the diversity among immigrant women becomes apparent, reflecting an array of social classes, or statuses, and family types. We begin with education.

Among the least-educated foreign-born adults living in the United States in 2008, women reported higher rates of no formal education and of completing no more than kindergarten, first, or second grade than did immigrant men. Above these grades, however, other rates of elementary and high school completion are quite similar across genders, with women slightly more likely than men to report completing some school grades and slightly more likely to hold a high school diploma or a GED and to have had some college. When it comes to holding associate's (two-year) degrees, the women outnumber men: 6 percent of the women, in contrast to 4 percent of the men, hold these degrees as their highest educational attainment. The foreign-born women also hold more bachelor's degrees than do foreign-born men, with 17 percent of adult women completing four-year degrees and 15 percent of men having done so. Although quite a number of immigrant women have completed graduate degrees, the men are slightly more likely than women to hold master's, professional, and doctoral degrees. Nevertheless, 6 percent of the

FIGURE 2.3. *Top-ten states of settlement: foreign-born women residing in the United States who immigrated as adults, 2008.*

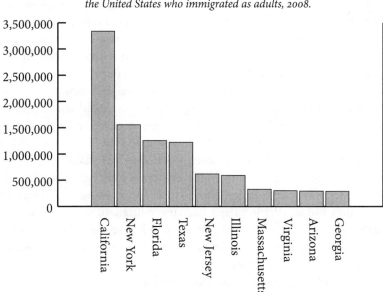

*Source*: Ruggles et al., "Integrated Public Use Microdata Series: Version 4.0."

immigrant women hold a master's degree; 2 percent, a professional graduate degree; and just over 1 percent, a doctorate. In comparison, 8 percent of immigrant men report holding a master's degree; 2 percent, a graduate professional degree; and 3 percent, a doctorate.

In comparison with native-born women, however, foreign-born women have slightly higher rates of completed graduate professional degrees and doctorates. Although there are numerically more native-born women who hold these degrees—due to the larger proportion of native-born women in the general population—foreign-born women hold 16 percent of all graduate professional degrees and 20 percent of all doctorates that are held by women in the United States. And the *proportions* of immigrant women holding bachelor's, master's, graduate professional, and doctoral degrees is roughly equivalent to the rates of these degrees among native-born women—with immigrant women being slightly more likely than native-born women to hold a doctorate. Just over 1 percent (1.3) of immigrant women have a doctorate, whereas under 1 percent (.06) of native-born women report holding a doctorate. At the lower levels of education, however, there are higher proportions of immigrant than native-born women who have not finished early grades.

For example, approximately 5 percent of foreign-born women have had no schooling at all, in contrast to less than 1 percent of native-born women. Comparably, 7 percent of the immigrant women had completed sixth grade only, in contrast to less than 1 percent of native-born women. And higher proportions of native-born women completed high school as their highest degree (26 percent) than had the immigrant women (20 percent).

Recently, scholars have documented a gradual but striking increase in the educational levels of new immigrants to the United States over the decades. Our data here help explain this change through the lens of gender: the broadened access of education that has become available to women globally—despite continued barriers—and women's desire to take advantage of educational opportunities in their home country or by immigrating. In 2009, UNESCO reported that between 1970 and 2007, there was a sixfold increase in the number of females in higher (tertiary) education, while the numbers of males rose by fourfold.[47] And globally, one in five students (female and male) who choose to migrate to another country for their university education heads for the United States.[48]

Another indication of women's educational achievements is their fluency in the English language. Immigrant women's reports of their level of English fluency show roughly the same rates as those of immigrant men. Just under 15 percent of the women and 12 percent of men say that they speak "only English," and 25 and 26 percent of women and men, respectively, report that they speak English "very well." Another 15 percent of women report that they do not speak English, in contrast to 12 percent of men. Among those who say that they speak English "not very well" or "well" the women's rates are slightly below those of men.

### Employment

A majority of women who immigrated as adults are employed; just over 54 percent reported that they are in the labor force, although this contrasts with the 80 percent of immigrant men who stated that they are currently in the labor force. Given that such a large percentage of these women are young adults, they may be either pursuing a postsecondary degree or taking time to raise children. And given women's tendency (as a group) to outlive men, a larger proportion of women are retirement age. The range of occupations that immigrant women hold spans the gamut of those that are also reported by the native-born; the women report 333 occupations (according to Census Bureau classifications). The most common occupation among foreign-born women is in the domestic sphere, or "housekeepers, maids, butlers, stewards, and lodging quarters cleaners." Nevertheless, this is the occupation of only 5 percent of all immigrant women and 9 percent of all immigrant women who are in the workforce. As we will see in chapter 5, it is highly possible that this estimate of household workers is low, given estimates from other sources and given the hidden nature of household work and the lower likelihood of undocumented workers to be counted. Quite high on the list is the medical profession, as the second-most-common occupation is "nursing aides, orderlies, and attendants" and the third is "registered nurse." Additionally there are 67,558 immigrant women physicians, roughly half the number of immigrant men in this field. And one of the more common occupations of foreign-born women is that of teacher.

A review of the occupations in which immigrant women work reveals that they are populating both extremes of the service economy—as well as many positions in the middle. For example, they are employed as cleaners, sales clerks, and waitresses, on the one hand, and in positions that require higher education, such as teachers, professors, accountants, managers, and administrators, on the other. At the general level, therefore, these numbers demonstrate that foreign-born women are contributing to the workforce needs of an economy that has moved from a manufacturing to a service base. They are filling the positions that are in the lowest status and pay scale, as well as those that demand the mental labor required by an information society. The profession of social work, for example, employs 32,386 immigrant women. There are key exceptions to this trend, which are important to note here. For example, "assemblers of electrical equipment" is one of the most common occupations; there are also 103,487 women working as machine operators and 63,038 graders and sorters in manufacturing. These women can also be found in other occupations that have historically been viewed as atypical for women: 96,775 are computer-software developers, 65,053 are computer systems analysts and computer scientists, and 27,377 are production supervisors or foremen. Additionally, 3,300 immigrant women report that they are members of the armed services, as do 19,584 immigrant men. Although farm work is not one of the highest employment sectors for immigrant women, we should not ignore the 94,747 who are farm workers, as well as thousands more in agricultural support or management positions, since farms are highly dependent on immigrant labor in the United States. This may, in fact, be another of the more undercounted groups of immigrants (in addition to domestic work), due to these women's mobility and remote locations from cities.

TABLE 2.1

Twenty Most Common Occupations of Foreign-Born Women in the
United States Who Immigrated as Adults, 2008

| Occupation | Number | Proportion of Immigrant Women in the Labor Force |
|---|---|---|
| Housekeepers, maids, butlers, stewards, and lodging quarters cleaners | 652,691 | 9.2% |
| Nursing aides, orderlies, and attendants | 524,413 | 7.4% |
| Registered nurses | 279,832 | 4.0% |
| Cooks, variously defined | 278,406 | 3.9% |
| Cashiers | 265,553 | 3.8% |
| Child care workers | 260,509 | 3.7% |
| Janitors | 260,166 | 3.7% |
| Retail sales clerks | 198,218 | 2.8% |
| Secretaries | 194,021 | 2.7% |
| Hairdressers and cosmetologists | 192,062 | 2.7% |
| Accountants and auditors | 166,099 | 2.3% |
| Assemblers of electrical equipment | 153,186 | 2.2% |
| Supervisors and proprietors of sales jobs | 152,459 | 2.2% |
| Managers and administrators, not elsewhere classified | 144,752 | 2.0% |
| Waiter/waitress | 141,073 | 2.0% |
| Teachers, not elsewhere classified | 129,309 | 1.8% |
| Miscellaneous food prep workers | 129,114 | 1.8% |
| Packers and packagers by hand | 128,517 | 1.8% |
| Primary school teachers | 122,150 | 1.7% |
| Subject instructors (HS/college) | 113,940 | 1.6% |

Source: Ruggles et al., "Integrated Public Use Microdata Series: Version 4.0."

Looking at another set of data, that from the annual group of new lawful permanent residents who arrive annually (or adjust their status from a different immigration category), these new entrants exhibit high levels of professional skills. Among the employed women who were new LPRs in 2007, 40 percent reported to be in "management, professional, and related occupations." Most of the remaining employed women are in service occupations (23 percent) and sales and office occupations (22 percent). Employed women represent 23 percent of the total adult women whose status is known, 10 percent are unemployed, another 32 percent are reported to be homemakers, and the status of the remaining 33 percent is unknown.

Historically, when New York City led the country in immigration numbers, it was the garment industry that was the center of immigrant women's employment, due to the fact that a strong command of English was not required and because many already possessed sewing skills before they arrived. Italian, Polish, Jewish, Russian, and other eastern European women could be found in this sector. The cultural memory of immigrant women's contributions and sacrifices in the garment industry has been sealed by the traumatic moment of the Triangle Shirtwaist Factory fire of 1911, in which 146 workers were killed. Garment work continues to employ immigrant women today, although much of textile manufacturing is now done abroad; in 2008, 130,869 women were employed as textile machine operators. In contrast to the past, however, Latin American and Asian women are now filling these positions, and Los Angeles has developed its own competitive garment industry.[49]

Although immigrant women have been ghettoized into labor niches at the lowest end of the pay scale, examples of women who migrated to the United States and became successful in high-skilled professions are not confined to the twentieth and twenty-first centuries. One notable female immigrant was English-born Elizabeth Blackwell, the country's first woman doctor, who immigrated with her family as a child in 1832. With her sister, Emily Blackwell, and another immigrant woman, Dr. Marie E. Zakrzewska, from Poland, Dr. Blackwell cofounded the New York Infirmary for Women and Children to serve women in the slums of New York City. The Blackwell sisters also helped found the Women's Central Association of Relief during the Civil War to provide training for nurses.[50] Dr. Zakrzewska, trained in midwifery in Berlin, moved to the United States and earned her doctorate in medicine. She went on to found the New England Hospital for Women and Children, the first hospital in Boston and second in the United States that was run by women physicians and surgeons.[51]

Immigrant women and both free and enslaved African American women were mainstays in the U.S. labor force from the founding of the country, but the past century generally has seen the arrival of women in new types of vocations and the overall growth in the number of women who are in the paid labor force. Between 1960 and 1990, foreign-born women's employment rates jumped from 48 percent to 68 percent.[52] Earlier in U.S. history, the female wage earner in the immigrant household was more likely a daughter than a mother. Today, however, as sociologist Nancy Foner observes, it is the mother who is employed, while the daughters usually are in school.[53] The historian Donna Gabaccia contends that immigrant women's adjustment to living in the United States is relatively easier today than in the past. Today, it is acceptable for women to be in the workforce. Earlier in U.S. history, female immigrants were disparaged for working—a practice that was necessary for struggling, impoverished immigrant families.[54]

### Family Status and Independent Migration

Regarding today's immigrant women's marital status, 57 percent of them are married with their spouse present. An additional 5 percent are married but with their spouses absent, 4 percent report that they are separated from their spouses, and the remaining 34 percent are single, of whom 9 percent are divorced, 11 percent are widowed, and 14 percent have never married. The majority of women (57 percent) have their own children living with them in the household, although we do not know if they have all their own children with them, as some women must leave their children behind for some time. This means that 43 percent of immigrant women live in a household with no children. Among those who do have children living with them, the plurality (46 percent) report that they have only one child with them, and an additional 33 percent have two children. In contrast with immigrant women of a century ago, these family sizes are remarkably small. In 1900, for example, 62 percent of first-generation immigrant Polish women under age forty-five were bearing more than five children. Women from other immigrant groups, including Irish-, Danish-, Norwegian-, Bohemian-, and Austrian-born women, lived in families that mirrored these same patterns. Between 39 percent and 44 percent of women from these groups also bore more than five children.[55] And in 1920, only 14 percent of foreign-born women who were more than fifteen years of age were single.[56] Today's existence of a higher number of single immigrant women (34 percent), in tandem with their relatively smaller family sizes, signals a major historical shift in the profile of immigrant women.

## Cultures, Structures, and Change

The interplay between global events and changes (contexts of exit) and the evolving culture and policy arena of the United States (contexts of reception) is reflected in the various demographic representations that census figures reveal and in the historical vignettes that we have reviewed. If we can extrapolate some general observations regarding immigrant women's contributions from this review, they would include the cultural and professional contributions of the leaders profiled here and the filling of job-market needs that span agriculture, manufacturing, and service. While women's options were constrained by immigration policies that restricted certain ethnic and racial groups and narrowly prescribed women's place in society, it is also the case that immigrant women have helped transform such practices and have benefited from new opportunities that changing institutions and cultural attitudes have made possible.

Among the features that immigrant women share with men is that they immigrate through both regular and irregular means—through official channels and through unofficial channels, forced and unforced. Within these two distinct routes of immigrating, however, there are specific gendered complexities that make the process different for women. We take a more detailed look at immigrant women's uses of these contrasting avenues in the next two chapters.

## II

## How They Come

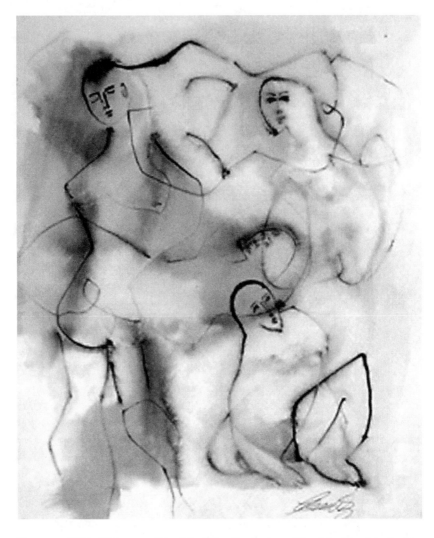

Figure 3.1. "Live 1," ink on cardboard, by Lilian Fernandez, a Miami-based artist who is profiled in chapter 8. One reading of this piece is that it captures the feelings of family unity and disunity that result in border crossings.

# 3

# "I Had to Start Over"

*Entering through the Front Door*

In 1970, *Anica* and her family left Romania, fleeing the persecution they experienced there as Jews. After spending a few months in Vienna, they arrived in the United States, settling in Baltimore. On a stopover in New York City, *Anica* saw the Statue of Liberty, which, she said,

> is the symbol of hope for every soul that can breathe behind the Iron Curtain. . . . It stands for freedom; you can go anywhere you want. It stands for opportunity; if you want to work, you might have to work like a dog, but you have the chance. . . . It stands for a dream. We flew over, and at some point my mother said, "Here is the Statue." . . . We were free.

When many Americans complain about undocumented immigration, the common refrain is, "They should have come here legally!" Yet that is often expressed with little awareness about how immigrants can come to this country legally, or through the "front door." In this chapter, we explore the stories of women coming to this country as "legal" immigrants. How do they come here? What are their experiences here? And how do American immigration policies facilitate—and sometimes inhibit—their aspirations? Before turning to the women's stories, however, we discuss some of the background that provides the context for their experiences.

Following a history of immigration policies that favored men of certain races and nationalities, U.S. laws now reflect broader principles and concerns. These concerns are shared by other industrialized countries and have become "orthodox." As Nicola Piper notes, "Industrialized countries in Europe, North America, and Oceania . . . admit permanent residents on the basis of three long-established principles: family reunification, economic considerations, and humanitarian concerns."[1] In keeping with these principles, there are three main avenues to legal immigration to the United States:

family sponsorship, employment sponsorship (economic considerations), and refugee/asylee immigration (humanitarian concerns).

Two less common routes are the diversity lottery, which allows potential immigrants from less-common sending countries to compete for coveted visas, and "nonimmigrant visas." Although it may seem odd to list "nonimmigrant visas" as a route to immigration, these can provide initial entrée for those who later adjust their status to a permanent one. For example, someone in the United States on an education visa may graduate and secure sponsorship from an employer, thus becoming a permanent resident. We use the metaphor of "front doors" to refer to these legal routes into the country.

The rates at which people use these various "front door" visas vary tremendously. Looking at 2008 data, we find that the most common legal route to immigration to the United States is to be sponsored by a family member already here: 66 percent of immigrants were sponsored by a relative. The rates of employment sponsorship and refugee/asylee immigration are roughly the same, with 15 percent of visas granted to each group. The diversity lottery, a mechanism that gives preference to immigrants coming from countries that do not already send large numbers of immigrants to the United States, is the fourth-largest category, with 4 percent of immigrants entering that way.[2]

None of these categories is a specifically gendered category. Men and women both can, and do, avail themselves of each of these categories, and the employment and refugee/asylee categories are very evenly balanced with regard to gender. Women and girls are, however, more prominent in the family-related sponsorship categories: in 2008, 58 percent of this type of immigration was female. The diversity category was least heavily female, with only 43 percent of those visas going to women and girls.[3]

## The Women's Stories

*Betty* grew up in Hong Kong, in a family of refugees from mainland China. When she was a young teenager, her cousin moved to the United States. This gave *Betty* an idea. She decided that she, too, would one day immigrate. At the same time, she was a student at a Lutheran school staffed by American missionaries, who also encouraged her dreams. Throughout high school, she worked hard, saved money, and researched American colleges and universities, seeing that as her ticket out of Hong Kong and to America. She completed high school and came to the United States with a university scholarship. Although she was shocked that the actual campus was not as beautiful as in the brochures, she immediately knew she wanted to stay here. "I felt very at home, very welcomed," she explained.

FIGURE 3.2
*Gender breakdown of immigration categories, 2008*

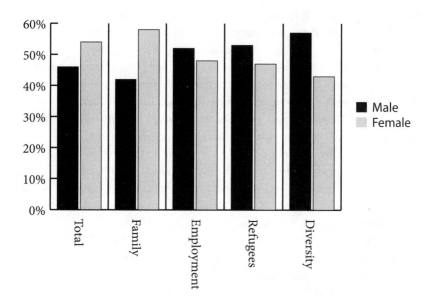

FIGURE 3.3
*Major immigrant categories, 2008*

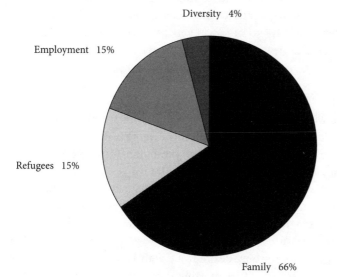

*Anica, Betty, Rosalinda, Xia-Hwa,* and *Zareen* are all women we interviewed about their experiences immigrating to this country. They, and the others we discuss in this chapter, all came in through the front door, that is, "legally." How did they come here, what were their experiences once here, and how were those journeys shaped by American immigration policies?

In the past, immigrant women were portrayed as passive, particularly with respect to family-sponsored immigration, presuming that men make the decisions regarding immigration and brought or sent for wives, mothers, or daughters. However, when we listen to the words of immigrants who have been through family- or employment-based immigration or who have come here as refugees or students, it is clear that women are agents in this process, making decisions, facilitating other family members' immigration, and being sponsors themselves. Indeed, *Betty* came despite initial opposition from her father, and other women also defied both the odds and their relatives to immigrate. Thus, it is important in examining immigration to consider women as sponsors as well as those who are being sponsored and to recognize immigrant women's agency: they are not passive participants in this process.

In examining the stories of these women who have entered the country through the front door, whether it is through family- or employment-based immigration, as refugees, or as students, we see how much overlap there is among these categories. *Betty* initially came here as a student but later regularized her status through employment, and her experience of moving through more than one official status is not unique. In addition, although we generally treat the categories of "documented/legal" and "undocumented/illegal" as distinct, many women's experiences involve serial moves between these statuses. The experiences of the women interviewed display a complex and multilayered picture.

## Reasons/Motivations for Immigrating

How did the women come to the United States? First, there had to be a motivation, particularly in cases in which there were great obstacles to their immigration. The motivations and obstacles combine to make up the "context of exit" they experienced, and those contexts were varied among the women we interviewed. When immigrant women spoke to us of their reasons for coming to the United States, they spoke of seeking opportunities, both educational and economic. Refugee women specifically focused on political freedom, and, for many women, family was a decisive factor. For some women of the latter group, desire to be with family was a pull to the United States, with marriage either drawing them here initially or, at times, allowing them to stay in the country after they entered through other means. However, for a few women, family problems, such as divorce or the death of a family member, served more as a push to leave their home country.

## Educational Opportunity

> Even if you go back after your education, it is looked up to, that you got an American college degree.
>
> —*Natalia*, Colombia

*Natalia* was a top student at her private school in Colombia. She also did very well on her standardized American college entrance tests and so received a full scholarship to a small liberal arts college in Florida. She felt that it was just assumed that the top students would go to college in the United States and that an American university degree carried with it a certain amount of prestige. Her parents approved of her decision to attend college in the United States, even though they realized very early on that she would want to stay in the United States after graduation. "I knew I wanted to stay, from the start. They had a pretty clear idea of that after my first semester." Likewise, Shana Castro, from Brazil, had parents who were supportive of her studies in the United States, and she describes coming to the States to study as her "family's dream." Although Shana was studying in the States at the time of our interview with her, she had originally entered the country on a visa to work as a nanny. For her, although education was the main reason for her immigration, it was not the vehicle that allowed her entry to the country. Instead, she had to work in a field through which she could gain legal entry, and only later was she able to pursue her educational goals.

*Xia-Hwa*, however, had to work very hard to convince her parents that she could travel halfway around the globe from her home in Taiwan to attend college in Oregon. Coming from a culture in which, according to her description, girls are unwanted, she was grateful to her grandmother for planting the seed in her head at an early age that she could indeed achieve as a girl. She remembered telling her father of her plans to study overseas:

> And so I had a talk with my dad, right before the finals, like, "I would like to go study abroad." He said, "You know we can't afford that." I said, "Well, if I can find a way for support, would that be OK?" And he said something like, "Yeah, you can try." And later on he admitted to me that he thought I would just try it and come back. And I'm sure—he thought I would get married.

Although men who plan to come to the United States for their studies may also need to convince reluctant parents, in cases such as *Xia-Hwa's*, parental reluctance was clearly tied to gender. Her father expected her to get married and, if she worked at all, to work as a hotel receptionist or flight attendant. Given these very traditionally gendered plans, he felt that higher education, particularly in a foreign country, would be a waste.

Some of those who came to the United States for educational opportunity did so for graduate school, as did *Dama*, who came here from India. In *Dama's* case, her engineer father, who had studied in the United States in the 1940s, encouraged her sister and her to pursue graduate studies in engineering in the United States.

In a 2002 research report on immigration in Baltimore, Maryland, Bruce Morrison suggested that if the city wanted to draw more immigrants, it should focus on, among other things, encouraging area colleges and universities to attract more foreign students. Morrison argued that not only are such foreign students, if given the chance, likely to stay in the country (and, perhaps, the city where they were educated), but also they would be exactly the type of immigrants from which the city could benefit greatly: highly educated and readily employable.[4] The experiences of the women we interviewed suggest that many foreign students do indeed stay in the United States. As we have seen, some of these women came, as Morrison envisioned, for college or graduate school. We also interviewed women who studied in the United States while in high school or who came after graduating from college to attend language institutes to improve their English.

Learning English was a central reason for other women's migration. *Teresa* and *Rosalinda* both came here after completing university.[5] Both women initially came here on tourist visas. When *Teresa* came from Argentina, she initially intended to stay with her sister in Chicago for just one month. However, she fell in love with the city and got her visa changed to a student visa so that she could stay longer to study English. *Rosalinda* traveled to California from Colombia and took English classes there. In California, staying with family friends, she felt that because she was surrounded by people speaking Spanish, she was not making progress. She then decided to move to live with a cousin in Seattle, where most of the students in her English classes were Asian. She felt this was a better learning experience, as she had no choice but to use her English to converse with her classmates. Both women transitioned from education visas to employment visas, and *Teresa* later gained her permanent residency through marriage to an American.

## Economic Opportunity

Education was not the only type of opportunity these women sought in the United States. Some women, and their families, came seeking economic opportunity, perceiving that they would have more ability to earn money and be socially mobile here. *Celia* noted that, in her native Panama, she was working as a teacher, making only ninety dollars per month. And *Victoria*, who came as a young woman with her parents from Argentina, noted, "We had some relatives, and they were insisting we come, because we'd have a better life here. So my parents decided to come."

In other women's experiences, this type of opportunity was tied to a specific job, as when *Ella* left Guatemala to work as a nanny for an American family, or when *Deborah*'s mother came on an employment visa from Zambia as an attorney, with specific specialties in demand here. Liliana Petrova initially came to the United States from Bulgaria as a college student on a temporary (J1) employment visa and was placed in Atlantic City, New Jersey, making saltwater taffy. She was sent to live in a "dirty house with horrendous conditions. There was a leather couch covered with cuts." She said, "We're legal here, and we're treated like we're illegal." She was not allowed to sit while making the taffy, and she earned five-fifty per hour after taxes. She was supposed to use this money to pay back the two-thousand-dollar plane ticket that was a condition of the job, but she could not figure out how she would do so in only three months. She complained to the owner, but she was threatened with deportation. Liliana took the situation into her own hands and put together a work schedule that involved three shifts a day in order to make ends meet. She decided to apply for an educational visa and finish college in the United States—a path that carried its own struggles, as she worked at a bar to pay for her degree. These are cases in which the women entered the country initially on an employment-related visa, sponsored by their employers. In many other cases, women who initially came to pursue their education were able to stay due to sponsorship by an employer. Therefore, even when employment was not key to the reasons behind a woman's initially coming here, it was indeed key to her staying here. However, as discussed later in this chapter, making that transition, for example, from student to employment visa, is not always easy.

## Political Freedom

Women who came to this country as refugees[6] were drawn to the United States by the promise of freedom—both in general and specifically as women. *Anica* is an example of a woman who was seeking freedom in general, not connected to her gender. In 1970, *Anica* and her mother escaped Communist Romania, arriving in Baltimore. As Jews, they suffered from the lack of both economic and religious freedom living behind the Iron Curtain. As a young woman at the time, *Anica* did not specify feeling any restraints on her life specifically as a woman but more generally as a person living in a totalitarian regime.

For other refugees, however, gender was central to the freedom they sought in the United States. Both Nadia and *Zareen* were initially excited about the Iranian Revolution of 1979. Both had been living abroad, in the United States and Italy, respectively, for a year or more prior to the revolution, and both returned to Iran in order to be involved. *Zareen* noted, however, that gradually her hope and optimism that the revolution would be a positive force dissipated. She said the changes were gradual, but one year, ironically on International Women's Day, the new government started to attack women and construct more "antiwoman" policies. As she made clear in her description of her state of mind at the time, the status attached to gender was absolutely central to the oppression she felt in Iran at the time:

> I felt paralyzed. I couldn't work, do my job. I couldn't express myself artistically. I couldn't be a woman, you know, just a woman, you know. "Cover yourself." . . . I lost all rights, even rights I had during the Shah's time. When I say "I," I'm talking about the whole—women. As a woman it was unbearable, and the violence was extremely high. It was a dark time. And, as it says in the poem, "indeed we live in dark ages." And I always remember that at that time of my life.

Although *Zareen* managed to avoid arrest, the government shut down the women's magazine she coedited, as well as the women's organization with which she worked. She shared her memory of watching most of her friends get arrested and depicted the experience of living and working "underground" as a way to stay safe.

*Nadia* was not as lucky; like *Zareen's* friends, she was jailed for her political activism. "I was jailed in Iran for one year. After that I felt it was not a safe place for me and my children." Having been separated from her children, then aged two and eleven, while in jail, she knew that upon her release from prison she would have to get out of the country. As discussed later in this chapter, in the section on the process of immigrating, refugees were among those women who faced the most harrowing and treacherous journeys to their new country.

Familial Motivations

Family-sponsored immigrants are by far the majority of immigrants, and family reunification is also the category that is the most female. So it is not surprising that families figured prominently in these women's accounts of their immigration. Although family members had long had preference in U.S. immigration policy, the 1948 War Brides Act was a major step toward today's strong emphasis on family-sponsorship immigration. Two women in this book fit this model, and several others immigrated after marrying American men abroad. Some women married after they immigrated, some were out of status (without papers) when they met and married their husbands, and others came with or to join other family members: parents, siblings, and the like. In addition, family-related issues sometimes figured into women's stories about why they came to the United States, as in cases in which family problems were a push for the women to leave their home country.

*Johanna* met and married her American husband while he was stationed with the U.S. Army in Germany, and *Celia* met hers more than forty years ago while he was stationed in the Canal Zone in Panama. *Paula,* mentioned earlier, met her husband when she returned to the United States to visit friends from her time as an exchange student in Idaho. After they met, she returned to Colombia to finish her degree, and she and her boyfriend dated long-distance. She was able to do an internship in California while an undergraduate at university in Colombia. During this internship, she and her boyfriend lived together and got engaged. She had to leave California, however, in order to return to Colombia to complete her degree. Today, when she reflects on her rationale behind immigrating permanently, she said, "We just sort of found out that the only way for us to be together was for me to move here. So that was part of the drive."

Marriage to an American man, for these women, was not simply a pathway to the United States. Some of the women found it a means by which to gain, or regain, legal status. *Deborah* immigrated to this country from Zambia as a college student accompanying her mother. Her mother later returned to Zambia, and when *Deborah* ceased attending school, she fell out of status. She was out of status when she met, dated, and married her husband, a U.S. citizen. He later sponsored her so that she could regularize her status. *Sonya,* likewise, was out of status when she met and married her American husband. *Sonya's* immigration was initially for medical reasons. She obtained a special visa to receive specialized obstetric medical care unavailable in her home country of Jamaica. An oversight after the baby was born caused her status to lapse. Like *Deborah,* she also lived for many years as an undocumented immigrant prior to meeting and marrying her husband.

Though it was marriage to Americans that allowed *Deborah* and *Sonya* to regularize their status, they were both very concerned about not wanting their husbands to think that this was the reason for marrying them. In fact, *Deborah* laughingly noted that if she had wanted to marry solely for immigration purposes, she could have married a gay male friend. In both these cases, the women had migrated prior to meeting their future husbands, for reasons having nothing to do with family reunification: education and medical treatment. Neither woman ever intended to be an undocumented immigrant. Both were very concerned that they not be seen as taking advantage of their husbands for immigration purposes. This is one example of how the categories "legal" (or "documented") and "illegal" (or "undocumented") are not as clear-cut as political rhetoric would lead one to believe. Rather than being two completely separate groups of immigrants, many woman move between these two categories throughout their time in the United States.

Marriage is probably the most publicly visible family-based reason for immigration. We found that divorce or loss of a family member could also be the impetus to leave the old country. *Linda* came to the United States from Guatemala in 1980 with her then eight-year-old daughter. In her description of why she came, she highlighted hardships she experienced after divorce from her husband:

> Yes, it was not an economic problem, because my parents, my ex-husband, had a lot of money. But I came here for emotional reasons. I finished everything. I was very depressed, with the problems I had with my husband, and I divorced him. I didn't want to know nothing more about him and his family. So I thought, I have a cousin here, in California, so I thought I was going to change, you know, the environment, change country. . . . So I thought it was good to have a change.

Some women immigrated to escape abusive husbands or to get away from the stigma that divorce carries in certain countries. However, in *Linda*'s case, she did not mention either situation. Instead, she seemed to find immigration a way out of a postdivorce malaise. *Beatriz* also sought a change of scenery to help her cope with familial loss. Her mother had already passed away, and she was very much affected by the subsequent death of her father. In her case, a doctor in her native El Salvador suggested immigration to the United States. "Well . . . my father died. I was very upset. I didn't feel well. The doctor asked me to come here for a while, to feel better. . . . I decide what I want to do, the doctor suggest to me to come, to change, and so [that's] why I come." These are clearly family-related reasons, but not in the way we traditionally think of immigration and family reunification. In addition, just as many immigrant women are sponsored through family-based policies, so do many immigrant women use these policies to sponsor relatives, again demonstrating their agency. Both these processes, however, are largely embedded in the norms of the society; when women want to do it for themselves, they may be defying cultural expectations, and thus agency becomes more important.

## Process of Immigrating

While the preceding discussion has separately looked at women who migrated for educational, work-related, and familial reasons, that discussion has made clear that some of the same women immigrated for more than one of these reasons. Thus, it is challenging to sort women narrowly into these three categories. A woman might come to the United States initially as a tourist, become a student, get hired and move to an employment visa, and then gain permanent residency through marriage, as was the case with *Teresa.* Or she might come in as a student and move to a temporary employment visa, as did *Natalia,* or gain permanent residency through work, as did *Dama,* who subsequently became a naturalized citizen.

When asked about whether the process of converting from a student visa to permanent residency was complicated, *Dama* said that it was not. Some of the women described a fairly easy process of getting the proper visas. Both *Celia* and *Johanna,* the military wives, explained that the army handled the paperwork for them. And even though *Linda* was an undocumented immigrant from Guatemala when she got married, when she was asked about the process of getting her green card after getting married, she said, "No, it was not hard; it was easy." She noted, however, "It was more than twenty years ago, so it was not as hard." *Paula* also described a time-consuming but relatively smooth process: "So we talked to a lawyer. . . . He told us, 'Here's what you need to do. Here's the first form that you need to fill out.' So we filled that out, we sent it in, and then I went back [to Colombia]. And then the rest of the paperwork he did when he was here." Once her husband processed paperwork here, the INS sent it to the embassy in Colombia, where she was given a list of what she needed to do. "I remember I needed to get some vaccines, health tests. I did that in Bogotá. And then you go to the embassy, and they go through all your papers."

Some of the women, however, recounted a more problematic process. A few of the women immigrated to work as nannies or housekeepers. In those cases, their employers sponsored them, and their residence in this country was contingent on them continuing to work for the same employers. That went fine when, as in the case of *Gwendolyn* from Trinidad and Tobago, the employers treated them well. However, when some of the women wanted to change employers, they faced the prospect of either falling out of status or having to return home. *Linda* was working as a housekeeper on a special visa that diplomats could get for servants. However, the visa tied her to those employers. When she later tried to get permanent residency, she was hampered by the fact that her diplomat employers had not paid Social Security taxes on her wages. "I waited for four years for my green card, make a lot of papers, . . . pay them a lot of money, because Immigration say I never pay income taxes."

As noted earlier, many women transitioned between student and employment visas. Some of the women described a relatively smooth process. However, *Betty,* who came to the United States from China to study engineering, conveyed some of the obstacles this process can entail.

> The company, they would not hire you unless you had the permanent visa, and you can't get one without employment. So it's like the chicken and egg. But I was still going along with interviews, because I had really good grades by then. . . . Actually, I graduated first of the class. . . . . And at that time there was such a strong feeling that I would love to just continue for a Ph.D., but then there's another part of me that's like, "No, I should really get a job, secure my residency." So every opportunity I get, trying to look for employment.

She signed up for an interview with one company. Having lived in Hong Kong, she has an English first name, and she said that she thought that led these particular interviewers to think she was American. She got the interview and describes being very lucky:

> They were really pleased with me, and they were looking for a woman engineer—and of course it's double minority. And during the interview day, I asked them, I said, "Just so that you know, I do have a lawyer working on my residency, and that would be OK with you, right?" And they said, "Oh, we shouldn't even have allowed you to come in." But then they decided they would offer me a job on the contingency that I would get the visa. That's all it takes is someone willing to—so that's how I got my green card.

She and many of the other women were able to solve this "chicken and egg" issue, getting offers for jobs as engineers, piano teachers, or lawyers from employers willing to go through the paperwork necessary. Unfortunately, this is a hurdle that many women are unable to overcome.

Liliana, the Bulgarian woman discussed earlier, after finishing her bachelor's degree, found a position in financial planning for an energy company in New York. The company applied for her employment visa for her, but Liliana felt limited by the constraints on her visa. After moving to a bank position, she recalled, "I kept pushing: 'I want my green card.' That opens doors for loans, pretty much everything else. My new company will reimburse me for my master's." Liliana is an ambitious self-starter, juggling her studies toward an MBA degree at New York University with her banking position. She felt that she would be able to pursue more options and undertake more challenges as a lawful permanent resident.

Women also struggled with navigating the immigration system when they were the sponsors of, rather than being sponsored by, relatives, particularly children. These were often the most emotional portions of our interviews. These women initially immigrated alone, generally to work as domestic workers, enduring long waits before finally reuniting with their children. During this time, their children were in the care of other relatives, and the women pressed on, knowing that the income they were able to send home was crucial to improving their children's lives. Despite this material benefit, these mothers missed their children terribly and worried about them. *Ella*, from Guatemala, described crying herself to sleep at night, due to missing her children. When asked how many children she had at the time of separation, *Ella* answered, "Three. . . . This time my son was very young, my littlest was two, and the other two . . ." At that point, her voice died out before listing their ages. Upon being asked if it was a trying time, she answered, "Yeah, it's very, very, very—I cry all night, all night."

*Gwendolyn*, from Trinidad and Tobago, had a much smoother time both being separated from and then reuniting with her children. As she relayed the reunification experience, "I did two [children] in the first two years. The other two [children] I did the next year. Within three years, I had all four here. . . . I decided to take the older ones first, because I think they needed to be with me more than the younger ones. They were teenagers, and they were supposed to be [with me]." She described the transition to living together again as quite smooth, noting that such transitions are harder in cases in which the separations are longer. As she noted, "We missed each other a lot, but they were looking forward to joining me and each other."

These are examples of immigrant women who were very active in the family-reunification process. Clearly, when women sponsor relatives, they are significant players in the family's migration process, actively pursuing the means at their disposal either to stay together or to rejoin family members who have been separated due to immigration. Women made use of a combination of family-, employment-, and education-based policies, making it difficult to think of these categories as completely distinct subgroups of immigrants. However, it is much easier to think of refugees/asylees as a clearly separate category. Unlike other immigrants, for refugees/asylees getting *out* of the home country may have been trickier than getting *into* the United States, and there can be an extended time spent in a third (or fourth) country en route.

*Nadia,* a refugee from Iran, endured much to leave Iran, including temporary separation from her children. Unable to travel to the United States directly from Iran, she first had to go to another country. "I went to Turkey— I *walked* to Turkey!" This was a considerable distance from where she was in Iran and covered often hostile terrain. She had to pay smugglers to help her escape, and men routinely took advantage of the women refugees in their care.

> It wasn't good that much, especially the guy wants to have sex with me, . . . which they do with women in a bad situation that they are in. . . . I said no, because he said that "I want to marry with you." And I said, "OK, as long as I go to Istanbul, then you can come." . . . And I keep walking in villages. And I said, "If you come over there [Istanbul], then we can decide what to do"—which he came, and [once in Istanbul] I said I would go to the police "for what you did with lots of young women. I'm sure all of you did"—and they didn't know what to do . . . When I was in Istanbul, he came over there, but Istanbul was a different situation!

Legal scholar Chaloka Beyani makes clear that experiences such as *Nadia's* are far from unique among refugee women: "Refugee women are often faced with specific abuses from which they need protection. The most pervasive and widespread are rape, sexual abuse, sexual extortion, and physical insecurity during flight and in places of refuge."[7] Once settled in Istanbul, *Nadia* felt safe enough to threaten her smuggler with police involvement, and he left her alone. Despite feeling relatively safer in Turkey, *Nadia* still did not feel entirely secure, as she claimed that the Turkish government cooperated with the Iranian government and sometimes sent back political activists.

During her year and a half in Turkey, she did her best to help other Iranian women, foreshadowing her later work in a domestic-violence shelter in the United States.

> I started to make a shelter, without knowing that was what I was doing. Because I saw a couple of Iranian women that they don't have a place, they don't have money. . . . So one of my friends over there gave me his apartment. . . . He said that I could have this apartment for more than a couple of months. I just told a couple of Iranian women that didn't have money that they could come stay with me. . . . So for that time they were in Turkey, at least they had some safe place that they didn't need to pay money and stay with me. . . . As long as I was in Turkey I tried to help other women. . . . Most of them had a political problem, just like me. And I thought that's a situation that I can do something for them.

She then had to go from Turkey to Italy to find out if she could get refugee status to go to the United States. Because the situation in Iran was well known throughout the world, she was able to prove she had been imprisoned in Iran, and she was able to show that she would, indeed, be in danger were she to return to Iran. She therefore gained entry into the United States as a refugee.

*Svetlana,* who migrated here with her husband and children from the Soviet Union, had a challenging time moving from asylum seeker to asylee. Upon arriving here, she and her family submitted their application for asylum. *Svetlana* said it was an emotional thing to do, because "it is very hard to write it down—at the moment you want to forget." However, the family did submit the application. It was 1991, which turned out to be a problematic time to apply for asylum.

> [During the Soviet era] the Americans wanted to put pressure on the Soviet Union and used immigration as a trump card. Then it changed just like this, and no one really cares, because we are not needed [for foreign policy]. One year before, people got citizenship. The U.S. just declared through its policy that Russia was now safe and democratic.

*Svetlana* and her husband were scholars. In addition to tutoring students in English, they also had been involved in translating banned books from English into Russian. These banned books would be passed around surreptitiously. "People would read it and pass it on. If they catch you passing it, you would get ten years in jail." Initially, it seemed as if *Svetlana*'s family would be successful in its bid for asylum. Despite the fact that the interviewer knew little about the USSR, after *Svetlana* and her husband explained their tenuous position in their home country, the interviewer agreed to process the applications. The initial interviewer seemed convinced and led the couple to believe that their application was successful. "She took to our daughter. A few months later we received a book about Christmas for our daughter and a note: 'Welcome to America.'" Unfortunately, this kind interviewer was not the person who ultimately got to decide their fate, and the family had to wait about a year to learn the outcome. To their surprise, the decision was not what the family expected. "Finally . . . we heard. . . . They said, 'We will start deportation proceedings.'" Eventually, *Svetlana*'s family successfully challenged this decision. *Svetlana* attributes their success to endorsements from many people in their town.

> We won the case; we had community support. By that time so many people knew me. I gave talks in camps and schools, etcetera, about Russian fairy tales and women in the Soviet Union. Somebody said, "Get a petition." I didn't realize this American thing [of a petition]. More than three hundred people signed the petition. The judge was from the . . . area [the area of the state they live in]. I think he saw how we had contributed to the community.

So, although *Svetlana* and her husband were successful in their quest for asylum and now are citizens of the United States, they had to overcome certain bureaucratic obstacles in their path to do so, obstacles that were subject to the winds of international political change. The story illustrates how an immigrant's legal status is not so much "owned" at a personal level as it is a mechanism of political and legal structures that are manipulated in distant offices with opaque and transitory rules. *Svetlana* is now a Ph.D. student at a university, planning a career in academia.

### Experiences as Immigrants

Clearly, the women's journeys here followed diverse paths. When we next ask the question "What were their experiences here?" we see a similar diversity in their "contexts of reception." In 1966, Everett Lee wrote of women immigrants with verbiage that more accurately reflected the world of forty years ago: "wives accompany their husbands, though it tears them away from environments they love."[8] Some of the women with whom we spoke did, indeed, accompany husbands. However, none of them displayed the sort of passivity implied in Lee's statement. *Nadia* particularly exercised tremendous personal agency not only to get herself safely out of Iran but also to help other women in her situation. An important insight that arises from examining the women's descriptions of their immigration process is that these women were active, not passive. They exercised agency in the face of a legal and bureaucratic structure that seemingly is set up to make their task of immigrating as complex as possible. We see this agency, as well, again and again in the women's descriptions of their experiences as immigrants. There are clearly many similarities between their experiences and those of male immigrants. But the women themselves highlighted the centrality of their gender, particularly when describing their positive experiences in this country. While the women enumerated difficulties related to discrimination and status dislocation, many also felt that they were able to experience a great deal of personal growth due to their immigration.

## Discrimination Faced as Immigrants

> Every day I feel that I'm refugee—or foreigner. Every day, with looks, with everything, I feel that.
>
> —*Nadia*, Iran

> I've had people dismiss me because I have an accent and make assumptions about me.
>
> —*Victoria*, Argentina

The women we interviewed frequently recounted experiences of discrimination. Sometimes the experiences were concrete actions, such as when *Xia-Hwa*, a Taiwanese woman who speaks English with almost no detectable foreign accent, arrived to see an apartment for rent. When the landlady saw that she was Asian, *Xia-Hwa* was told that the apartment had already been rented. But often, the discrimination is less concrete: the experience of being ignored or seen as less intelligent because of a foreign accent or of seeing darker people such as oneself portrayed only as terrorists on television. *Nadia* particularly pointed to the effects of 9/11: "I didn't like it. And I want everyone to know, yeah, I'm Iranian woman, I'm in this country, this is me! But even that was so hard to all the time want to show yourself that this is my—I'm proud of myself, I'm good, I'm here." Communities of immigrants across the United States felt the need to retreat from public visibility after 9/11.

In addition to the specific effects of the 9/11 attacks, many of the women traced such discrimination to their status as immigrants, though, as with *Xia-Hwa's* experience with the potential landlady, it seems that race was also a decisive factor. It can be difficult for immigrant women of color to determine whether discrimination is on account of race or nativity or is a combination of both. *Teresa,* a slim, fair-skinned, blonde woman from Argentina, could more easily single out her immigrant status as the source of difficulty. Initially, she said she had not experienced any barriers at all, noting that perhaps the absence of discrimination was because of the color of her skin (i.e., being white). She did, however, follow up, noting that there had been a slight disadvantage in that before she knew English well, people doubted her intelligence.

Some women were quite surprised at the centrality of race in the United States. *Josselyn,* from Ecuador, noted that she had been sheltered from thinking about race prior to arriving in the United States. While a college student in New Hampshire, a friend warned her, "Be careful: you're dark, not Anglo." She reflected on this comment in the interview: "I didn't know race was an issue in this country! I was raised very sheltered. Maybe it was a blessing, because I didn't feel different than anybody else. But I was perceived as different: I was the only girl with black hair." Despite this assessment, however, she generally described her time here as positive and did not recount any specific instances of being discriminated against.

### Status Dislocation

> It's kind of a shock; when you finish your education, you think you're going to go into this professional environment.
> —*Paula*, Colombia

> I felt as if I had to start over. I felt my experience was not valued.
> —*Shanice,* Trinidad and Tobago

Immigrants commonly experience status dislocation, or the lowering of their occupational and/or class status, purely on the basis of discrimination: an employer who will not hire them for the positions they are capable of filling due to prejudice. At other times, however, status dislocation can occur based on language difficulties or problems having one's credentials recognized in the new country. *Paula* had just finished a degree in international business in Colombia when she moved to California to be with her American husband. At the time, the only work she could find was in a flower shop, working in the back in cold conditions and on her feet all the time. *Shanice*, from Trinidad, was a UK-certified accountant, but those credentials were not recognized in the United States. It was not until she found work with a Filipino boss who was familiar with British credentials that she felt her work was valued. *Zareen* was from a wealthy family in Iran, and upon arriving in Iowa, the only work she could find was as a babysitter. She said that this was a humbling experience, as it made her realize how hard her family's servants had worked for years, without her truly appreciating what they did:

> The best advantage that I got: my very, very rich experiences. I became a good human being. I know I am a very good human being. I read a good quote by Buddha. Buddha said, "Life is suffering, aging is suffering." He has a long line full of "this is suffering," etcetera, but that what you get from that is it makes you be a good human being."

## Personal Growth

As *Zareen*'s words suggest, by no means did the women have universally negative accounts of their experiences as immigrants. For many of the women, their experiences in the United States brought about tremendous personal growth. *Zareen* noted that her work as a babysitter when she initially arrived in the United States expanded her world. While she is now a successful playwright, she felt that the hard times she had to go through were ultimately useful. Similarly, *Natalia*, who came to the United States from Colombia for college education, felt that she was exposed to people and experiences she would not have been if she had stayed at home:

> The society where I grew up in—obviously my parents are well-off. And I grew up in this sort of bubble, very sheltered, and I only interacted with a certain type of people. And coming here, especially coming to [a public college in Florida], . . . I met people with all sorts of backgrounds, which I hadn't had a chance to do back home. So it was super eye-opening for me. It was amazing. I was like, "Wow!"

Other women felt that growth had occurred through increased independence. *Gwendolyn*, from Trinidad, said that at home, she had relied very heavily on her husband. Having divorced him and immigrated here, she said that she had to deal with things on her own and not rely on a man. Through this experience, she became a stronger person.

Women who are mothers felt that, though they themselves had to suffer much, the success of their children made it all worth it. *Ella,* who came to the United States from Guatemala to work as a nanny, initially left her children behind. She recounted a great deal of difficulty with missing her children, until she was able to send for them. As she pulled out her son's business card, *Ella* glowed with pride, dabbing at her eyes as she spoke:

> Well, the truth is I suffered a lot. It was very difficult, but I think it was worth it. But if I had another opportunity to do it again, I would do it again, because it is worth the sacrifice to get your children ahead. And I am very happy because my son has now two professions, as a lawyer and accountant, and my other daughter is also an accountant, and my youngest daughter, Sophia, just graduated from the best university in New York, which is Columbia University. And she continues to study to get her master's. Well, this is what makes me happy, because it was worth it, to make a sacrifice to come here and fight and work hard—'cause you do work hard here.

## The Policies

These women's experiences need to be understood in the context of the policies that governed how and whether they would be able to immigrate. In the case of immigrant women, immigration policies are crucial to understanding the structure that shapes their lives. At times the policies facilitate their actions, as when someone is able to immigrate because she "fits" the criteria for a policy, whereas at other times policies take the shape of obstacles that make women's chosen paths more difficult. In this section, we consider policies related to family-sponsored and employment-based immigration, as well as refugee/asylee policies, and examine them through the lens of gender.

*Gwendolyn* immigrated to the United States as a young Trinidadian woman decades ago. She came to work as a nanny and was sponsored by her employers. Although this is a profession rife with exploitation, *Gwendolyn* remembered having been treated quite well by the employers and was clearly devoted to the children in her care. In fact, during her interview, she showed us pictures of the family's children over the years and was proud to note that, even as young adults now, they continue to visit her and keep in touch. Clearly, *Gwendolyn's* bond with them is strong, as she was their nanny through almost their entire childhoods. Now in her sixties, she no longer works as a nanny, though she does offer day care for a few children at a time in her tidy row home in northeast Baltimore.

The irony in *Gwendolyn*'s situation is one common to many immigrant women in domestic work, particularly in child care. When *Gwendolyn* left Trinidad to take care of an American family's children, her own children remained in Trinidad with *her* parents. As she and other women describe it, in order to provide for her children, she had to leave them, travel hundreds of miles away, and take care of other people's children. However, *Gwendolyn*'s story had a happy ending, due to family-reunification immigration policies. Within two years, she had sent for her oldest two children, and the following year the other two joined her. She feels luckier than many other immigrants, because she was able to bring all four of her children to the United States within three years of her arrival. She went on to raise them very successfully and bragged about their educational and professional accomplishments. *Gwendolyn*'s experience thus involved both employment- and family-based immigration.

Because family-sponsored immigration is the most common, as well as the most heavily female, method of immigration, we first look at the policies related to it. Next, we explore employment-based immigration policies, and then those relating to refugees/asylees. For each type of immigration, we examine what the current policies are, how they came to be, and in what ways they are gendered. We conclude with discussion of possible directions for such immigration policies.

### Family-Sponsored Immigration

Policies that favor family members for immigration are meant to allow these individuals to live together in the same country and to minimize the separations immigrant families must endure. *Gwendolyn*'s experience of having an easy time sponsoring her daughters bears out this intention. On the other hand, her experience with sponsoring her brother was very different. *Gwendolyn* worked hard to attain her citizenship, with the intention of being able to sponsor additional family members, which immigrants with lawful permanent resident status cannot do. Immediately upon gaining citizenship, she petitioned to sponsor her brother. Although siblings of American citizens are among the favored categories of immigrants, *Gwendolyn*'s brother was still awaiting his approval for immigration ten years after initially applying. This story illustrates one of the more frustrating aspects of family-reunification policies: though intended to bring family members together, too often they keep them apart.

Receiving countries generally favor family members in some way in their immigration policies. Most of these policies are ostensibly gender neutral, but they have a strong impact on immigrant women *as women*. Policies meant to favor family members of citizens and immigrants can help determine whether a woman can immigrate to a country and, once there, to what extent she will be able to have family members, including children, join her. The centrality of such policies, however, can also make it very difficult for many people to immigrate, particularly to countries that prioritize family ties very highly, such as the United States.

Currently, family-sponsored immigrants represent 59 percent of the total flow of immigrants to the United States.[9] Gamze Avci notes, "family has become a new 'magnet' pulling migrants to host countries."[10] Thus, this type of immigration is key for immigrants themselves, as well as for policymakers and scholars focusing on immigration. There is reason to believe, as well, that it is particularly important for immigrant women and those studying immigration and gender.

Katharine M. Donato and Andrea Tyree argue that family-based immigration, particularly the sponsorship of spouses and parents, has contributed to a predominantly female sex distribution of immigrants to the United States.[11] This is due, they argue, to a greater likelihood of men to sponsor wives than for women to sponsor husbands, as well as a preponderance of mothers in the group of parents sponsored. In addition, Donato notes that research on Mexican-immigrant women has found that having family ties in the United States was more influential in the immigration process for women than for men.[12] It is possible that this is the case with other immigrant groups as well.

As mentioned in chapter 2, family reunification became a centerpiece of American immigration policy with the 1965 Immigration Act. From the beginning, these policies were complicated and contentious. This is partially because family-sponsored immigration policies must set forth some understanding of "family," and the definitions set forth then have an enormous impact on citizens, immigrants, and would-be immigrants. As Mark Fine argues, "There is no single correct definition of what a family is. Rather, there are multiple definitions in the literature, and these are necessarily related to the values of those who supply the definition. The choice of any particular definition is not a trivial matter, as this decision has important implications for many individuals."[13] Family-sponsored immigration policies must be understood in the context of this statement. In enacting these policies, governments make statements about what types of relatives are seen as worthy, and not worthy, of gaining entrance to their country. Although many of the women we spoke to were able to bring children here because of these policies, or were themselves sponsored as spouses of Americans, some women cannot make use of these policies because their relatives fall outside what is considered permissible. These policies spell out specific, often narrow, definitions of "family." The United Nations notes that, "at a minimum, where national provisions exist for family reunification, 'immediate relatives' of nationals are always eligible."[14] Who, however, is an "immediate relative"? Most people would agree that spouses and minor children are, and they are indeed considered as such in U.S. immigration policy. Even most American critics of family-based immigration agree that spouses and dependent children should face fewer obstacles in immigrating than others do.[15] Yet one woman we interviewed, who did not want us to mention her sexuality in relation to the rest of her story, had to remain a full-time student in order to stay in this country on a student visa, because her same-sex partner can neither marry nor sponsor her.

Minor children are one of the main family-reunification categories, and many of the women we interviewed had sponsored their children sometime after their own arrival. The assumption that children belong with their parents, particularly their mothers, is so strong that this is perhaps the most difficult type of immigration-related family separation, and some of the women teared up while recalling being far away from their children. Although Hania Zlotnik notes that there is no conclusive evidence that the children involved are harmed due to the temporary separation resulting from a parent's immigration, she also argues that "so ingrained is the view that women are the main caretakers of their children . . . that even the women themselves have doubts about migrating and are ready to accept responsibility for any negative effects on their children."[16]

The United States, unlike many other countries, differentiates between citizens and permanent residents in family-reunification policies. That is, citizens can sponsor more types of relatives, and with greater ease, than can permanent residents. For example, citizens can sponsor their parents, but lawful permanent residents cannot. Although none of the parents of the women we interviewed had come to join them here, *Dama*, after obtaining citizenship, did arrange for her father to be able to join her. He chose not to move here permanently and preferred to remain in India, however. Similarly, citizens, but not permanent residents, can sponsor adult siblings, and as mentioned earlier, as soon as *Gwendolyn* gained her citizenship, she applied for her brother to immigrate. However, quotas on this category make it a lengthy process, and she was still awaiting his approval ten years later.

So one way in which family-related immigration policies help shape the experiences of immigrant women is in determining who can and cannot be sponsored. This shapes not only whether a woman will be able to immigrate here through family sponsorship but also, once here, whether she can sponsor the loved ones she wishes to bring. More recently, however, these policies have set up another possible roadblock for women wishing to sponsor relatives. Since 1996, the United States has had stringent financial obligations for sponsors, who now must earn 125 percent of the federal poverty level. Given the gendered and racialized nature of poverty in the United States, this requirement is more likely to prevent women of all races and men of color from sponsoring relatives than to prevent white men. Philip Martin noted that in 1999 "in Juarez, Mexico, the U.S. Consul reports that a majority of applicants for immigration visas fail to show that the incomes of their U.S. sponsors exceed 125 percent of the poverty line."[17] None of the women we interviewed had tried to sponsor relatives since this change in the provisions, but a few noted that it has gotten much harder to do so in recent years.

### Employment-Based Immigration

Some people who criticize family-based immigration complain that those who come over may not have any skills or training needed for the American workplace. Because the criteria by which they enter are based on family relationships, it is not necessary to show that they have the ability to secure employment in the United States. The financial requirement was one attempt to address this situation, to prove, at least, that the immigrant is not likely to require support from the government. However, those who criticize family-based immigration frequently encourage more emphasis on employment-based immigration. If the standpoint is that only immigration that can clearly benefit the receiving nation should be encouraged, employment-related immigration is the easiest to justify. A sponsoring employer has to show that there is a shortage of Americans to fill a job, and so it is clear that the immigrant is filling a demonstrated need.

Interestingly, immigration policy has shifted greatly in relation to employment. In 1885, one of the earliest federal immigration policies had to do with contract labor. There was a widespread concern that native labor was being undermined by immigrant labor brought over by unscrupulous recruiters. At that time, having a job lined up prior to immigration could be reason to be denied entry into this country. Now, having an employer willing to sponsor you is one of the surest ways to immigrate. The 1965 Immigration Act made employment qualifications a centerpiece of U.S. immigration policy.

Probably the most well-known employment-related visa is the H1-B, which is for those working in "specialty occupations." Each year, employers in need of immigrant labor apply for these visas, and demand frequently outpaces supply. Although a few of the women we interviewed had come in through employment visas, many others who entered through other statuses later gained permanent residence through sponsorship by employers.

## Refugee/Asylee

We interviewed women who arrived here as refugees from Iran, Romania, the former Soviet Union, and Vietnam, fleeing religious persecution, political persecution, and war. Whether or not a woman gets labeled a "refugee" depends on how that term has been defined in national, and international, law. According to article 1 of the convention on refugees adopted by the United Nations High Commission on Refugees (UNHCR), a refugee is someone who, "owing to well-founded fear of being persecuted for reasons of race, religion, nationality, membership of a particular social group or political opinion, is outside the country of his nationality and is unable or, owing to such fear, is unwilling to avail himself of the protection of that country."[18] Although this definition seems fairly straightforward, what is less straightforward is what constitutes a "particular social group." Especially relevant for this book, our discussion here involves the question "Does gender count?" Although *Zareen* was fleeing multiple types of persecution in Iran, it was her work on a woman's magazine that resulted in her having been imprisoned there. Many other women face persecution *as women* and seek refugee status here as a way to escape such conditions. Yet, until fairly recently, gender-specific persecution was not considered grounds for granting refugee status. As Judith Kumin notes, "When the fathers of the 1951 Convention—all men—drew up what would become the Magna Carta of international refugee law . . . they did not deliberately omit persecution based on gender—it was not even considered."[19] Kumin argues that governments began considering women as a protected social group in the 1980s, but this became more common in the 1990s, especially when the UNHCR issued its "Guidelines on the Protection of Refugee Women."[20] Natalie Oswin notes that this document "emphasizes the fact that gender-based persecution exists and should be recognized by 'refugee-receiving' states as a basis for asylum."[21] Chaloka Beyani observes that, according to the UNHCR, "States, in their exercise of sovereignty, are free to adopt the interpretation that women asylum seekers who face harsh or inhuman treatment due to the values of their society may be considered as a particular social group."[22] However, just because states are free to do so does not mean that they always do. Although women have always been a constituent of refugee flows, it is only recently that their refugee status has been determined on the basis of their gender.

In 1996, in the *Matter of Kasinga,* the U.S. Board of Immigration Appeals for the first time granted asylum based on gender as a ground of discrimination. A young woman sought asylum arguing that if she returned to her home country, she would be forced to undergo female genital mutilation. This decision turned the tide for women seeking asylum in the United States, as it set a precedent for finally recognizing women as a "particular social group." In addition, women from countries with state-sanctioned violence against women, such as Afghanistan under the Taliban, have had success seeking gender-based asylum. However, it has been harder for women fleeing domestic violence in their home country to gain asylum on those grounds—a situation that leaves many women unable to escape harrowing circumstances. Women who face this situation have had a more difficult road; during the 1990s, Guatemalan native Rodi Alvarado Peña migrated to the United States to escape the repeated brutal attacks by her common-law husband, a former soldier who threatened to kill her.[23] Rodi applied for asylum on this basis, alleging that she could be seriously hurt or killed if she returned home. Her case shuffled through various levels of the immigration appeals system for years, and at one point she was ordered deported. In 2009, the Obama administration reversed the Bush administration's position on such asylum requests and stated that under certain conditions a woman could be granted asylum due to fear of abuse. This included recommending asylum for Alvarado, setting a precedent for other individuals like her.[24]

The right to gain asylum status on the grounds of gender violence and harm is a definite step forward for women. However, Oswin notes that there are some problems with this approach. One issue is that gender has come to be seen as exclusively female, and other claims to asylum or refugee status come to be seen as male: "By explicitly focusing on women's experiences of gender oppression, a stereotype that women 'own' the 'genderified' category of oppression is created."[25] Oswin points out that this view neglects to acknowledge that men, too, are held to particular gender norms and can face harm for not living up to them. An additional issue is that to successfully press a claim of asylum, the woman in question generally needs to be portrayed as a passive victim. "Carving out territory for refugee women within mainstream legal realms has been one way that feminists have successfully redressed their invisibility within refugee discourse. To do so, however, they have been required to paint a monolithic picture of these legal subjects as passive, dependent, vulnerable victims in need of protection."[26] This also involves the refugee claimants' having to "be extremely emotional so that they would be believed to be classic, passive, pitiable victims."[27]

Although gender is now accepted as grounds for refugee status, many women continue to be granted refugee status or asylum based on well-founded fear of persecution due to membership in other social groups: religion, ethnicity, and so on. It is important to continue to acknowledge women's refugee claims as women, but it is also important to acknowledge that often the persecution women face due to membership in these other groups is very gendered, as in *Zareen*'s case. In addition, in recognizing women's claims to refugee status, it is important to simultaneously acknowledge their agency, rather than paint them as purely passive victims. As seen in the stories of the refugee women in this chapter, even in the direst circumstances women worked to make their situations as tolerable as possible.

## Policy Recommendations and Reflections

We asked many of the women we interviewed what could be done to make the lives of immigrant women easier. Many pointed to the government and described the difficulties they had experienced navigating the immigration system. At the time of this writing, "comprehensive immigration reform" seems somewhat of a pipe dream. It is hard to imagine in the current political climate the kinds of far-reaching reforms the authors and some of the subjects of this book might prefer. Some of the women noted, however, that an important step would be simply to have the existing policies work better. It is well known that the immigration bureaucracy suffers from an enormous backlog. It is one thing not to be able to sponsor a relative because he or she is not one of the allowable family members or not to be able to get an employment visa because there is a surplus of workers in a given field. It is quite another thing to have to wait years to sponsor an allowed relative or not to be able to get a needed employment visa because somewhere along the way one's papers were lost in the system. So, at a bare minimum, a policy recommendation would be simply to make the system easier and quicker to navigate and more transparent.

Some proposals for immigration reform have included a reduced emphasis on family reunification. Although this may seem like a gender-neutral position, the fact that this is the most female category of immigration suggests that such a move would have a disproportionate effect on potential immigrating women. In addition, reductions in family-sponsored immigration would hamper the abilities of women already here (whether immigrant or native) to sponsor family members including spouses, children, and parents. Standing in the way of families being together seems counter to the "family values" that both major American political parties like to tout, and we would urge policymakers not to make such changes.

Although it would be easy to focus solely on the trials and tribulations these women faced, a recurring theme across their stories was the freeing nature of having moved to the United States. In some cases, this had to do with having left extremely oppressive situations at home, as with *Anica*, who escaped Communist rule in Romania, or the women who fled Iran and Vietnam. And sometimes the women indicated that their feeling of freedom had something specific to do with American culture. *Betty*, from Hong Kong, is an accomplished painter, and she said she feels that American culture fosters innovation, rebellion, and creativity. She clearly noted that in her particular artistic genre, in Hong Kong she would have been pushed to follow tradition blindly, as opposed to defying it, as she does in the United States. She stated that, in her opinion, "immigrant artists tend to do bolder, more creative work," due to this melding or tension between tradition and innovation.

*Dama*, from India, said, "I feel that I'm outside the boundary anyways, so I don't have to follow any of the rules." This quotation makes it sound as if she is a rebel, or lawbreaker, rather than the very law-abiding engineering professor that she is. However, she argued that, as a woman, as a mother, as a wife, she would have had more rules and expectations to follow had she either stayed in India or been an American-born citizen living here. This statement may seem counterintuitive at first glance, but *Dama* explained. She argued that women she knew who had been born here had "to conform to certain social values," whereas, she said, "I don't have any social pressures pulling me back. . . . I never felt like I have to behave in a particular way."

The picture we get when we look at how these women came in the "front door" has nothing in common with the passive women Everett Lee depicted. Although they may indeed have loved the environment they left in their home country, they certainly were not torn from it, weeping, by unfeeling husbands. And the front door was not necessarily always an open door. These women's stories depict how they often had to wait, scratch, peek in, and push at the door. The policies, as well as normative structures and institutions that govern gendered roles, make the passage through the front door complex and not always smooth. And women, by embracing these roles and sometimes by resisting and challenging them, create new ways of "entering" their new life. Although they encountered many structural obstacles, they employed their personal agency to surmount them, to be "bolder, more creative," to persevere, and to grow through change and suffering. In so doing, they have established lives in which they bring their diverse experiences to bear on adding to and improving their new communities, through counseling clients at a domestic-violence shelter, writing a novel of their family's saga, running a restaurant, providing child care, teaching university students, doing construction work, creating paintings, or serving as a state legislator, for example, vocations and avocations we turn to later in the book, where we examine what these women do once they are here. First, however, we examine the experiences of those women who enter the country through the "back door," using methods other than the legal ones.

# 4

# "I Had to Leave My Country One Day"

*Entering through the Back Door*

Reyna Gómez was perched on a cozy sofa in her small Miami, Florida, apartment, eagerly and passionately reciting the details of her biography: "It was hard to come here. I had a good life in Honduras, working in a school. It was a rushed decision; I had to leave my country one day. They tried to run me over, kill me, so I had to leave. I didn't want to come." Her journey to her eventual home in Florida took her over the Guatemalan border, across El Salvador, and through the hot deserts of Mexico—a journey she described as "a very hard experience": "I never thought I would experience something so terrifying." Reyna continued walking across Mexico on this journey to the other side, fending off advances of the *coyotes* who were arranging her passage and weighing her current troubles against the risk of returning to more certain violence in Honduras. Her perseverance paid off, and she found herself face to face with the mighty Rio Grande river—the one remaining obstacle between her and the solid ground of the United States. Although Reyna was familiar with the river's *mythical* grandiosity, as she stood and surveyed the opposite bank in a dim and distant horizon, the river's actual *physical* scale caught her completely unaware: "I have heard about the Rio [Grande] River, but I thought it was just a little stream. I couldn't believe it."

Reyna remembers the waters' oppressive darkness, obscuring the rushing currents that repeatedly pulled her toward the muddy bottom. As she frantically treaded to keep afloat, her eyes caught the sight of a fifteen-year-old girl, seemingly frozen from fear, midriver. She reflected, "She reminded me of my daughter, so I couldn't leave her behind. It's like leaving my daughter behind. So I just went underwater, took her by the waist, and pulled her up." Reyna's dive made so much noise, however, that the nearby border patrol took notice. Reyna pulled herself up on the river bank through layers of mud and roots so deep that she continued to feel as if she was being submerged by the elements. She helped the girl to the banks, and, resigned to her new fate but with no alternative options, Reyna surrendered to the border patrol and asked their help.

As she dug further into her memories to convey the painful details of her saga, Reyna began to cry. At that moment, the entire life-or-death sojourn appeared to have been in vain. How did the border patrol answer her pleas for help? By rounding up Reyna and her cosurvivors of this tortuous swim and delivering them to a detention center near Brownsville, Texas. Clearly, these agents were performing their required duties. Reyna, however, described a place that sounds more like a site of punishment than a temporary holding center: "They held us there for two days. We were in wet, dirty clothes. It was super cold: like a *freezer*. They gave us one blanket for two of us. Two times a day we got bologna on bread and juice. We made a system; men wouldn't eat their morning food and would give it to the children." At the time, the border patrol practiced a policy of "catch and release." They freed both Reyna and the girl; Reyna eventually made it to Miami, where she pieced together a living through several strenuous low-wage jobs; today she works as a labor organizer. Her story continues in chapter 9.

Despite the public image of the undocumented immigrant as male, irregular immigration to the United States also has a female face. Just as there has been a feminization of immigration through the American front door, similar claims can be made about the growing number of women entering the United States through back doors: swimming rivers, crossing deserts, or overstaying the terms of a valid visa—the latter of which accounts for approximately 40 to 45 percent of undocumented immigrants.[1] Immigrants who enter through irregular means can be said to occupy two extremes of the continuum of agency in the immigration process. On one end is the woman who is coerced or forced and thus the least free; her agency is, therefore, severely restricted. At the other extreme is the woman who has crossed a border without documents on her own initiative. This is among the most voluntaristic activities that a migrant might take given its risks—an immigrant who crosses a border taking her life into her own hands without structural support from a system.

The material in this chapter is based primarily on interviews with advocates and service providers in the immigration rights arena and on secondary research sources, supplemented by stories from our interviews with individual immigrant women.[2]

## Gender and Irregular Migration

Estimates of undocumented immigrants are necessarily rough, but those who document trends in unauthorized immigration, such as the Pew Hispanic Center, observe that numbers had risen gradually from approximately 8.4 million in 2000 to an estimated 11.9 million by 2006.[3] These include individuals who crossed borders without visas as well as those who entered with legal documents and fell out of status or overstayed visas. The former include asylum seekers, who constitute approximately 10 percent of undocumented individuals who enter each year. Among those working in the United States without documents were approximately sixty individuals who lost their lives in the attack on the World Trade Center on September 11, 2001, many of whom were employed at the Windows on the World restaurant. The Pew Hispanic Center estimated that in 2006, 42 percent of all unauthorized migrants in the United States were women.[4] Despite a public moral panic over undocumented migration during the decade, however, the unauthorized population actually grew more slowly between 2005 and 2008 than in previous years, and by 2008, fewer people entered the United States each year irregularly than regularly.[5] In 2008, there were an estimated 8.3 million workers in the labor force who were undocumented.[6] Comparisons of these workers reveal distinct gender patterns. Among working-age *unauthorized* immigrant men, higher proportions of these men (94 percent) are in the U.S. labor force than *authorized* immigrant men (85 percent). Among women, however, higher proportions of the *authorized* (66 percent) are in the labor force, versus 58 percent of the *unauthorized*; an additional estimated 29 percent of unauthorized immigrant women report that they are responsible for raising children at home.[7]

On the surface, it appears that the pattern that has been called the "feminization of migration" does not apply to the unauthorized, since the majority continue, in fact, to be men. And certainly, it is this gender imbalance that makes the undocumented population in the United States the exception to the general global trend. Nevertheless, the overall gap between male and female immigration rates has narrowed over the years, leading us to conclude that a dynamic of feminization is in process among the unauthorized as well. There is also a geography-specific explanation for this observation: Mexico is the largest sending country of immigrants to the United States— both documented and undocumented. The proximal location of Mexico influences the higher numbers of undocumented immigrant men who, in their role as breadwinners, remain either temporarily or semipermanently estranged from their families at home. This dynamic strongly influences the gender imbalance in these numbers.

Like the unauthorized passages of men, women's are forced or voluntary, intentional or unintentional, with or without family. And parallel to men, the women residing in the United States may have been living with authorized documentation at one point but fallen out of status due to any number of reasons. In addition, an undocumented woman may be a member of a mixed-status family, which describes a large number, if not the majority, of immigrant families: some members are documented, while others are not. As of 2005, the best estimates were that 64 percent of children in families with an unauthorized adult were born in the United States and thus are citizens.[8] Only 11 percent, or 725,000 families, had only noncitizen children.[9]

Women (and men) who are unauthorized to live and work in the United States fall into three broad groups:

1. Those who crossed a border without authorization and are ineligible—or do not realize they are eligible—to take advantage of one of the available visas that would regularize their status (these include individuals who came as children with their parents).

2. Those who came without authorization and have applied to adjust their status to receive asylum, a T visa, or some other means to remain in the country in an authorized status but are awaiting a decision or a court date.

3. Those who were once authorized but have fallen out of status, which could have happened for several reasons: a woman may have overstayed the expiration date of her visa (often dubbed a "visa overstayer"); she may have lost a job that sponsored her work authorization; an employer or educational institution was delayed or made mistakes in processing paperwork; immigration authorities made mistakes or had processing delays; or she lost a family-member sponsor through death, deportation, or divorce. Stories abound across the country of immigrants who have fallen between the cracks due to one of these scenarios.

We review these varied means of irregular migration here, with a focus on the gendered experience of this side of the migration experience. Included is a survey of trends in the practices of detention and deportation, a net in which asylum seekers, described in the previous chapter, also get caught.

## Smuggling

Accounts of experiences similar to the one reported by Reyna are found not only in communities of Mexican and Central American immigrant communities but also in communities from Asia and other continents. *Smuggling* refers to a situation in which a migrant consents to be taken across a border; it is an act of (relative) free will and usually involves payment of some form to smugglers.[10] Certainly, examples abound of individuals who resort to smuggling who are less than free, such as those involving children or pressure by other family members. Given the societal contexts of patriarchy and imbalances of power that continue between women and men, the agency of a woman's consent to be smuggled is not an unbounded, free act.

As Reyna's story illustrates, a growing number of women have been risking such desperate acts. Border crossings carry some relatively predictable gender dynamics. The *coyotes,* under whose wing Reyna found herself throughout her passage, are predominantly men. Reyna's experience with the advances of these *coyotes* was not an isolated one. Women who cross the border from Mexico through the services of a *coyote* report that rape and sexual abuse are so common that the *coyotes* or "border bandits" publicize their exploits by displaying the victim's underwear on "rape trees."[11] In 2009, a study of Latina immigrant women in the southern region of the United States reported that 89 percent of these women state that passage to the United States is more violent for women than for men.[12] Once they cross the border, they will likely also be met by men rather than women. Robert Lee Maril's study of the Texas-Mexico border patrol indicates that an overwhelming majority of these agents are men, due to the hours required, difficulty with balancing work and family, and a work climate that is not always female friendly. In the three stations that Maril studied, he estimates that there has been little change in the proportion of female agents since 1999, when it was reported that only 5 percent of agents were women.[13] Further, a post-9/11 volunteer militia who call themselves "Minutemen" and patrol unauthorized crossings into the United States are—as indicated by their self-identification—primarily men.

Whether an individual consents to be smuggled or crosses a border independently, the historical context of American immigration policy plays a pivotal role. The long history of seasonal migrants from Mexico, for example, described in chapter 2—which has included more than one official era of U.S. government recruitment of Mexican workers—created a culture of circular migration. Changes in immigration policy often have unintended consequences, such as opening the door for more unauthorized passages. Although the 1965 reform of the immigration system opened the door to more non-Europeans, for example, it put a cap on visas that had previously been available to Mexicans. Despite the visa cap, the jobs remained, their employers continued to have the same needs, and the streams of workers that those job positions drew continued, relatively unabated.[14] Needs for workers continue to drive such flows, including emergent crises such as the 2005 devastation wreaked by Hurricane Katrina in New Orleans, Louisiana, and the surrounding vicinity. Streams of undocumented migrants, including a strong Honduran contingent, responded to the need for postdisaster rebuilding. Those responders, however, continued to live in fear of immigrant sweeps[15] and were subjected to the types of labor exploitation that have become commonplace in day-laborer employment stories across the United States.

As border crossing became riskier for unauthorized immigrants, many of those seasonal migrants chose to remain in the United States rather than continue their circular lives. Their families joined them, and they settled down. In situations in which those circular migrants were men, this meant that more women migrated than in the past.[16] In the book *Beyond Smoke and Mirrors,* researchers Douglas Massey, Jorge Durand, and Nolan Malone date this change from circular migrants to settlers from the 1986 legislation called the Immigration Reform and Control Act (IRCA), which resulted in stricter border controls. Pierrette Hondagneu-Sotelo, however, questions this characterization of Mexican emigration history. One provision of the IRCA legislation, for instance, was that of amnesty for undocumented immigrants residing in the United States. Equal numbers of men and women applied for that amnesty, leading Hondagneu-Sotelo to conclude that women had been joining men in unauthorized migration long before 1986.[17] Nevertheless, some pockets of circular migration such as agricultural labor remained male dominated despite this increasing feminization of border crossing. In the 2006 documentary film *The Guest Worker,* for example, a Mexican woman, who was married to a man who had been a circular migrant to the United States for forty years, ruminated over how strange it was that her house had no men across much of the year.[18]

Examples abound of women who were smuggled across other borders into the country as well. In 1998, a Texas nursing-home owner was convicted of running a ring to bring nurses into the United States. Capitalizing on a nationwide shortage of nurses, this ring drew licensed nurses from the Philippines and South Korea; all these women paid a fee and assumed they were being placed in legitimate positions with legal visas but were mistreated and underpaid upon arrival.[19] Despite the quasi-voluntary nature of smuggling, since the migrant technically consents to the act, examples of exploitation and years of indebtedness to smugglers abound; thus, this act of free agency may not result in the free range of choices for which the migrant had originally hoped. Individuals often feel enslaved to their debts and to their perception that returning home is not an option, for a range of reasons.

## Human Trafficking

> Human trafficking. Selling women and children as sex slaves? It's outrageous! This isn't one hundred years ago. Nowadays women can go to the moon.
>
> —Kieu Chinh, Vietnamese American actress

It is a warm July day in 2007, in Los Angeles, California. Two recent college graduates who voluntarily established an office for the Polaris Project in Los Angeles are seated in their sparse downtown office—a small room in a suite of offices occupied by another organization. Their goal is to offer services for individuals in labor enslavement—and hopefully help them to freedom. The two women enthusiastically recount their daily excursions to scout out potential victims of trafficking in the city's streets, handing out flyers, getting word out about services, and publicizing their hotline. Both women are daughters of Asian immigrants and know from past cases that have been uncovered that there are active networks within both Asian and Latin American communities of their city that are keeping people in conditions of servitude. They had also noticed a growing African residential population that is vulnerable to such abuses. Although they have yet to definitively root out any networks themselves, citing the frustration of finding victims willing to come forward, they enumerate the cases that have been uncovered to date. Just to the south of them, for instance, in San Diego, the sheriff successfully uncovered an extensive operation in which Mexican women and girls were smuggled into agricultural fields for sex work.[20]

Human trafficking is not the most common back-door means through which foreign-born women enter the United States, but it is a persistent, largely invisible global trade, in which the United States plays a key role. By no means is this a new practice; in 1910, the U.S. Senate passed the White Slave Traffic Act to combat what was perceived to be a growing problem, which was known as "white slavery" in that era—white women being kidnapped and forced into prostitution. The moral panic that ensued over this reported practice may have exaggerated the extent of the problem at that time. Today, the U.S. government has once again gotten involved in attempting to combat the problem, which is defined more broadly than in 1910, encompassing other forms of forced labor in addition to prostitution. The U.S. government defines *trafficking in persons* this way:

> The term "severe forms of trafficking in persons" means—
>
> (A) sex trafficking in which a commercial sex act is induced by force, fraud, or coercion, or in which the person induced to perform such act has not attained 18 years of age; or
>
> (B) the recruitment, harboring, transportation, provision, or obtaining of a person for labor or services, through the use of force, fraud, or coercion for the purpose of subjection to involuntary servitude, peonage, debt bondage, or slavery.[21]

The trafficking of individuals for the sex trade or other forms of labor has become the second-largest criminal business in the world—and the fastest growing—garnering an estimated eight billion U.S. dollars annually. One reason that this trade *is* so lucrative is that each human can be "resold" over and over—and, in the case of sex work, "leased out" multiple times a day; drugs (one of the other two "commodities" in the global underground market, in addition to guns) can only be sold once.[22] The rapid growth in transportation and communication technologies, including the Internet, are effective support mechanisms that help fuel the expansion of this industry.

Given the secrecy and hidden nature of this business, estimates of the number of victims both domestically and globally are extremely rough. Based on the knowledge to date, however, the U.S. Department of State estimates that between six hundred thousand and eight hundred thousand people are trafficked across international borders each year and that 80 percent of these are women and girls. Although much public attention has focused on foreign-born victims of trafficking, the trafficking of *native*-born women, men, and children is also extensive within the United States and within the borders of other countries and is integral to the larger trafficking portrait. In fact, the definition of *trafficking in persons* used by both the U.S. government and the United Nations includes the practice of trafficking within state or national boundaries. The United States is one of the top-three destinations in the world for international traffickers and the top destination in the Western Hemisphere; the other two major destination countries are Japan and Australia. Records and reports from locations across the United States suggest that a roughly estimated 14,500 to 17,500 foreign nationals may be trafficked into the country each year.[23]

In contrast to smuggling, in which individuals consent to be transported across a border on their own initiative, trafficking involves coercion, deceit, or force. Among those who are trafficked transnationally into the United States, most hail from the world regions of Africa, Asia, Latin America, and eastern Europe—and they may transit through other regions before arriving here. India, Iran, Mexico, and Turkey are among transit countries through which people are trafficked to another destination. According to research of the U.S. Department of State, there are only three countries in the world that have been identified as being free of sex trafficking, all three of which happen to be in Africa.[24] Women living in countries that have experienced major or sudden political or economic dislocations are particularly vulnerable, such as the countries that were part of the former Soviet Union. In fact, one 2001 publication about trafficking was entitled "The Natasha Trade," using a common Russian woman's name.[25]

The advocacy, legal, and investigative-journalism communities have been collectively piecing together a portrait of trafficking patterns within the United States. We are using these front-line accounts to summarize the portrait here. The major known trafficking hubs in the United States are located in California, Texas, New York, and Nevada (Las Vegas).[26] The Office of the Texas Attorney General reported in a 2008 study that 20 percent of trafficking cases in the United States occur in the state of Texas, with a great deal of activity centered in Houston.[27] Trafficking is making an appearance in other states that are the more recently growing gateways for new immigration, including Ohio, North Carolina, Maryland, and Virginia. A national study found that ninety cities across the fifty states and two territories had uncovered cases of forced labor.[28]

It was the 1995 discovery of 109 Thai and Latino women and men employed as garment workers in a Los Angeles sweatshop that propelled the issue of human trafficking into the public eye in more recent years in the United States. The workers (the majority of whom were women) were required to sew from dawn until midnight and sometimes as long as twenty-two hours per day, seven days per week, within a building surrounded by a razor-wire fence where they also resided. Most made less than two dollars per hour. When the operation was exposed, the traffickers were prosecuted; five major companies, including Mervyn's and Montgomery Ward, that sold merchandise produced in the sweatshops agreed to a two-million-dollar settlement to the workers.[29] A shocked U.S. Congress drafted new federal antitrafficking legislation. The Trafficking Victims Protection Act of 2000 represented the culmination of this awakened Congress, backed by years of advocacy by antitrafficking activists. The act created the new T visa, which allows trafficking victims to stay in the country legally for three years and then apply for a green card. The act was reauthorized in 2003 and 2008.

One recipient of the T visa was South Korean college student You Mi Kim, who had answered an ad for a hostess job in California; the travel broker who interviewed her gave her a promise that no sex would be involved. Upon arrival in California, she was told that she owed the men twelve thousand dollars for her passage, and she would not be free until she paid. Despite her resistance, she was set up with a call-girl service in Koreatown in Los Angeles. You Mi Kim was eventually able to free herself from this work and find more respectable employment, but she now refers to her years in the brothels as slavery. Since she agreed to testify against her traffickers, she was able to receive the T visa.[30] Soon after You escaped, several dozen Koreans who operated this network were charged in a federal indictment called Operation Gilded Cage, spanning both Los Angeles and San Francisco. Although the 2000 Victims of Trafficking and Violence Protection Act created twenty-year prison terms for sex traffickers, the brothel owner was given one year in prison and ordered to pay a fine consisting of the one million dollars in profits that he had made.[31]

In the same year, a trafficking case was uncovered in New York State. Behind closed doors of a multimillion-dollar house in an upscale neighborhood on Long Island, a wealthy couple had kept two Indonesian domestic workers, Varshna and Samirah, in a situation of forced labor for more than five years. In exchange for their work as full-time live-in laborers responsible for the family's cooking, cleaning, and other services, the two women received two hundred dollars per month and were not allowed to leave the premises. The owners of the house also attempted to control these women through physical abuse. When the news broke about the abuses that the two women suffered, New Yorkers expressed shock and outrage that this was happening in such an unsuspect environment in their own backyard. The employers have since been sentenced to prison for this enslavement.[32] Similar cases of abuse of foreign-born domestic workers abound both in the United States and across the globe.

Human trafficking is routinely disguised behind apparently legitimate businesses such as modeling agencies or beauty salons.[33] Massage parlors are common fronts for brothels where foreign-born women are held and forced to offer sexual services for massage clients. Newspaper reporters are among those who have uncovered such practices, leading newspapers such as the

*New York Times,* the *Boston Globe,* and the *Los Angeles Times* to refuse to sell advertisement space to any massage parlors. In April 2009, the activist Katherine Chon, who cofounded the antitrafficking organization Polaris, critcized the *Washington Post* for selling advertising space to massage parlors despite its own reportage of this same phenomenon. The *Post* reportedly made an estimated two million dollars from such sales in a peak year that spanned 2002 to 2003. Chon's blog post *"The Washington Post:* A Paper Pimp?" exposed this practice and called for readers to voice their opposition. This exposure was an example of the extent to which this underworld business had reached its tentacles into more legitimate institutions.

## Marriage "On Order"

Among the legitimate institutions that intersect with trafficking is the quickly growing mail-order marriage business. Marriage to an American citizen is a legal, regular means of entry into the country, but it warrants a discussion here because of certain dynamics that overlap with human trafficking and smuggling. Like human trafficking, mail-order marriages have a long history in the United States, dating at least to the American Revolution. A new growth in this industry in postindustrial times is related to the development of new communication technology such as the Internet and cellular phones. As of 2005, in fact, there were a reported 590,000 Internet websites that offered the choice of mail-order brides from around the world—for a fee. International marriage brokers advertise available women through websites and catalogs to men who primarily reside in industrialized countries and are known as "consumer husbands." In the United States, one estimate is that four to six thousand marriages per year are the result of this business.[34] Advocates have suggested, however, that these are underestimates.

Despite the legality of this option, activists and observers cite the business as one that, when abused, could border on human trafficking. After all, it involves a financial transaction for a woman who, many consumer husbands hope, will provide them with a more obedient, sexually available partnership than what they believe they would get from the more independently minded American women. Marriage brokers promise to potential clients that their offerings are "old-fashioned" or have "traditional values." Many services promise money-back guarantees, just like any other consumer purchase. The website GoodWife.com introduces its services in the following way on its home page: "We, as men, are more and more wanting to step back from the types of women we meet now. With many women taking on the 'me first' feminist agenda and the man continuing to take a back seat to her desire for power and control many men are turned off by this and look back to having a more traditional woman as our partner."

The women who are advertised as potential brides tend to hail from the same regions of the world as those who are trafficked, such as Asia and the countries of the former Soviet Union. The Natasha Club is the name of one Web-based broker, for example. One bank teller who worked in an area of Baltimore where a large Russian community had settled observed, "I see very young Russian women coming in to open bank accounts with much older American husbands. It makes me wonder." Researchers and activists have documented high levels of domestic violence within the mail-order marriages across the country, and at least one resulted in the murder of the bride. The highly publicized investigation into the murder of Russian-born Anastasia King resulted in the conviction of her American husband, Indle G. King Jr., in 2002. Indle had exchanged his first mail-order bride for Anastasia; disappointed a second time, he chose a different way to dispose of his "purchase."[35]

Unlike trafficking, of course, a woman chooses to sign up for these programs, usually adding her photo to a catalog from which men will select their brides-to-be. Culturally, some women may view this as an extension of their own, legitimate cultural practices of arranged marriages—and compared to those practices, this one may be viewed as offering an additional layer of freedom. For example, the couple's families are not necessarily involved, there is no expectation of a dowry, the woman has the right to refuse, and she has the opportunity to move to a country that likely offers both better financial opportunities and more rights for women. There are reports of families who pool their money to help a woman get to the United States, in the hope that doing so will allow them to follow eventually. Certainly there are reports of successful, satisfactory marriages through these brokers; however, advocates have reported a pattern of dashed hopes for many women. For example, a level of dependency on the native-born partner might develop in these relationships, particularly if the bride's English skills are limited and she is not familiar with her legal rights, resulting in an imbalance of power in the marriages. Further, at a global level, as the mail-order marriage business has grown, illegitimate versions of the practice have mushroomed, involving coercion and deceit and leading to a hybrid underground business labeled "bride trafficking." In fact, one service that the brokerage programs offer is a tour for the potential consumer husband: small groups of men are visited by several hundred women, who are circulated through in batches. This practice has been exposed as another variant of sex tourism.

Despite differences between trafficking and the (legal) mail-order marriage business, the two share similarities when it comes to human agency. The trafficked women whose bodies and labor are exchanged as commodities may appear to fit squarely into familiar articulations of "free-market" capitalism, with the consumer simply paying what the market will bear—whether it is for sexual pleasure or a new shirt—as with any other good for sale. On the other hand, the exchange is actually one that goes on over and beyond those bodies. These bodies are more akin to raw materials for the final product of the labor and are exchangeable as soon as one's body is deemed less functional, rendering each woman's individuality as erasable. Those who register themselves as potential brides place their bodies—and, in fact, their entire foreseeable futures—on the market. Overall, they have little agency in the exchange. As expressed by the frequent request for "traditional values," a central commodity being bought and sold is also that of culture. That commodity, many consumer-husbands claim, has been traded in by American women in the name of equality and independence; thus, American women's agency is derided in the bride-ordering discourse, in which the term "feminazi" is bantered around.

## Losing Status

In addition to domestic workers and mail-order brides, thousands of other immigrant women enter the United States on valid visas but fall out of status for a number of reasons. Like men, many women choose to stay following the expiration of their visas in the hope of remaining in the country longer. As we have written, women make up a higher proportion of the foreign-born who enter the country to study on a student visa or to work on a nonimmigrant visa than ever before in history. Although many of them are aware when they become unauthorized, others are not, for example, if they are dependent on an employer to file paperwork for them and something is amiss or if their application is stuck in a backlog at the U.S. Citizenship and Immigration Services.

For years, immigrant women (and men) were subject to a restriction that was nicknamed the "widow penalty." If an immigrant was married to an authorized immigrant or U.S. citizen on whom her or his immigration status depended, that legal status disappeared when the spouse died. Despite years of complaints about this policy, Congress did not move to reverse it until October 2009, when this practice was officially abolished.[36] With a growing number of immigrant men and women serving in the U.S. armed forces and deployed in the wars in Iraq and Afghanistan, some spouses left stateside found their immigration statuses in jeopardy. In 2007, for example, U.S. officials began deportation proceedings against a Dominican woman, Yaderlin Hiraldo, who was married to Alex Jimenez, an American serving in Iraq. Alex had petitioned for a green card for Yaderlin while in Iraq, but the paperwork was still in process when he deployed. As deportation proceedings were moving forward, Alex was missing in Iraq and presumed captured. News of Yaderlin's plight fortunately reached the ears of her senator, John Kerry, and the government dropped deportation proceedings. Yaderlin never did get to celebrate her husband's homecoming, however. His body was eventually found in Iraq, and in 2009 Yaderlin attended his interment in Arlington National Cemetery.[37]

Parallel to the risk of losing status upon the death of a spouse, a divorce or marital separation could jeopardize an individual's status. Until recently, a woman whose status was dependent on the status of her marriage partner (whether that partner was a citizen or noncitizen) risked losing legal status upon leaving the relationship.[38] If the woman needed to leave because she was a victim of partner/family violence, she faced a choice between danger at home and the vulnerability of being undocumented. Advocates who learned of this dilemma, including news of women who were killed by partners because they felt that they could not take this risk, led to new legislation contained in the Violence Against Women Act (VAWA) of the Violent Crime Control and Law Enforcement Act of 1994; VAWA was reauthorized in 2005.

### The Culture of Enforcement

In the 1990s, the U.S. government began expanding its enforcement measures regarding immigration law. And after the events of 9/11 particularly, that enforcement intensified further to aid the war on terror. The former Immigration and Naturalization Service (INS) was folded into the newly created umbrella agency, the Department of Homeland Security (DHS), and was renamed the U.S. Citizenship and Immigration Services. Although many people in the immigration rights arena had criticized the INS for its bureaucratic mishandlings and delays, they nevertheless expressed strong hesitation over the prospect that an agency responsible for immigration *services* would be located in the same arm of the government responsible for *enforcement*. What followed, in fact, was an escalating culture of securitization that targeted the far corners of towns, cities, and states where the undocumented were suspected to reside.

In 1996, the Antiterrorism and Effective Death Penalty Act and the Illegal Immigration Reform and Immigrant Responsibility Act became federal law. Under these laws, a wider list of offenses was defined as grounds for deportation than had been the case in prior years. Immigrants also lost the right to ask a judge to overturn a deportation decision, and they could no longer be released on bail.[39] Whether or not a noncitizen immigrant was authorized to be in the United States, she could, under these new laws, be detained for a minor misdemeanor, such as shoplifting. She could also be detained for a misdemeanor or felony for which she had already served a sentence.[40] As a result, the number of immigrants taken into custody and deported rose considerably. Government raids of workplaces also began to escalate. U.S. borders—especially the one shared with Mexico—became more militarized. All of this translated into more deportations and more immigrant women, men, and children in jails and prisons. In chapter 3, we discussed the increasing requests by women for gender-based asylum. The heightened securitization culture has meant that those women are more likely to be escorted directly from airports or boats to detention centers until their cases can be tried. As the securitization culture deepened, the drive for more detention facilities fueled a booming private enterprise. In 2006, one-half of the sixteen federal detention centers for immigrants were owned by two private companies, Corrections Corporation and GEO Inc. When then-president George W. Bush cleared the way for more federal dollars to go toward immigrant detention, the companies enjoyed a sharp increase in their stock values; GEO's stock more than doubled between February 2006 and May 2007.[41] In January 2009, in the midst of the largest U.S. stock-market decline since the Great Depression, GEO proudly announced the opening of a new 192-bed expansion of a detention center in the state of Georgia.[42]

Complaints mounted from immigrants and advocates during this period that people suspected of working without documents were given criminal-level treatment and subjected to potential abuses of prison facilities, away from public scrutiny. Such reports led the New York Times to point out in 2006 the "nearly impenetrable maze where immigration and criminal law meet."[43] Immigration law and criminal law come under separate legal codes. Immigration law is primarily a *federal* domain and is considered a *civil* law. And criminal law exists in both federal and state statutes. With immigration law constantly changing, adding to the confusion, it is the judges who must attempt to untangle the maze. The Detention Watch Network reported that "[b]y the end of 2009, the U.S. government will hold over 440,000 people in immigration custody—more than triple the number of people in detention just ten years ago—in a hodgepodge of approximately 400 facilities at an annual cost of more than $1.7 billion."[44] The Department of Homeland Security operates a number of detention facilities, in addition to those owned by the private companies discussed in the preceding paragraph. Due to the large number of detainees, however, DHS also places individuals in more than 312 county and city jails.[45] Of those four hundred thousand people in detention, an estimated 10 percent are women.[46]

While detention predominantly affects men, the impact of the enforcement frenzy on women may carry added dimensions, particularly if they are primary caretakers of children. In January 2009, for example, a Latina named Ciria Lopez, while driving a car with her two small, U.S.-citizen children in Maricopa County, Arizona, was stopped by a deputy sheriff sporting a black ski mask. She was taken into custody for an unpaid traffic ticket, and her children were left behind. After paying the ticket, she was detained for being undocumented. This deputy worked for Sheriff Joe Arpaio, labeled the "toughest sheriff in the West" for requiring inmates to pay for their meals and work in chain gangs.[47] A growing number of counties across the United States had implemented a federal program called 287(g), giving local law enforcement the authority to hand over suspected undocumented immigrants to immigration officials. Complaints over this program arose in response to this sheriff's activities as well as those of other police departments across the country, with charges of racial profiling usually accompanying the protests. Although immigration rights activists had hoped that local police could be added to the federal antitrafficking forces, many of them decried this new dispersion of responsibility to enforce immigration civil law, particularly since it is extremely difficult for a nonspecialist to determine the precise legal status of immigrants. In addition, immigrants who are in the process of waiting for a court decision regarding their asylum would not be in possession of the appropriate documents but are legally entitled to remain in the country until their case is decided. We interviewed one woman who escaped Iran following the revolution, for example, and her asylum process took about two years; it was another five years before she received her green card to work legally.

The enforcement culture has its supporters, however. The passage of immigration bill SB 1070 in Arizona during 2010, which empowered police to question people whom they suspect to be undocumented immigrants, drew support and potential copycat legislation in other states, even as it was being challenged in federal court. Although immigrants and advocates have organized rallies to protest racial profiling and detention practices, in fact, they have regularly been met by groups of protesters favoring stronger restrictions on immigration. Although such protesters tend to characterize men as the potential criminal threat, the enforcement net has caught many women, as well as children, through home and workplace raids and border stops.

## The Wait Inside

Most of the conditions and activities within detention centers are outside the public eye, but a number of stories about women being held inside began to surface as attorneys, journalists, and human rights specialists were able to visit those facilities. The journalist Mark Dow reported in his book *American Gulag* the stories of several women in detention at the Krome Detention Center in Miami, Florida—many of whom were seeking asylum. One African woman, he explained, spent one and a half years in detention before she received her asylum papers. She had fled to the United States to escape her country's military, which had threatened to kidnap her. During her time in detention, however, she was shackled to another detainee, strip-searched, and verbally abused and threatened by those in charge. She had exchanged one life of threats for another.[48] Other observers documented reports of sexual abuse at the same center.[49]

Additional investigative research into the conditions that faced women in detention in Wisconsin[50] and Arizona[51] uncovered patterns of distress that were gender based. One woman, for example, was detained in Arizona because her abusive husband reported her status to Immigration and Customs Enforcement (ICE). For eight months she was allowed no communication with her children and was unable to speak with any agency to have the children taken from her husband's care—despite her worry for her children's safety.[52] Among other cases that were discovered was a woman detained in a workplace raid and separated from her six-month-old child until she was released—only to find herself in a custody dispute for her own child. The judge viewed her action of crossing the border without documents and then working without documents, which landed her in detention, as unfit behavior for a mother. The judge wrote in his decision, "Her lifestyle, that of smuggling herself into the country illegally and committing crimes in this country, is not a lifestyle that can provide stability for a child."[53] In 2009, other reports of similar situations were emerging from across the country, suggesting a pattern of women losing their children simply due to their immigration status. The judge's use of the term "illegal" reflects the tone of the culture wars at the time, when this label was playing a particularly volatile role—blurring the boundary between civil and criminal offenses.

Women who escaped to the United States in the hope of being granted asylum may have already experienced imprisonment for their political views or group membership in their home country. Iranian artist Roya Pazooki, for example, who resides in Atlanta, spent four years behind bars in Iran. When such women find themselves imprisoned once more in the country where they hoped to gain their freedom, they may go through a confusing déjà vu at best or a return to a traumatized emotional state at worst.

Across 2007 and 2008, ICE closed three detention centers after reports of deaths of detainees, which critics blamed on inadequate health care. One of the cases that captured public attention was a young Chinese man who had overstayed his visa and was denied medical attention for his cancer and fractured spine.[54] After such centers close, however, challenges continue, as families have a difficult time locating their detained family members, who get transferred to other facilities, sometimes in a different state. Immigration cases can take years to settle; it is not uncommon for detainees to wait for months or even years in such centers. Those who are fortunate to get released are not authorized to work legally while they await the decision on their potential deportation.[55]

## Deportation

With the escalation of home and workplace raids and detention came a rising number of deportations. One thread in the public debates has been a discussion over mass deportation of everyone who is unauthorized. The U.S. government must pay for these deportations, which Immigration and Customs Enforcement estimates would cost at least ninety-four billion dollars, if the government were to deport all who are living in the United States without documents.[56] One "documented" immigrant weighed in on this question on an Internet blog: "It could not be done short of some Hitler Like Pogrom. You cannot find, manage, and remove that size group. If you could, you would have mass dislocations in various sectors of the agricultural, building, meat cutting & other sectors of our economy."[57]

ICE has already attempted to make a dent in the number of the unauthorized population. Between 2007 and 2008, aboard the Flight Repatriate Airlines, which ICE operated, 367,000 people were transported from twenty-three U.S. airports to locations that spanned the globe.[58] Many of the deported people left U.S.-born children and other family members behind. Across ten years, an estimated one hundred thousand parents of U.S.-citizen children were deported.[59] It was reported in 2008 that U.S. hospitals, bypassing government deportation procedures altogether, had begun to directly deport undocumented patients who had been admitted for treatments—whether the ailments were serious or more routine.[60] Mass sweeps caught some legal immigrants and even U.S. citizens in the net, and complaints arose over accidental deportations of citizens.

As deportations intensified, a journalist reported that Evelyne, a thirty-five-year-old Haitian asylum seeker and mother of a five-year-old daughter, was caught by surprise as authorities entered her Miami, Florida, home and attached a monitoring bracelet to her ankle. She was ordered to leave the country within one month. Evelyne had escaped Haiti years earlier, after her brother was killed, and was awaiting a decision on her asylum application; until this morning visit, she had received no word that her application was denied. She and thirty thousand other Haitians in the same situation got a temporary reprieve that same month due to the spate of hurricanes that had destroyed huge swaths of Haiti. But Evelyne did not know how she could return to Haiti following that reprieve, as her mother's house was destroyed in the storms.[61] By 2010, ICE was exhibiting visible internal divisions over the rush to deport, with decision-making on future directions caught in limbo while the issues were hotly debated on campaign trails during the midterm congressional election season.

## Reflections and Policy Solutions

Our review of policy approaches to the victimization that often accompanies irregular migration begins with human trafficking. Since human trafficking is a violation of U.S. federal law, local law-enforcement officers were until recently not empowered to investigate and charge traffickers. The office of Immigration and Customs Enforcement of the Department of Homeland Security has overseen this responsibility, but it does not have the personnel in adequate numbers and locations to address the scale of the problem. From the other side, frustrated local police officers may have been aware of trafficking rings but had no authority to pursue the traffickers. Grassroots activists concerned about this problem, partnering with sympathetic state legislators, addressed this enforcement gap by lobbying to make human trafficking an offense under state law. As of 2009, thirty-four states had passed their own statutes criminalizing human trafficking in some form. This includes states in all regions of the contiguous United States as well as Alaska and Hawaii.[62]

Advocacy organizations devoted to addressing the problem have become a growing presence at local and national levels. The activist Joy Zarembka, daughter of a domestic worker from Kenya, devotes her professional career to fighting human trafficking and helping domestic workers escape their conditions and get restitution, through her organization Break the Chain Campaign.[63] Other Washington, DC–based projects that are devoted to ending human trafficking are the Protection Project and the Polaris Project.[64] The Protection Project of the Foreign Policy Institute at the Johns Hopkins University School of Advanced International Studies has built an international network of human rights scholars and activists to advocate for policy change, raise awareness, and conduct research.

International activist attention to the issue has also grown; as a result of these activities and pressure from governmental bodies such as the U.S. Department of State Office to Monitor and Protect Trafficking in Persons, new legislation to combat trafficking has begun to appear in countries across all continents. In 2006 and 2007, for example, Israel, the United Arab Emirates, and Malaysia joined the growing list of countries that have passed laws against human trafficking.[65] The growing coalitions of groups devoted to tackling human trafficking, however, have created strange bedfellows: feminists, Catholic Church leaders, government officials in the conservative U.S. government under George W. Bush, and other grassroots groups.

Despite such coalitions, vocal immigrant-rights dissent regarding governmental approaches abound. Critiques of the U.S. government interventions into the issue, for example, have included charges that the government was mixing agendas and using its annual Trafficking in Persons (TIP) Report, which ranks countries according to their antitrafficking initiatives, to punish countries with which the United States disagreed on other issues. Regarding this charge, the consequences for countries who rank low on their TIP are quite serious, including ineligibility for "nonhumanitarian, nontrade related foreign assistance."[66] Since the antitrafficking zeal primarily targets sex work, it potentially ignores nuance, such as areas of the world where sex work is legal and carries certain state protections; it does not address the larger structural situation of the low wages that women earn globally, making sex work a "fallback" option.

Rhacel Salazar Parreñas has exposed the U.S. antitrafficking initiatives as unintentionally undermining options for women to migrate freely. For example, the U.S. government listed Filipino workers entering Japan as entertainers as individuals at risk of human trafficking, and after 2004, such applicants had to show that they had trained in the entertainment arts for at least two years. This requirement (an increase from the prior rule of six months) resulted in reducing the numbers from eighty thousand Filipino entertainers in Japan during 2004 to approximately eight thousand in 2006. Some feminist migration scholars viewed these trends and asked whether antitrafficking campaigns are masked attempts to undermine women's global migration and to create a climate of fear to keep women and girls inside and within the bounds of socially acceptable behaviors. Parreñas goes further, arguing that practices such as raising the entrance requirements for entertainers in Japan could inadvertently *encourage* more trafficking, as women who do not meet this requirement resort to more desperate means to emigrate.[67] Activist watchdog initiatives are needed to expose such intended and unintended consequences of international, externally imposed laws if the ultimate goal is women's freedom from restraints of whatever form.

Legal scholar Shelley Cavalieri, for example, has critiqued the reference to slavery in activist and governmental approaches as potentially legally inaccurate since some women do not self-identify using this term; some women may have even had more than a vague clue about the situation they were getting into when they answered an ad for an overseas position, thus complicating the characterization of these women as passive victims. Cavalieri suggests that in describing trafficked sex workers, a middle ground must be found between viewing women in sex work as totally coerced or totally consenting, especially given the complexities and changing dynamics of the situation when migration is concerned.[68] Further, as the Polaris activists articulated in the story reported earlier in this chapter, the boundaries between some employment situations and that of trafficking can become blurred.

On September 27, 2007, a long-awaited visa became available: the "U" visa. Although this visa is officially classified as a "nonimmigrant" visa—in other words, it resembles some employment visas in that it does not confer permanent lawful status—it opens the door to a more permanent status. Placed into the legal code in 2000, this visa offers lawful resident status to victims of crime (with some restrictions on eligibility) for up to four years, with the possibility of an extension. Among the twenty-six types of criminal activity to which this visa applies are rape, human trafficking, incest, domestic violence, sexual assault, prostitution, sexual exploitation, female genital mutilation, and involuntary servitude—crimes with very specific applications to women and women's bodies or criminal acts to which women are particularly vulnerable.

One reason that the U visa was long awaited is its relationship to the very promising Violence Against Women Act (VAWA). Under VAWA, a woman (or man, girl, or boy) who was the victim of interpersonal-relationship violence can remain in the United States, even if she or he separated from the abuser on whom her or his own immigration status depended. Since VAWA applicants had been formally requesting U visas since 2003, attorney Julie E. Dinnerstein for years called the U visa her "imaginary friend."[69] In fact, almost nine thousand people—the number who had applied for the visa as of May 2007—could have referred to it this way. Among immigrant advocates, the visa does have critics, however. Since the regulations require the arrest of the perpetrator, some women recoil from this option. Compliance with VAWA has also been wanting. In 2010, for example, the National Organization for Women's Legal Momentum project was investigating reports of immigrant women who left violent partners and were denied the right to federally subsidized housing because of their loss of status.

Several individual women gained national visibility as symbols of the country's immigration rights campaigns. One of those was Mexican-born Elvira Arellano, single parent of a U.S.-born child. In August 2006, after she was issued a deportation order, she took refuge in a small storefront Chicago church and spoke out for the rights of the undocumented. One year later, however, immigration authorities arrested her while she was speaking at an immigration rally in California and deported her to Mexico.[70] In 2008, Elvira was replaced both physically (in the same church) and symbolically by Flor Crisostomo, a young woman arrested during a workplace raid. Flor described her actions as civil disobedience and announced, "Here I am, and here I'll stay until the government fixes these broken laws."[71] Echoing the strategies of the U.S. civil rights movement, Elvira and Flor were drawing on more-universal human rights norms and a tradition for which their new home country is particularly known, that of civil disobedience. Activists and officials have joined forces to oversee the largely unregulated mail-order marriage business, particularly following such reports as the Anastasia King murder. Individual states have passed their own regulations to oversee the industry; the U.S. Congress passed the International Marriage Broker Regulation Act (IMBRA) in 2005, requiring criminal background checks on all consumer husbands. Perhaps predictably, this law drew the ire of vocal consumer husbands who feared getting stuck with American-born women as marriage partners. Results from IMBRA might also benefit from activist watchdogs, as mentioned earlier in the context of human trafficking, to ensure that potentially appealing paths to migration are not fully plugged. Here, we must be mindful of social class differences; whereas a woman with a law degree may be able to secure an immigration path through employment visas, other women may look to a marriage option as their only resort.

While much work lies ahead to resolve the issues related to irregular migration—and defenses against such migration—it may be the intersection with gender where one of the leading edges of policymaking can be found. Given the vulnerability of women in the situations depicted here, advocates have devoted targeted efforts to tackling such problems as deportation risks for partner-violence victims, trafficking, the widow's penalty, and irregularities of mail-order marriages. Many of those advocates would say that the victories have been hard won and slow, but the steady progress on these fronts has been evident. And although these new protective policies are in place, advocates have noticed broad gaps in compliance and enforcement, and many immigrant communities are unaware of these remedies.

## On Bodies, Borders, Business, and Agency

With the popular mail-order marriage business, women who have entered the country through marriages to U.S. military personnel met in their home countries, the traditional tendency of men to be the leaders in chain migration, and due to certain immigration policies, many immigrant women across the country are in a dependent status to their husband's immigration or citizenship status. Thus, despite the fact that the common-law tradition of coverture has been abolished, vestiges of a virtual coverture culture continue to exist, due to these continuing gendered relationships and roles.

One theme that permeates the arena of irregular means of entry for women is the woman's physicality—quite often, she is viewed as a body that is the object of surveillance, the subject of uncontrolled fertility, the source of sexual pleasure, and the target of control. Ironically, it is the cultural *de*valuation of a woman who is foreign-born that explains her *value* as a commodity to be bought and exchanged. The late philosopher Michel Foucault analyzed the practice of surveillance in modern societies as a key mechanism for maintaining power over citizens. He also argued that there is a strong relationship between physical bodies and social hierarchies of power.[72] Foucault's argument is applicable to the situation of the irregular migration of women, using the lens of intersectionality: it is not only a woman's gender that renders her physicality as a site for purchase and control but also her exoticism—her national origin and even its related culture—that seemingly multiplies this imagined persona as simultaneously weak and threatening.

As the women profiled here, such as Reyna, have attempted to counter or escape their treatment in the vulnerable places in which they found themselves as unauthorized immigrants, a style of agency appeared that is distinct from the border-crossing or visa-overstaying actions. It could be labeled a "triumphalist" type of agency. This defiant act of agency, however, sometimes overlaps with the acts of intentional violation of (civil) law—such as the women who have taken up sanctuary in churches. These acts of civil disobedience were also moments of confrontational dialogue with the constraints placed on them by social structures both in their home country and in the United States: these women are fully aware that they have no tenable options in either country. A growing number of women migrating irregularly have found themselves "stateless," as Hannah Arendt called it—lacking a legal home anywhere.[73] Many, therefore, are contesting accepted definitions of a rigid binary between "regularity" and "irregularity" and moving the discussion to new levels through the use of other binaries: just and unjust, humane and inhumane, or fair and unfair—all within a knowledge of the current limitations on their options in any country, based on their gender.

Of the women that we interviewed for this book who found themselves in an irregular status, a move into a position outside the rights and protections of legal residency was often a last resort, sometimes accidental, and always undesired. We met a number of women who overstayed visas or arrived without documents prior to the current securitized era, when the deportation/detention risk was not as great; these women smoothly transitioned once they were able to secure visas. They went on to build their futures as productive community members and economic contributors. Should the U.S. government decide to reverse course and offer more predictable paths to green cards and citizenship for those who continue to live in the shadows, our research did not uncover any examples of potential social or economic risks to communities or to the nation as a whole from such a solution.

We have highlighted here the particular vulnerabilities that face women who migrate irregularly and the intended and unintended gender dynamics of this underworld. When policy change is targeted toward specific abuses, however, it risks marginalizing or victimizing women further, even when it is well intentioned. Such targeted approaches require (1) a more systemic context in which to be more effective: that of broader, fuller immigration reform to expand the number of available legal entry options; and (2) progress at the level of international relations to reduce the risks of terror attacks.

In the next chapter, we meet women who are occupying some of the most vulnerable places in our society and economy, where an irregular status carries one of the highest risks: the hidden world of domestic work.

# What They Do

# 5

# "I Am Not Only a Domestic Worker; I Am a Woman"

*Immigrant Women and Domestic Service*

*Sarla,* an immigrant from Nepal who worked there as an accountant, spoke contemplatively of her entrance into domestic service through an unexpected route and the dilemmas and questions she faced after coming to the United States in 2003:

What do I tell you? We got trapped coming here. Our name came in the diversity lottery. Everyone said we were lucky. We gave up our life there [in Nepal] and came [to the United States]. We never anticipated a life like this. It's a result of our sins in a previous life! . . . Soon, the money we had brought almost finished. My husband was having difficulty finding work, children had to start school. . . . We were looking for odd jobs. My daughter looked up this job in the Indian newspaper. . . . After the interview, they [prospective employers] told me I had to live in. This was not mentioned in the advertisement. Had I known, I would not have applied. But they liked me for their child, so they said that if I stay during the week, I could go home on the weekend. I came home and told my family, . . . and my children said, "It is okay, take the job, we will manage." It felt so wrong to me to leave my children and do child care. I was torn. But there was no option. . . . I had never thought I will become a domestic worker, but I said to myself, "I know how to do this work, and I will not let my family suffer." So I took up the job.

*Bettina,* who migrated from Argentina, reflected on the path that led her from her home to her life caring for children in a household in the United States:

The woman I used to work for in Buenos Aires had a brother in USA. When he got his second child, she wanted me to go there because they trusted me. The situation in Argentina was not good at the time. . . . I had worked for this family and knew them. So I agreed to come. He did not get a work contract; when I got the visa he said that he will get the work contract later, and it was very easy to get it. . . . He also promised to bring me back in a few months to visit Argentina.

After reaching here, it took me two months to have any reaction. I had not called home for a month. . . . I don't remember what happened in the first few weeks—there was so much work. . . . I just hit the ground, not like I got a day or two. I had to take care of the two children right away. . . . It wasn't until a few weeks that I hadn't looked into the mirror that I saw hair on my lips and my thick eyebrows—I was shocked to see myself. Like I didn't care and gave myself up, like I was on autopilot or something. I just gave myself to work. . . . I came from a big city, but what made me nervous was that I didn't know anything here, I could not speak English, did not understand anything.

*Bettina*'s and *Sarla*'s narratives are reflections of the globalizing world where women are emerging as important economic players and where domestic service is evolving as a notable form of paid labor for women across national borders. Both of these women represent the everyday modes within which women face and challenge the structural impacts of global capitalism. In the context of the international migration of women, domestic service embodies intriguing contradictions. On one hand, it has been a propeller of the autonomous migration of women, as an occupational category whereby women become primary contributors to household and national incomes. These women who leave their families and the shores of their native countries are decision-makers, risk-takers, and entrepreneurs in their own right. Yet, on the other hand, this feminization of migration and women's avatar as an economic entity is happening through women's increasing participation in domestic service, a gendered occupation that, being labeled as woman's work, undermines its economic value. The fact that domestic work is historically and traditionally characterized by notions of servility and subservience and is marked by its exclusion from the formal labor market in modern economies makes it one of the most potentially exploitative labor categories.

Globally, the past few decades have witnessed changes in the interrelated phenomena of international immigration patterns and labor-force participation of women. The direction of these migration flows is characteristically

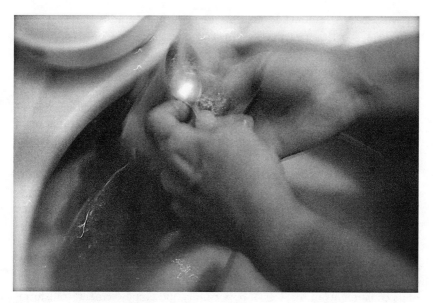

Figure 5.1. Domestic worker (Photo by Lisa Lenker)

from "developing" countries to the developed parts of the world, launching women into economic activity that ensures smooth functioning of the global capitals in the destination countries and survival of the native families of the women in their homelands, as well as of their families that migrate with them. It is estimated that about one hundred million women, mostly from the world's low-income countries, leave their homes each year and migrate abroad in the hope of finding a better life.[1] According to the International Labor Organization (ILO), the service sector is emerging as the largest employer of women worldwide, and within the service sector are "sub-sectors that are traditionally associated with 'female roles,'"[2] represented largely by domestic service and caregiving jobs.[3]

In the United States, female migrants have outnumbered male migrants since 1970.[4] In 2000, about 32 percent of all female noncitizens in the United States were employed in service jobs,[5] and a large number of female migrants turn to domestic work as a means of supporting themselves and their families back home.[6] Domestic service can be singled out as a foremost employer of transnational immigrant women.[7] Nicola Piper points out that "domestic service has become one of the most important legal avenues for migrant women today."[8] The salience of domestic service as an occupational niche for women as a response to growing demand in postindustrial economies is illustrated by the fact that several countries have instituted special visa categories and policies to regulate and facilitate this exchange of labor. This exchange of women's labor and services, however, occurs within the context of inequality between nations as well as local hierarchies of global cities. It is what some scholars call the "reproductive labor"[9] of immigrant women such as *Sarla* and *Bettina* in middle- and upper-class households that helps to maintain and uphold the economic and familial arrangements in American cities.

Domestic service is situated at the intersections of gender, race, ethnicity, and social class, within the context of global capitalism and transnational mobility. Women, located at these variable intersections, rather than being merely driven and defined by them, constantly reconfigure these axes through their endeavors and reincarnate themselves through their struggles. "Immigrant–woman–domestic worker" makes for a vulnerable configuration. Women such as *Sarla* and *Bettina* take this configuration and turn each of its constituents into places of opportunity and empowerment, transforming it into an occupational niche and a platform to organize for rights.

Who are these women such as *Bettina* and *Sarla*, whose prime identity becomes that of a "domestic" in the United States? Where do they come from? Why do they become domestics? What is their reaction to their work and lives? Do they have any other aspirations? What are their lives like both as domestic workers and as women? And are they doing anything to change their situation? What is the context of policy within which this occupation operates? These are some of the questions we explore in this chapter.

### Contextualizing Domestic Service in United States: Past to Present

Domestic service in the United States has historically transferred across lines of the sociocultural hierarchy, and the ethnic groups primarily responsible for domestic service have varied from one historical era to another. Until the Civil War, the terms *domestic servant* and *slave* were almost interchangeable; people who were considered slaves, both men and women, performed the range of household-related chores. Domestic service became predominantly a female occupation in the period after the Civil War, forming the single most important category of employment for women. In 1870, for instance, more than 52 percent of all women wage earners had been domestic servants.[10]

During the early decades of the twentieth century, native-born white women primarily provided domestic service in smaller towns and rural areas. In bigger urban cities, white European immigrant women, particularly Irish, Scandinavian, and German females, replaced native-white women as household workers.[11] Due to the processes of urbanization and industrialization, between the close of the nineteenth century and the end of World War I, a range of white-collar jobs opened up for white women in different professions and trades. During this period, the great European wave of migration also declined, leading to a paucity of white immigrant women entering domestic service. This had significant and long-term impacts on the way domestic service was structured, making it increasingly segregated along the race and gender divide.

As a response to this situation, the migration of African American women from the South to the North increased during this period,[12] as they filled in the domestic-service positions made available by the upward mobility of white women, whether native-born or immigrant. The number of white women who participated in domestic service decreased by one-third between 1870 and 1920, while that of African American women increased by 43 percent,[13] reaching up to 78 percent in 1930 in places such as the District of Columbia.[14] Domestic service, for white women in general, was seen as a bridging occupation during the transition from early adulthood into married life. For native-born black women both within and outside the institution of slavery, domestic service was an intergenerational occupation, and it was considered a dead end with little hope of mobility.[15]

In the West and Southwest of the country, domestic servants included both immigrant women—primarily Mexicans and Asians, including first and second generations of immigrant Japanese women—and native-born women of Mexican, African, and Native American descent.[16] Mexican women domestics were predominant in this region during this period, and the trend has continued to the present time.[17]

The increase of African American women in domestic service in most parts of the country continued through to the middle of the twentieth century. In 1950, more than 40 percent of employed African American women worked as domestic servants, which was ten times the number of white women working as domestics.[18] A landmark shift in this picture of domestic service occurred after the civil rights movement, when African American women rejected domestic service in order to realize opportunities that became available to them after the Civil Rights Act of 1964. The subsequent decades of the twentieth century saw a decline in the proportion of African American women in domestic service, from 16.4 percent in 1972 to 7.4 percent in 1980 and then to 3.5 percent at the end of the 1980s.[19]

The latter part of the twentieth century, therefore, saw the passing of domestic-service jobs from African American women to more recent immigrant women, especially in global economic centers such as New York, which are characterized by stark income disparities among their inhabitants. High incomes, as well as the growing presence of dual-income couples in the upper and middle professional classes, build a substantial demand for domestic-work positions in these cities. The availability of a cheap labor force in the form of a population consisting of immigrant women of color has been filling this emerging need.[20] For instance, in Los Angeles, the presence of Latinas in domestic service grew from 9 to 68 percent from 1970 to 1990—a period that saw the proportion of positions held by African American women domestics decline from 35 to 4 percent. According to a report by Domestic Workers United, 95 percent of the domestic workers in New York are people of color, and 93 percent are women.[21]

This transfer of a labor-market niche from African American women to immigrant women of color is analogous to the process in earlier eras, with one of the least valued occupations—that of domestic service—being passed on to the most disadvantaged segment of the female population with the least number of options. The Domestic Workers United report further mentions that U.S. census data show a 24 percent increase in the size of the New York domestic workforce from 1990 to 2000, despite only a 10 percent growth in the workforce overall. It also estimates that in New York City there are more than two hundred thousand domestic workers, "who sustain the city's families and homes."[22] Studies also point to the fact that one of the major occupational groups that immigrant workers, especially the new immigrants, represent is private household services.[23] Maria de la Luz Ibarra argues in her study on Mexican domestics in Santa Barbara, California, that although the census data show that private household workers in the city grew from 342 in 1980 to 644 in 1990, "anyone who lives in the city knows these numbers are low, and their principal usefulness, therefore, is simply to show a growth trend." She further notes that during that decade, "based on Census data, the number of domestics in Santa Barbara grew at a rate of 5.5 times that of the general population."[24]

Neither a "dead end" with little or no hope of mobility, as it had been for African American women, nor a "bridging occupation," as it had been for white women in the early twentieth century, domestic service exists as an occupational ghetto which immigrant women of color try to live in as well as to transcend. These women have become an indispensable part of the informal "shadow economy"[25] of urban life: a social reality, entrenched in public imaginations to the extent that domestic service in contemporary U.S. society has become almost synonymous with images of immigrant women. Women domestic workers in everyday parlance in America are known by synonyms such as the "Filipina," the "Latina," the "Domestica," or the "Maid."

In the following sections, through the apparently disparate stories of women currently working as domestics, we look at the interplay of common denominators such as gender, immigration, race/ethnicity, and class and at the agency of these women as they work in private households in the United States of America. We learn about women's pathways into domestic service, their lived experiences as immigrant–women–domestic workers, and their transitions into the public sphere to address their life and work situations. Through the meanings they give to their experiences, we also learn how they navigate the present and craft a future within circumstances that are often paradoxical.

## Pathways: Immigration and Domestic Service

Pathways to immigration and domestic service for women, as is apparent from stories such as those of *Sarla* and *Bettina,* are diverse and intertwined. Most of the women we interviewed said that they immigrated to the United States with a hope to improve their life circumstances of poverty or to escape situations such as personal violence or political-economic unrest in the home country. Whereas for some of the women,[26] domestic service was the key reason and/or channel to come to the United States, about the same number of women came with an ambiguous understanding and knowledge that domestic work was a plausible option to fall back on for survival and to earn a living.[27] For some others,[28] domestic service was not a planned or desired direction but emerged as the only viable option for sustenance for them as immigrants in the country. At least one woman also mentioned being smuggled or trafficked into the United States for domestic labor.[29] Whether the women came as part of the family or came alone, domestic service became the medium for them to become primary supporters of their family units or to contribute to the family's survival.

For immigrant women workers, the visa category and the type of immigrant status they hold influence their ability to be legally employed in the country. Some women responded with ambiguity to questions regarding their immigrant status; their stories also indicated fluidity or a likely slide between documented and undocumented status over the course of time. So how is this fact important in the context of domestic service? In the United States, as in many other countries, domestic service is part of the informal economy, and therefore labor legislation is not likely to be enforced. As a relatively unregulated occupation, employment and work arrangements are conducive to multiple forms of abuse of the worker by the employers and intermediary agencies or brokers. An unregulated occupation such as domestic service provides a way for undocumented immigrant women to be employed, but outside the view of authorities. The informality, however, excludes these workers from much labor legislation and protections available to workers in the mainstream labor force.[30] The possibility of abuse is amplified if the worker is undocumented.

The overlap of these aspects—an occupation located within the informal economy and a workforce characterized by ambiguous immigrant status— combined with the gendered nature of the work and the workforce, consigns domestic service and immigrant women domestics to an interlocking cycle of stigma, vulnerability, and susceptibility to exploitation. This confluence gives rise to and breeds what Pierrette Hondagneu-Sotelo has called the "under the table" economy, which operates usually to the disadvantage of the worker.[31] For immigrant women as workers, therefore, the variations in immigrant status are quite consequential and, as their stories indicate, significantly affect their experiences of being a domestic.

Although both *Sarla* and *Bettina* entered the country on legal visas, there was a critical difference between the kinds of legal status each had. *Sarla's* green-card status through the diversity lottery assured her a determinant, long-term status leading up to the possibility of citizenship. Her search for employment was evidently a part of the survival strategy of her new immigrant family. As a new immigrant, *Sarla* came to domestic service as the most viable option for paid work *after* she migrated to the country. For *Bettina*, who said she "came as a domestic worker," the immigrant status was somewhat tenuous; her story indicates that she entered the country as a documented person on a tourist visa. Given the regulations of the tourist-visa category, she was not allowed to work and consequently fell under the category of an irregular worker. Her visa was also time limited and needed to be renewed or changed within the requisite time period for her to maintain a documented immigrant status in the country. Whereas for *Sarla* or for *Gracia,* who came on a family visa as a dependent of her daughter and entered domestic service to contribute to the family income and to become self-sufficient, employment as a domestic worker was not the medium or condition to ensure residence in the country, for *Bettina,* in contrast, the ability to stay in the United States was contingent on her employment as a domestic in the hope of getting a work visa. By extension, she was dependent on her employer to maintain her documented immigrant status in the country by renewing or changing the visa, an experience that resonates in many other stories of women.

The stories of *Rashmi, Stella, Meenu,* and *Malathi* indicate that employers bring workers on short-term temporary visas on the premise of arranging a work visa or a green card. These assurances, the women said, are seldom clearly stated or fully explained by the employers. Thus, such individuals often enter the country on a tourist visa without adequate information about its implications for them as workers or as temporary immigrants. People may also enter on a "domestic worker" visa, as domestic service is an occupational category with a designated visa by the U.S. Citizenship and Immigration Services.[32]

It was not uncommon for the women we interviewed to be uninformed about intricacies of visa-related documentation, or, as they called them, "the papers." *Rashmi,* recalling her ignorance of these matters, said that she only came to learn that her visa had lapsed and the implications of its invalidity when she wanted to visit her family in India and was told by the employer that if she left, she may not be able to return. *Bettina* and *Malathi* said they continued to work for their first employers despite bad treatment because at the time of hiring, the employers had promised to get them the requisite work visa. They were hesitant to ask the employers, and when they did ask, they were threatened or given vague answers until the time the visa on which they entered the country actually expired. Women in such situations are concerned about the consequences of seeking help for these matters unless they can fully trust that the person offering assistance will not report their status.

Although somewhat aware of the risk of sliding into an undocumented immigrant category, the women who entered on valid visas did not realize the connotations of their status on work and life until they lost their documented standing. *Khursheeda* came to the United States on a one-year travel visa from Bangladesh; she explained, "I have no papers now; had one-year visa, then no money. Nobody told how to extend visa . . . at the agency.[33] I came to know I have no [legal] papers anymore; therefore, I am doing this domestic job. I can't go home [to her home country], because my family depends on the money I send. I am always worried."

While the unregulated structure of domestic service and the resultant hidden nature potentially make it an oppressive form of labor, this invisibility as workers also makes it possible for women to stay under the radar of immigration authorities and labor regulations. For instance, women on dependent visas, such as *Kiran*, who came as a student spouse,[34] may resort to domestic service, even though they are not permitted to undertake other types of employment, as an expedient measure to tide themselves over through periods such as the completion of a spouse's education, in the hope that the spouse will land a professional job with a work permit or green card. *Kiran* recounted that although domestic service provided a viable option for paid work, it made her and her family's legal situation tenuous during that time, as she was always "afraid of being reported." The choice, she said, was "not easy."

As these stories attest, domestic service emerges as a complex domain of survival and challenge for immigrant women in myriad circumstances.

## *Navigating the Maze: Networks and Connections*

Given the informality and hidden nature of this labor sector, household jobs are often arranged through informal channels. These circuits are generally sealed and somewhat hidden, requiring personal networks to break into them. Despite the growing demand for domestics and babysitters, the women we interviewed mentioned that for a new immigrant, these jobs are not readily accessible, and finding a reliable job as a domestic may be challenging. *Gracia* used the metaphor of a maze to describe the process of an immigrant woman seeking household work, and she said that knowing someone with contacts was "the key to the right door." Employment is often organized through word of mouth to maintain the informal arrangement for the benefit of both the employers and the workers, who to varying degrees disregard labor legislation in the arrangement.

Most of the women emphasized the value of having reliable networks in the new country in order to find household work. Those who came without a prearranged job as a domestic invariably acquired their jobs through personal networks. *Kiran* got her first job when a woman whom she knew was returning to her home country; she referred *Kiran* to work in her place. *Khursheeda*, like *Sarla*, found her job through an advertisement in an ethnic newspaper, and her brother helped her find references. *Majida*'s first job came from referrals through her friends' circle. *Gracia*'s daughter helped her find her job through agencies in which she had been employed. *Rosita* started her first job as "helping" at the house of her husband's friend. And *Nina* found her job through her church network.

The presence of a relative or acquaintance, or the development of a support network soon after arrival, proved to be a lifeline for these women in an alien country. *Khursheeda* told about finding her first job after arriving from Bangladesh: "[My] brother help me, and in less than a month I had a job; he help me in preparing for interview because he knew how things work here. . . . If he did not help me with speaking English and reading, I would have never found a job or make sure it is safe to work here."

Sixty-eight-year-old *Gracia,* who was sponsored by her daughter when she came from the Philippines, found it "easy to find a job even at the old age," as her "daughter and son-in-law knew a lot of people and agencies" and helped her find a job suitable to her capability. Even in cases when the job is arranged through an employment agency, as *Gracia* explained, "someone who knows the difference between the quacks and a reliable placement agency and how to apply and fill in forms and understand the conditions" is important. Upon arrival, the existing networks were found to be like a buffer from the exigencies of adjusting in a new world.

*Rosita* and *Nina* highlighted the role of wider, community-based networks such as the ethnic community or religious congregations such as a church. *Nina,* who came to the United States as part of family reunification from Ukraine, found that while her family was there for personal, emotional support, all resources during the initial days were provided by the church community. This network also provided references and referrals for her to find household work with "kind employers," who she said were good to her.

Women domestics universally emphasized the need and value of affiliation with a community well disposed to their life circumstances and informed about the nuances of this occupation. They explained that networks were crucial in more ways than just in finding employment. Women actively sought supportive networks, which fulfilled a range of emotional, social, and professional needs. Being members of these circuits helped women find jobs and learn about employers, facilitated their ability to change jobs, and kept them abreast of the market value of labor time. The networks were also instrumental in understanding the "work" in domestic service and ways to deal with employers. Of foremost value to women were the insights that they developed, by sharing experiences, to identify exploitative aspects in their work.[35] Networks also kept them connected to their homeland and oriented them to the new role of this occupation and to life as an immigrant. *Rosita* remarked, "If I had not met other women, I would have forgotten I am not only a domestic worker; I am a woman."

### Contested Meanings: The Nature of Domestic Work

The quest for a reliable workplace points to the unique location of domestic work at the intersection of the private and the public realms. Located within the private homes and the personal domain of an employing family, the work and work relations in domestic service are clearly marked by aspects such as personalism and informality. The personalistic demands on workers include expectations of emotional labor. Although the personalism of this labor arrangement is sometimes favorable for women domestics,[36] often, given their unequal status and the insecurity of their job, the informality negatively affects the bargaining power of the workers.[37]

Unregulated hours, nondefinition of work, lack of clarity of role, and the expectation to perform whatever is asked of them were only some examples of work conditions that the women cited in interviews.[38] *Bettina*, like many of the other women, expressed her bewilderment at the "ever-stretching list of tasks to be done" and, at the same time, the embedded exploitation in the personalistic nature of the job. She said,

> For immigrant women—for them it is not like one job: within one job, you have twenty other jobs. They hire you to care for children, then they ask you to walk the dog or clear the office. . . . They add this and that, and we don't say something, because we are scared. . . . This happens a lot. . . . When I was new, I never said anything. It seemed like just another thing to do in the house.

She also mentioned how employers consider domestics "to be on call." She said, "Her [the employer's] schedule changes, so she calls me according to her shifts or in emergency. . . . So *I* cannot have a schedule. . . . I am all over the place because my schedule changes so many times a week. I cannot set up my life, and therefore I forget." Her statement relays the lack of control the women have over their time as domestics. It depicts how their work is arranged around the convenience of employers and how the personalistic nature of the job assumes their availability beyond work hours.

*Bettina* was not alone in this experience. Statements of other women workers indicated that employers prefer to hire immigrant women because of their vulnerabilities, which leads to deference and subservience. Employers try to maximize control of the work performed by the domestic and exercise personal control over her, especially in care jobs or live-in work. These personalistic expectations and negotiations operate within the context of a market economy that is largely disadvantageous for immigrant women workers.

When new in the country and new to the occupation and lacking awareness of the labor market, women are taken advantage of in several ways. To quote *Sarla,* "The first work I started, I was even shy to ask about money. She [employer] said three hundred dollars a month, and I agreed. I had no idea of appropriate wages; one dollar is equivalent to a lot of money back home. At the end of the month when I got the money, I was happy to get it."

In a study conducted by Human Rights Watch in 2001, the average hourly wage of live-in domestics in the United States was found to be $2.14, which is far below the federal minimum wage; from this wage, the employers sometimes deducted payments for board and lodging. The median workday for these workers was fourteen hours.[39] Another study of domestic workers, conducted in New York in 2007 by Domestic Workers United, did not find much change in these conditions: 41 percent of workers earned low wages, and 67 percent did not receive overtime pay, while nearly half the respondents of the study worked fifty to sixty hours a week, and live-in domestics worked up to one hundred hours per week.[40] California researchers have reported that 90 percent of domestic workers who worked overtime did not receive overtime pay. Further, 31 percent reported working more hours than agreed, and 22 percent were paid less than was initially agreed.[41]

Interviews reveal that many of the women only became aware of wage disparities after some time on the job, with an increase in networking and meeting other workers doing similar work. *Rosita,* in recounting her experience, demonstrated how women challenge such presumption on the part of employers when the situation allows:

> One day I came to work, and some people also came to fumigate the house. So I could not work, obviously, but had come to work, as they had not informed me to not come. . . . They only gave me ten dollars for the whole day. . . . This was not the only time they did this. They would ask me to stay on if there was any work to be done, but they never paid me for that time. . . . Then, that day, I said, "Forget it." I left the job. They were after me for some time to return to work, but I had decided, . . . because I was active in the church, I knew a lot of people who could help me.

*Rosita's* resolve to give up her job, as she mentioned, was possible only after she had acquired confidence and had built networks that assured her that she would find other jobs. Until such a stage arrives, women bear such conditions of employment as underpayment or nonpayment of overtime or extra work despite the regulation that requires overtime pay for domestic workers in some states, such as California.[42]

## Domestic Work as an Immigrant Woman: Weighing Advantages and Disadvantages

Most of the women we interviewed engaged in an ongoing and personalized assessment of the multiple aspects of domestic service and tried to make these aspects work for them. They integrated experiences and identities from their earlier lives to give meaning to the present circumstance of being immigrant women engaged in domestic service. *Bettina* said, "There are some advantages: e.g., salaries are higher here [in the United States]. . . . We live in an age when everyone works, both men and women; therefore, there is an increase in demand for immigrant women; therefore, there is a source of work that we can depend upon."

Although the women characterized domestic service as assuring them a source of livelihood and the ability to support themselves and their family, for most domestic workers, it is not a secure, sustained source of income. Living under a constant fear of loss of employment and compromising on challenging work conditions was a commonly reported experience. *Kiran's* statement was not atypical: "I found a job; there were three families in one big house with different units. I worked there for very little money, . . . lot of work. . . . I was not used to standing and cleaning for up to ten hours, but I had to work."

Several women conveyed that given the circumstances, they preferred domestic service to other forms of employment. *Bettina* mentioned that once they have some experience, the salaries they can obtain or demand in domestic work can be higher than other corresponding job options available to women in the informal service sector. *Gracia* added, "I would suggest women to do this work because it is easy—not easy but easier than many other jobs. . . . It is safe when you are old like me, and salary is good. When people need you, they give money." And *Nina* said, "No, it was not difficult to do this work. In our country, girls are taught to do housework. So I knew how to clean and cook. I could do this job without going to school again."

Although most of the women had limited options for other forms of remunerative work, their responses revealed a studied decision-making process in which they weighed the available options. *Stella* said,

> I would like to do other jobs—like work in a restaurant—but in that you have to be there every day, even Sunday. In that job there is no flexibility. I like to be active in son's school and in other things like coming to CHIRLA.[43] Working in houses can be flexible. Sometimes they need you to work more, so when you need to do something, you can ask to leave early if you have worked with them long.

She added, "I would tell women to do housework if they really need money. . . . Even if they don't know English, they can work. It is like being self-employed. If you can finish the work faster, you can go home faster."

*Kiran's* family members minimized their social interactions when she started work as a domestic, since her husband was doing graduate studies at a university and all their friends were members of the educated middle class. *Kiran* said, "I had to stop thinking about how they [her employers] treated me sometimes or what others thought. . . . This was all I could do."

## *"Yes It Is, but It's Not": Child Care as "Work"*

In evaluating this occupation, women also disaggregated the cluster of varied activities within domestic service so that some activities stood out as more preferred than others. Although harder to obtain as immigrants, requiring reference checks and strict scrutiny of the worker, babysitting and child-care services were identified as most in demand and as having a higher value in both the wages and status accorded to the worker. *Stella* explained, "We are from outside here, and because I have no language skills, therefore no respect. But if I work as babysitter, they respect more. They shout less." *Majida* emphasized the greater stability in babysitting jobs: "If the child gets used to you, the employers want to keep you and adjust more with you." *Sarla* offered her insight: "If you look at the reality, being a woman in this situation is better. To earn what we get in child care, men have to stand and do hard physical labor for ten to twelve hours."

Internal contradictions in performing the "labor of love" were not lost on those who provided child-care services. *Kiran* said that she stopped working for the employing family only because their "child had grown up, and they started going to school, . . . and the family moved to Long Island" (away from the city). Therefore, *Kiran's* child-care services were no longer needed. With a sense of nostalgia and pride, *Kiran* said, "The child calls me 'Didi.'[44] . . . I go to meet the kid even after four years of leaving the job. . . . Takes me more than twenty dollars each time, but I go. I connect with my heart with them. . . . They also respect me. If I don't go, they ask after me." In her narration, the emphasis is on the relational aspect of her job and the continuity of a bond with the employer-family that goes beyond the labor contract and that *Kiran* valued over other aspects of her work experience. This personal dimension was, however, experienced simultaneously with the labor and time involved in the job. *Kiran* also reported, "There was no set time for work. If the child was crying, I stayed on till late. Sometimes they paid [extra] money, but not always."

This paradox of emotional labor—the gratification of a relational bond and, at the same time, the embedded exploitative aspects including unscheduled labor time and nonremuneration of overtime—is part of the experience reported by most women domestics engaged in child care or household work. At the same time, such bonds became crucial for emotional and psychological sustenance for women domestics in the otherwise isolated existence within the employers' house, especially for immigrant women who were away from their own family.

### Living-In as a Domestic

Live-in domestic work is disproportionately performed by the immigrant, and especially new immigrant, workforce[45] that caters to the growing demand for personalized, home-based child-care and household services among the middle- and upper-class professional families, as a cheap, vulnerable labor force. The live-in form of domestic service is unique because of its location within the household of the employer, where the overlap of "workplace" and "home" blurs the boundaries of work and personal life for women domestics. Their membership in the employing household is often limited to performance of personal-emotional labor, without the rights or status of being a "part of the family."[46] *Rashmi*, who came to work for people introduced to her through her family circuit, spoke of this experience as part of her being a live-in domestic:

> I was told I had to take care of children and help in cooking. I did not think what it would mean to live so far away in someone's house. . . . After I came here, the very first day, I felt out of place. I ate alone. I was not even a guest. It was different: they did not treat me like a servant, but no one talked to me like you talk to people in the house. I was someone who worked for them.

*Rashmi*'s statement exemplifies the work relations and living conditions of the live-in context.[47] *Rosita* mentioned experiencing sexual assault, and *Malathi* and *Sarla* also alluded to it. *Malathi* spoke of her experiences as a live-in worker: "I have had three surgeries. . . . They used to hit me on my back and pull my hair. . . . Once I fell and bled and got stitches, and I had no health insurance. . . . When I wanted to leave, I was threatened by employers."

*Malathi*'s narration about physical abuse, *Meenu*'s experience of being "asked to stand out in snow at night [as punishment] because the baby was crying when employers returned home," and *Bettina*'s story of overwork to the extent of not finding time and energy for self-care or being able to make a phone call to her family to inform them of her whereabouts are testimonies of the myriad forms of abuse commonly experienced by women domestics in live-in work.

*Stella*, speaking from her experience of living in the United States for several years and working as a domestic, said, "The situation has not changed. Women keep coming and keep working in homes. When they come, mostly they live in. That's hard work. They are on call all the time. But they can't do anything. They have to find a job and a place to live."

The susceptibility to abuse is faced by women not just due to factors such as a precarious immigrant status. In fact, these experiences of women on designated domestic-worker visas such as A-3, B-1, and G-5 are a result of the conditions placed on the workers by the visa itself, leading to extreme forms of control and abuse of workers. Human rights groups are challenging such exploitative legal provisions, yet the exploitative conditions persist. A report by Human Rights Watch indicated that domestic workers on employment-based visas cannot change or leave exploitative employment, as they face the situation of losing legal status if they leave their job.[48] Even if a domestic worker files a complaint, employers of domestic workers on these visas often enjoy diplomatic immunity and escape legal reprimand under U.S. criminal, civil, or administrative jurisdiction.[49]

Like child-care jobs, live-in work is taken by many immigrant women because it is one of the few options available to them given their life context, but many attempt to move on as their conditions change or their bargaining power improves. *Sarla*, for example, started out with live-in work and eventually moved on to day jobs. Despite the added travel time, long work hours, and aspects such as travel expenses and house rent, most women preferred day jobs to being a "24/7 worker." Day jobs allowed women their personal worlds and social networks at the end of the day. Most of the women interviewed opined that the availability of a public-personal realm where they could retain autonomy over their lives and labor, away from the confines of the employers' house, made it the more desirable option. This trend is similar to the historical preference of African American women to shift to day work and to what Romero has referred to as the professionalization of domestic service among Chicano women domestics in Denver.[50]

### Their Worlds: Immigrant-Women-Domestics

A common thread that runs through the stories of these women is their commitment to support their family in the United States or back home; and with this motivation, they met challenges, but they also reported a pattern of continually shaping these challenges into opportunities. In doing so, these women experienced domestic service through the specifics of their circumstances. Despite the shared status of being immigrants engaged in domestic service, their diverse backgrounds gave their experiences different subtexts and their struggles and accomplishments different meanings. For *Nina,* a pharmacist from Ukraine who never thought of domestic service as part of her future in the United States, "a job is a job. You go, you clean. Sometimes it's bad luck with who you get as employers, . . . like weather." For *Kiran,* coming from a middle-class background in Nepal, where she had employed domestics, it was a longer journey of acceptance of this occupation: cleaning bathrooms for her was "degrading and defiling" in the beginning; but later, she viewed a household job as a job she could "do as a woman" and something that she was "proud to be very skilled at." For *Gracia,* at sixty-eight years of age, household work was a "way of self-reliance even in old age," doing what she had done all her life: "caring and cooking." *Rashmi,* a widow from India, found a rationale for being away from her children to provide for them. Even though she was torn and conflicted at times about living in her employers' household and being a surrogate mother to her employers' children while she lived away from her own, she coped by focusing on how this work allowed her to provide financially for her children. For *Sarla,* taking care of children was a familiar role in her extended family back home, making babysitting an acceptable form of labor, like caring for her nieces and nephews. Women who had worked as a domestic in their home country had comparative insights as workers in this occupation: *Stella* found it easier than being a domestic in Mexico, but in contrast, *Meenu,* while finding the chores easier to perform in the United States, found the nature of domestic work and the inherent relations to be the same in India and here: "no end to work, no talk of money."

Amid the women's hard work and their ability to find ways to sustain themselves, there was a detectable theme of a sense of alienation due to the ongoing and seemingly unending struggle of precarious living and arduous work. *Josefina,* an immigrant from Paraguay, remarked, "The first thing to take into account is that no one is in a foreign country just for the fun of it. It's very difficult to leave family and friends. . . . I came here thinking it's a place of opportunity and the 'First World.' . . . But I don't see any humanity here."

The stigma associated with the overlap of immigrant status and the low status of domestic service was a universal experience that the women shared in the interviews. Equally significant was their awareness regarding their role as domestics within the macro socioeconomic context. *Josefina* said, "Women left their homes behind to provide for their families, . . . to make a better life. . . . They come over here, do work people here don't want to do, or they wouldn't do it themselves in their home country." *Stella* commented on the labor-market situation: "Earlier you could leave a job and get another job easily. Not now, because industry is saturated now. There are so many women to work, it is hard to find work now." *Meenu* added, "There is no advantage of being an immigrant in this country. It is worst to be an immigrant woman. They say women are respected here. As an immigrant woman, all you have is to clean others' dirt. That's what it is to be an immigrant." *Bettina* said, "First of all, we have to confront language barrier; second, since we are immigrants, people look down their noses with disdain. . . . We come here to work, but we are seen and treated as slaves."

For women who now work as a domestic but had pursued a different profession in their home country, the experience was far from pleasant or expected. Yet their responses reflect the ability to adapt to the realities of their new life as immigrants. *Rosita* said, "I was an accountant in Mexico, . . . had some other women to come and do work for me in Mexico. I did not think I will have to do this work in USA, but money is money. If I can earn, all work is okay." The resilience of women such as *Rosita* in such circumstances is evident, as they actualized their gendered role into a marketable skill set. *Lucia* said,

> I had been a teacher, but no way could I teach here. So I took what I got, . . . a job to work in the house, to do cleaning and washing and cooking—what other women used to do for me back home. . . . They say woman are not strong. But I am working here, and . . . I never thought like a woman. When I left my country, I told myself, "I have to go and work, and I will do it." And here I faced all kinds of things, but I am here.

*Bettina* summed up the dichotomy felt by most women about their situation: "I like this work, although, if there was something else to do, I would do. . . . But this is an advantage to immigrant women. If it didn't exist, what would we do? . . . I don't feel ashamed; this is devalued work, but it is still respectable."

Women such as *Josefina,* who came to the United States to escape violence in her home country, Paraguay, and *Rashmi,* who left her country to find a way out of destitution for her and her children, do not want to return. Many women, such as *Malathi, Khursheeda, Meenu,* and *Rashmi,* have not seen their children and family in years. Hondagneu-Sotelo uses the term "transnational motherhood" to characterize the situation in which domestic workers care for the homes and children of American families while their own children remain "back home" in their societies of origin. This arrangement, she says, "signals new international inequalities of social reproduction."[51]

Women continue to work, albeit as undocumented immigrants and with very restricted lives in the United States because of that status. Most want to find a life beyond the one that they currently experience, since they followed their dreams to move here, and they are striving hard to attain those dreams.

### Beyond Being a Domestic

With regard to these women's personal lives, most of them did anticipate that the need for them to financially support their family, either back home or here, would continue in the future. *Rashmi* mentioned that her children are grown up, but she still supports them and her in-laws. *Khursheeda* supports her family in Bangladesh, and *Gracia* sends money to her daughter and grandchildren in the Philippines. For those with family here in the United States, such as *Nina, Sarla,* and *Kiran,* their role as provider also seems likely to continue. These women seemed to have developed an acceptance of domestic service as their occupation, at least for the present moment, and depending on their social location, they found a rationale and meaning in their work. *Kiran* said, "After coming here, I earned money . . . after all, despite all troubles. Feels good! I became bold. Earlier, all I could was to carry out my duties at home. Now I spend from own hands, for myself also."

Like *Kiran,* others also found personal growth and enhanced self-reliance through and alongside this work. *Sarla* shared this sense of autonomy and said that although she may not need to work once her husband gets a job, "I like to work and earn my own money." Further, these women aspire to use their experience of working and living as an immigrant to contribute in various ways to their home society. *Stella* mentioned that she saves money: "[As] part of a group of Mexican people, we raise funds for projects in my hometown, like to improve drainage, for school supplies for children, etcetera." *Gracia* has a personal, familial aspiration, as the oldest in the family; she is saving money to organize a family reunion to meet all her grandchildren in the Philippines. *Sarla* exudes determination in saying, "I do not want to keep doing babysitting job. Want to start my own business—open a store." And *Kiran* wants to go back to her country and set up an organization to help women—something she used to do before migrating. *Rosita* dreams of going back to her country and owning a poultry farm. Despite the prolonged struggle and feeling somewhat trapped in the domestic work and/or the immigrant situation, these women retained their ambitions and dreams. As *Nina* indicated, "Realistically, I doubt I will ever go back to school, but I want to tell that I want to do it." And *Bettina,* with much optimism, stated, "I know for myself that I will always be a domestic worker. But I know a domestic work[er] who is now teaching math and Spanish in schools. So it can change for some. Keep your eyes on the prize."

*Meenu* and *Majida* are pioneers in their own right. *Meenu* freelances as a masseuse and earns extra money. *Majida* described her arrangement: "On the weekend, I teach new immigrants—women—language and life skills. When I came, I needed so much help. I want no one else to suffer as I did." *Majida* and *Meenu* are proud of these alternate identities that they created for themselves and of their ability to find creative ways to survive and grow amid struggle. They are able to craft lives that are wholesome as workers and as women, and they are also trying to give back so other women are enabled in whatever ways are possible.

### Becoming a Force: Organizing as Workers

*Majida,* though she is exceptional in the extent of her commitment, is not alone in joining the ranks of volunteers in organizations to expand a support network for women. An important milestone in women's stories was the contact with an organization, typically following adverse events in employment. Given their isolated working conditions, the existence of such organizations that help women understand and address abuse was crucial. Yet the reach of the networks remains limited, due to the same reasons of domestic service's being located in the isolation of private homes. The increasing membership of women domestics such as *Gracia, Rosita, Sarla,* and *Stella* allows smoother flow of information among women and between organizations and women, which often happens informally through ethnic or church networks and even surreptitiously in cases of abuse, such as for *Khursheeda* or *Malathi. Ingrid,* who had faced abuse as a domestic worker and went on to become an activist with domestic laborers, told about her initiative to reach out to women in different ways: "I go to the streets and distribute brochures: 'Know your rights. If you are currently under abuse, know that we can help you defend yourselves.' . . . Prevention is our main goal."

The movement for domestic workers' rights has come of age in the United States. Several organizations with which these women are affiliated were established by women domestic workers and are currently run by the volunteer support of women domestics.[52] These domestic-worker organizations address issues that arise from the intersection of gender and nativity and within a broad framework of rights and equity for immigrant women in domestic service. The mandate and sense of mission of these organizations to fight exploitation comes from an experiential base, which has been instrumental in taking the issues to the level of formulating employment contracts, articulating charters of rights, and demanding legislative reforms. An important part of their work is raising awareness of their rights as domestics and immigrants. *Stella's* statement affirmed this: "I saw a documentary about CHIRLA and then met [one of] their member[s] at church. I told this person that my employer didn't pay what she owed me. . . . Worker said that she will help me get my money. . . . I found so much support here. I want to give that same support to others. That is why I am at CHIRLA."

There was a pronounced sense of solidarity and pride in women's narrations regarding their engagements with activist organizations.[53] *Sarla* mentioned, "I wait for Sunday. . . . It's a reason to come out of the house. We have programs there, meet other women. I feel happy. Before I started going there, I was scared. . . . Now I know what is happening in the world. . . . We can ask each other, even learn how to talk to employers."

These public spaces available to women through such organizations are crucial for personal and professional growth, emotional and social sustenance, referrals, and political mobilization. The activities that women undertake at the organizations include enhancing their skills and building confidence to meet the varied challenges in their professional and personal life. They learn English, make friends, educate themselves about the legal issues around work and immigration, and learn to advocate for rights. Women also call these organizations their "home," their "refuge," and their "haven." They speak a language of rights that they have learned at the organizations, participating as volunteers and bearers of the movement themselves. *Malathi,* speaking from her position as a worker, said, "We are fighting through our organization for rights of women, and government should support us, so that people know that nobody is weak. Nobody should beat any woman. . . . We work for so many hours; we need food to eat, time to eat. We need a holiday too." And she added, "I worked here for so many years. Government has to help me get my papers so my children can come here and I can see them." *Rosita* added her experience: "Since I came to this organization, I don't have to suffer. I know my rights now. I participate in leadership organizing. We talk about work and about community. We also do campaigns for legalization of domestic work and immigrants who are working in USA."

These organizations are building coalitions nationally with other organizations, gaining local legislative victories for rights of domestic workers and aiming for changes in federal policy. An organizer at Domestic Workers United[54] said that the organization is also persuading employers to be a part of this rights-based approach to support and protect the rights of women domestic workers. Such advocacy to include employers in the campaign for domestic workers' rights became significant in contexts such as the recession of 2008–9, which resulted in job losses for women domestics who worked for families negatively affected by the recession. The plight of women domestics remains invisible in times such as the recession or economic downturn. *Rosita* spoke about the difficulties that an immigrant woman faces regarding the availability of jobs and the increasing vulnerability of domestic workers due to the skewed supply-demand situation, at least in some cities: "Now household workers are everywhere, in thousands. We need the government to recognize us as workers. Women are raped in houses. We need respect for their rights, as workers, civil rights, so that no one should steal their wages or do sexual assault. This workforce suffers a lot. Somebody has to do something."

Such narratives speak of the ability of immigrant women to respond to their immediate context and take up work as a domestic, as well as the motivation to join a larger cause to alter the situation that confronts them. Simultaneously, these are stories of individual courage and determination and collective responses to situations to which the state has been slow to respond.

### Immigrant Women and Domestic Service: Intersections of Policy

Domestic service constitutes a complex domain for consideration of policy recommendations. Andrew Sum and colleagues point out that this occupation is not captured by the monthly payroll survey of the U.S. Bureau of Labor Statistics.[55] Census data are only available for specific categories such as immigrant domestic workers on designated temporary visas[56] or household workers and nannies for whom employers pay taxes.[57] Consequently, despite the increase in the phenomenon of domestic service, the available data on this occupational category are scarce and elusive, and domestic workers largely remain underrepresented in official enumerations. This invisibility as workers perpetuates their manipulation, sanctions their exclusion from legal benefits, and makes assertion of their grievances and their rights tricky. Developing some measures to augment visibility in official enumeration of this workforce is a primary requirement for discussion and advancement of policies in this field.

Ongoing advocacy by groups around the country, especially in cities with higher concentrations of immigrant domestics, such as New York, Washington, DC, Los Angeles, and San Francisco, is mobilizing women domestic workers to organize for rights, to increase public awareness of the issues, and to garner political support to accomplish positive advances for relevant legislation. Media is playing an important role in bringing forth the hidden issues through widespread reporting of ill treatment and policy developments, as well as helping to organize events.[58]

These efforts are leading to measures that urge changes to the conditions of domestic workers, including those on special designated domestic-work visas.[59] As a result, a handful of new regulations and labor legislation—at the local, state, and federal levels—increasingly cover aspects such as hours, wages, and boarding costs of live-in workers and others in private domestic work.[60] However, implementation of these regulations is challenging, as few employers and fewer employees know of these provisions, and when employers are aware, invariably, most of them effectively ignore these regulations, while women's multiple vulnerabilities prevent them from realizing their rights as workers.

Efforts to consolidate this movement by expanding these successes to other states are under way. In 2007, organizations around the country formed the National Alliance of Domestic Workers, which aims to connect regional advances in order to develop protective measures in all parts of the country and to lobby for federal legislation for domestic workers.[61] In a concerted response to the reported cases of abuse of immigrant domestic workers, a group of nongovernmental organizations, collaboratively under the aegis of "Global Rights," took their grievances to the U.N. Human Rights Committee (87th session). The group's report invokes norms of international rights for women and for workers, stating, "Although U.S. laws should protect them, domestic workers find that they are often excluded from legal protections or that the laws are not enforced. This reprehensible abuse of domestic workers violates various articles of the International Covenant on Civil and Political Rights."[62]

This report is a step toward acknowledging that the issues faced by immigrant domestic workers are part of a global phenomenon, deserving attention to policies that transcend national borders. Countries such as Canada and the United Kingdom have set examples by reviewing their existing policies. Canada, for instance, initiated provisions that address both the labor conditions and immigrant status of workers: a "live-in care-giver program" introduced in 1992 includes a provision to allow the worker to change employers by informing the Ministry of Citizenship and Immigration and a provision whereby, after two years of nanny work, the worker can apply for landed-immigrant status.[63]

These examples merit consideration when reviewing policy development for women domestics in the United States. More importantly, the movements led by immigrant women domestics addressing issues relevant to them provide signposts for the direction in which policy needs to move. These women are no longer "disposable domestics,"[64] "doing the dirty work"[65] in private homes that is still not considered a "real job."[66] For the policies to be relevant and meaningful, voices of this invisible yet omnipresent collective need to be recognized and included in the process of policy formulations.

Figure 6.1. Rita Kalwani (Photo by Dawson & Associates Photography, Irvine, CA)

# 6

# "Mighty Oaks"

*The Entrepreneurs*

On a sunny March afternoon, Los Angeles–area architect Rita Kalwani presents the offices of KAL Architects, the firm that she built, owns, and manages. Rita moves glowingly from room to room, describing the models and drawings on display that feature both past and current KAL projects; she pauses to introduce her father, a member of her firm, who is intensely focused on a deadline. Rita migrated from India as a young woman, entered a U.S. university, earned her architecture degree, and then steadily built a career in a downtown Los Angeles firm. All along, she dreamed of starting her own company but had her hands full raising her children. As the years went by, she started to notice visible patterns of ageism toward colleagues in her workplace: as the younger people moved in, older workers were forced out. This began to make her uneasy about her future. It was at this point that Rita realized, "If you own your own company, this won't happen to you." With a battery of help from her husband, friends, family, and associates, Rita poured her time and energy into taking seminars and producing mounds of paperwork. Today, she reflects on the early days of her new venture and recalls, "Those first five years were extremely tough." Her labor resulted in her first design contract of her own—a government project—and this gradually dominoed into more. Her Orange County, California, firm has a strong regional reputation for its excellence. In fact, a local magazine ran a story about her success and nicknamed her "a Mighty Oak." As the presence of her father as a valuable member of her firm attests, Rita has been able to remain competitive without reproducing the ageist tendencies in her former firm.

Anecdotally, Americans notice immigrant start-ups all around us, from the local Chinese restaurants, which currently number more than forty thousand across the country, to the occasional surviving Jewish tailor shop that opened a century ago. Such anecdotes of the entrepreneurial spirit of new immigrants are supported by statistics as well. A long history of research literature has documented the existence of immigrant entrepreneurship in the United States as strong in comparison to such activity by the native-born. According to decennial census figures dating from 1880 to the present, immigrants have consistently been self-employed at higher rates than have the native-born.[1] Very recently, scholars have begun to comment on observations that the gap has been narrowing between these two groups and have attempted to explain this phenomenon.[2] Is the myth of the successful immigrant entrepreneur a thing of the past? Although we could speculate that we have entered a different economic epoch in which immigrant entrepreneurs either are *disadvantaged* because they cannot compete or are relatively *advantaged* because they are entering established businesses more easily, we should first examine these rates by gender. Doing so, we learn that while immigrant men's rates of entrepreneurship have leveled off, immigrant women's rates have been rising exponentially. A 2002 study, for example, reported that business ownership by minority women, predominantly foreign-born, "is the fastest growing business community in Southern California (and the nation)."[3] Research literature has not given sufficient attention to the intersection between migration and gender when it comes to entrepreneurship. As Ursula Apitzsch and Maria Kontos have written, "In women's studies, self-employment has been analyzed within the framework of the feminist discourse, while migrants' self-employment has been discussed within the ethnic business debate"[4]—and the two literatures rarely meet.

There are social, cultural, and economic reasons for the old, and continuing, trends of immigrant business ownership. Commonly, researchers suggest that there is a selection process that has to do with the experience of immigrating: someone who takes the initiative to move to another country usually mirrors many of the qualities of the entrepreneur: risk-taking, for example, tends to top the list. Although these studies have, in the past, focused on immigrant *men*, risk-taking is a characteristic that the women discussed in this chapter also share. As one of the women we interviewed explained, "For the immigrant woman, it is an even *greater* risk to leave one's home and culture."

The entrepreneurs discussed in this chapter have opened businesses in service industries (bed-and-breakfast inn, catering, clothing sales, insurance brokerage, hair salons, health-care services, home-based child care, home cleaning, immigration law, nail salon, organizational consulting for nonprofits, restaurants, transcriptions) and manufacturing/construction industries (architecture, engineering, packaged-dessert manufacturing/sales, and wheel manufacturing).

## Women Run the Shop

The idea that immigrant women might be the owners and originators of some of those Chinese restaurants—and their entrepreneurial equivalents, such as the Indian-owned motel, the Silicon Valley hi-tech firm, or the local real-estate agency—has yet to become conventional wisdom. In fact, another myth in the shared social memory of the immigrant entrepreneur in the American public imagination is that of the man who led the family's chain migration and brought his wife over to become a volunteer assistant in the shop. Although the reality behind this image is rapidly changing, as women open their own enterprises, we must also credit a number of foremothers: biographers have chronicled examples of women's start-ups throughout American history, illustrating that entrepreneurial women were right there, actively in the middle of the game, at every stage of the American economy's evolution.[5] These included both the immigrant and the native-born. Historian Barbara Howe has documented the businesses that immigrant women in nineteenth-century West Virginia tended to own, ranging from boarding houses and groceries to millenary shops, with forays into food and beverage production industries.[6]

Today, immigrant women entrepreneurs abound in every region of the United States. Statistically, the top-ten states where immigrant women make their business home are distributed across the Northeast, Midwest, Mid-Atlantic, Southeast, Southwest, and Northwest—covering every U.S. region.[7] Of all U.S. cities, Los Angeles has the highest number of entrepreneurs, followed by New York City and Washington, DC. Gradually, immigrant women are leaving behind the world of unpaid workers in their husband's business, and there is also a growing presence of immigrant women in fields that were once unusual or atypical for women. Several businesses owned by immigrant women are making their way into the lists of top-grossing firms in arenas such as technology. This growing pattern illustrates the broad impact of the yet-unfinished women's equality movements worldwide, as more of our new immigrant women bring a strong educational background or professional experience with them. This is not to discount the fact of continued struggles of women who arrive without such privileges or without the licenses or background that are recognized as transferable; yet such scenarios of relative disadvantage are also among the back stories of those who turn to innovative ways to make a living.

According to the 2000 U.S. decennial census, 575,740 foreign-born women who immigrated as adults reported that they were self-employed in their own incorporated or unincorporated businesses, which is the census category that researchers use to measure entrepreneurship.[8] As with other census data, our use of these numbers requires caveats. The category of *self-employed* may not reflect the type of new business creation that the term *entrepreneurship* often implies; further, we do not know which businesses are jointly owned with other individuals.

Although the decennial census and the American Community Survey are not strictly comparable, as we discussed in chapter 2, there was a notable rise in immigrant women's entrepreneurship rates between 2000 and 2008. In 2000, for example, 7 percent of employed immigrant men and 10 percent of employed native-born men owned their own business. Immigrant and native-born women's business-ownership rates were roughly equivalent in 2000, at 5 percent for each group.[9] By 2008, according to the American Community Survey, immigrant women's entrepreneurship rates had grown to 8 percent of all foreign-born women who were employed, 3 percentage points higher than the native-born women's rate, which was 5 percent, and only 2 percentage points behind that of immigrant men, which was 10 percent. The ownership rate for immigrant men was just below the rate for native-born men, at 10 percent for immigrant men and 11 percent for native-born men. Thus, these statistics show that we are seeing a historically new phenomenon: whereas the native-born were slightly in the lead among the men, it is the foreign-born who were leading for women.[10] Although immigrant men's business ownership outpaced that of immigrant women if we look at the raw numbers (1,234,120 men and 714,811 women), the entrepreneurship growth among women translates into the fact that 38 percent of all immigrant business owners were women in 2008. Further, 41 percent of all women business owners were foreign-born, according to these 2008 data. These census-derived estimates may even be conservative. The Center for Women's Business Research estimated that there were 553,618 businesses owned by Latinas in 2004 and 419,793 firms owned by Asian women. Even though these research figures also included the native-born, we do know that large proportions of Latinas and Asians in the United States are foreign-born.[11]

The Latin America and Caribbean region is the area of the world from which the largest number of these entrepreneurs hailed, followed by Asia and the Pacific Islands. All ten of the top-sending countries are located in Latin America, the Caribbean, Asia, or the Pacific Islands. The top sending country of entrepreneurs (141,103) was Mexico, with Korea in second place (46,213) and Vietnam in third (36,742). Strikingly, but perhaps predictably, these countries all represent the global South—the areas from which the majority of post-1965 immigrants migrated. Yet the global South was not the only region represented in the top-twenty countries. Poland, Canada, and Germany were in fourteenth, fifteenth, and nineteenth positions in the list.[12]

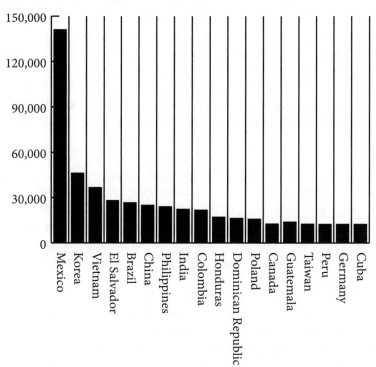

FIGURE 6.2

*Top-twenty sending countries of immigrant women entrepreneurs, 2008.*

*Source*: Ruggles et al., "Integrated Public Use Microdata Series: Version 4.0."

These numbers indicate that there is a quiet revolution of immigrant women's business ownership that is organically growing but is going relatively unnoticed in the culture at large. The Center for Women's Business Research estimated that business ownership for women of color—both native-born and foreign-born—was increasing at six times the rate of ownership by other demographic groups during the first decade of the twenty-first century. Eduardo Figueros, a community-oriented specialist who trains Latinos in entrepreneurship in the Los Angeles region to encourage self-empowerment, has noticed these trends firsthand. In 2007, he reported to us that he had been seeing a major growth in the number of women joining his seminars. In addition, Eduardo was noticing something quite new: women were gravitating toward businesses that have been considered atypical for women in the past. Fewer wanted to open food stands or sell handicrafts than in the past. Crossing the country to the East Coast, similar trends are evident. Anthropologist David Griffith echoed this observation of the growing entrance of immigrant women into business ownership in his report of a 2009 ethnographic study of local Latino shops known as *tiendas* across North Carolina; the study documented that as many as half these businesses were owned by women.[13] At the time of the study, North Carolina hosted the fastest growing Latino population in the United States.

Rachel Owens, cofounder of the Orange County, California, chapter of the National Association of Women Business Owners (NAWBO), offered her overview of the changes in both native-born and immigrant women's ventures:

> At the beginning, it was middle-aged white women, *all* in the service industries. After sixteen years, it has been a metamorphosis. In the last ten years, the businesses are across the board: manufacturing, detective agencies, lawyers, CPAs, aerospace, machinery, and construction. In the last five years, there has been a definite growth in minority businesses: primarily forty years old and under; many are thirty and under. I believe it's education, access to capital.

In the following narrative, moving from the numbers to the stories, we hear from these business owners as they relate their reasons for starting their ventures, their challenges, the meanings of their businesses, and their contributions.

### "Everything That Made Me Who I Am Was in Mexico"

What were the "contexts of exit" for these entrepreneurs? In other words, what led them to choose to leave their home country? Judith Rodriguez, who owns a home-based day-care center in Houston, first came to the United States in 1979. In recounting her story, she remembered, "When you live in Mexico, and everyone talks about the U.S., in your mind it's the promised land. My country has a lot of poor people. I saw a different way of living when I came here." While in Mexico, she was watching her marriage deteriorate, and her husband was exhibiting signs of abuse. Judith did not want to watch her children grow up to be like her husband. She realized, "My kids needed me." This determination drove her to pick up and move her children with her to Chicago to live with a cousin. Judith found the experience to be depressing at first, as she had cut off her own roots; she recalled, "Everything that made me who I am was in Mexico."

There are several recognizable patterns in these entrepreneurs' reports of their reasons for migrating. One was a need to escape trouble of some kind, whether abuse, family discord, or danger in their home country. Sometimes, the escape was quite sudden. Three of these entrepreneurs, for example, were refugees who escaped Vietnam, two as a result of the war in the 1960s and 1970s and the other more recently. Another business owner had been living under repressive political conditions in Romania before 1989. More than once, women cited domestic violence. One had dared to initiate a divorce in her home country decades ago. Her decision did not sit well with her relatives. She recalled, "Everyone in my family hated me. There had never been divorce in the family."

Whereas some of these women escaped trouble, several migrated for the educational opportunities and started businesses after establishing themselves professionally. A few of these women came specifically to set up their business; although this was not the norm for most of them, it is notable that some entrepreneurial ventures were preplanned. Maria de Lourdes Sobrino, the owner of Lulu's Desserts, was already a successful entrepreneur in Mexico and was looking to the United States as an investment opportunity. Her business was severely affected by the devaluing of the peso in the 1980s, and she suddenly realized that she needed to close her Mexico operation. Of the twenty-four entrepreneurs interviewed for this book, only a handful of them came with or because of a husband. Most of the entrepreneurs spoke of coming either alone, with their children, or with other family members. Two African entrepreneurs reported that they were (separately) vacationing in the United States, with no plan to leave home permanently. But they saw the opportunities here, and the plans suddenly changed. As one remembered, "I came here for vacation. I had no idea to stay. I found that here you can do everything you want. There is every opportunity to succeed in life. I called my parents and said I won't be back home."

Once these women arrived, they set about putting down roots and figuring out how they would survive in their new environment. Some worked low-wage jobs, others earned a college or graduate degree, and a few took training classes. Those who did not speak English juggled these new commitments with English classes. One entrepreneur remembered starting every day with her English language class, then working a full shift at one job and the next shift at a second job. Finally, she recalled, she regretfully had to give up her English classes because of lack of time. Judith, from Mexico, worked in a child-care center from seven in the morning to five in the evening each day and then studied from five-thirty to ten o'clock at night for her license to open her own center.

Even those with professional training in their home country often found themselves underemployed in the United States. This experience of status dislocation was true of a number of these entrepreneurs. One former teacher found herself cleaning houses after she arrived, and another teacher scrubbed animal kennels and worked as a live-in nanny for some years. This is not uncommon; Rhacel Parreñas's study of Filipino migrants found that the Philippines faced a teacher shortage, as teachers who emigrated made higher wages as domestic workers in other countries.[14] A woman with a strong educational background in Mexico who found herself waiting tables in the United States remembered, "The hardest moment was when I got a tip. I cried, because I felt like a beggar. I tried to give it back. They said no, and tears came down."

### "I Didn't Want to Punch the Clock"

The decision to take the leap and open a business is a risky one, even in the wake of closed or partially blocked doors in other avenues. What made these women decide to embark on such a risk? For the Kelly sisters from Ireland, one motivation was the desire for schedule flexibility. After arriving in Los Angeles, they had each found work in the health-care industry. But they were of childbearing age and wanted to raise children and spend time with their families. They also missed the lengthier European vacations. Further, they looked around and noticed that it was the insurance brokers who were making the money, and they decided that it would be smart to capitalize on that discovery and become brokers themselves. They began observing brokers and came to a realization: "Hey, we're better than them. . . . So we picked up the trade by literally going on appointments with brokers and listening to them going through medical and dental and 401(k) proposals." Today, Anne and Deirdre Kelly cannot stop talking about how happy they are with their flexible schedules. The sisters integrate their commitment to family issues and needs by promoting their business as family friendly for their clients. They use themselves as examples, in fact. A promotional flyer for their company sports a photo of one of the owners giving a kiss to her baby. They have built a reputation on this principle that attracts clients. "We go to the hospital when a client gets ill."

Another entrepreneur—while not abandoning her family responsibilities—actually chose to start her business in order to *reduce* her time in her household. Angela Chan reported, "I'm not a housewife type. After half a year, I was bored." She reported, "Chinese women feel like it's our responsibility to take care of children, even though I'm very liberal." She felt that she was defying cultural expectations to take a different path, but in the end, this did not deter her. She joined a Los Angeles business and eventually launched her own wheel-manufacturing company.

A repeated, prominent strand in these women's decision to start their own business was the desire for independence. As one put it, "I don't want to work for anybody. I didn't want to punch the clock." This woman, from Iran, started a hair salon. Another was shocked at the way she was financially exploited by her employer. Martine Divahe, from Gabon, learned African hair braiding in a New York salon. She recalled, "I was earning one hundred dollars per week, in *New York City*." It was clear to her, even as a new immigrant, that this level of income was vastly inadequate. Therefore, she decided to take her training that she got from her employer and set up her own shop. Previous research has uncovered a pattern of migrants starting businesses to repair their damaged self-esteem from underemployment and exploitation. This was likely true for several of these women. Child-care-center owner Judith remembered how roughly she was treated when she arrived from Mexico: "Every day was getting harder and harder. . . . I said, 'I'm going to swallow it and do what it takes to be here.'" From a supermarket-cashier job, where she was required to memorize the price of every product on the shelves, to poorly paying temporary jobs, to thirteen years of waiting tables in restaurants while she completed her education, Judith was determined to have "something different."

It would be easy to make the assumption that it was the inspiration of independent women in the United States that helped stimulate these women's courage to open their business. Interestingly, however, and more than once, the women reflected on the inspiration that they received from particular women in their family back home who were business owners. They spoke of these women as people they admired for their strength and independence. The Vietnamese restaurant owner learned her cooking skills from her mother's restaurant. Health-care business owner Shirley Nathan-Pulliam, from Jamaica, remembered, "I always wanted to start my own business." In Jamaica, she observed her aunt, a successful restaurant owner who raised her during several years of her childhood. Shirley's mother began a humble clothing business and later became the manager of a large department store. In fact, women's entrepreneurship is traditionally central to a number of cultures—and economies—across the world. One estimate is that African women produce 80 percent of food grown on their continent, that Asian women produce 60 percent, and that Latin American women produce

40 percent. Many of these women also sell their produce in the market—and thus are merchants as well as producers.[15]

The desire for challenge was also common among these entrepreneurs. Indian-born Rubina Chaudhary started her business on a dare. She had begun to use her newly minted MBA degree to run training seminars on business skills for other professionals, and one day, one of her clients from these seminars dared her to start her own firm. She took the dare and built an engineering company. Today, she runs the business side of the firm, and her husband, an engineer, works for her firm. Los Angeles resident Denise Davies, a Canadian, was similarly looking for challenge. Prior to arriving in Los Angeles, she had been running a school in Pakistan for many years; her first immigrant experience, therefore, was quite far from her current Los Angles abode. While in Pakistan, she began collaborating with an entrepreneurial friend to offer consulting services for businesses. As the World Wide Web was taking off in the West, Denise became fascinated with the idea of capitalizing on the potential for the Internet to boost her consulting business. She eventually relocated to Los Angeles to establish her new company.

Frustration and disappointment with the conventional workplace certainly motivated many of these women, but this was not true of all. Several of these women, for example, received their encouragement from supervisors in their workplace to go out on their own. In each of these cases, those supervisors were men. One of these entrepreneurs, Angela Chan, is a woman with a strong work ethic that served her well in her former workplace. She had been able to advance quickly in the business and kept taking on more challenges that previous employees were unable to handle. Her supervisor realized that she had the ability to run her own company. Angela recalled how little confidence she had early on, as she spoke broken English and was afraid of public speaking. Eventually, she found herself turning a company that was losing money into a profitable one, and the Securities and Exchange Commission interviewed her to learn how she was doing it.

### *"I Was Invisible to the Banks": The Quest for Capital*

If access to capital is one key to getting a business off the ground, how did these women garner the resources that they needed? Ghana-born Esther Armstrong, owner of the Sankofa African and World Bazaar in Baltimore, came across her business idea quite accidentally. She was working for a national corporation when she met a group of visitors from Ghana who were peddling traditional African clothing in the United States. The visitors left some of their unsold merchandise in Esther's basement when they returned to Ghana. One day, she had the idea to take these items to a flea market to sell, to test the waters and clear the clothes out of the basement. The clothing proved to be popular, and the experiment paid off. From there, she continued the flea-market circuit almost weekly, in her free time. Soon she needed to restock, so she began to send regular orders to Ghana. As this part-time hobby began to grow, the opportunity arose to take early retirement from her job, and she saw the opening that she needed to be able to support an independent enterprise. She took the retirement package and set up her own street-level shop. Several years later, she expanded the store and moved to a location with more street traffic, where she now sells brilliantly colored clothing, crafts, drums, and fabrics from Africa and other areas of the world. In one of our visits to her shop, a customer was on the mezzanine level trying on a traditional dress from Ghana for an upcoming special event; a store regular was hanging out by the counter engaged in a warm and animated conversation while finishing her purchase; and curious passersby were stopping in to survey the wares, which included expressive wooden masks staring down from surrounding walls.

These entrepreneurs found their resources through various types of capital, which can be divided into the typologies that French social theorist Pierre Bourdieu identified.[16] First is economic capital: some of these women, such as Esther, did not need capital to start their business. Firoza Diddee, who runs a medical-transcription company, also needed little capital. But most would not have gotten their business off the ground without funds. Several did so solely from savings—but those savings were not always built from high-wage work. One amassed a large savings account from working two full-time jobs simultaneously, earning minimum wage or below, and this savings allowed her to buy restaurant equipment and renovate her space. Ana Martinez, owner of a tamale catering business in the Los Angeles area, also used savings from her own independent tamale selling to start her business. Repeatedly, however, the entrepreneurs told stories of how difficult this capital was to come by. When they applied for loans, as one said, "it was as if I was nonexistent to the banks." And as another entrepreneur said, "Women are in the service industries. No one is going to fund the service industries." Yet another echoed, "When you're small, they won't help you!" Maria, owner of Lulu's Desserts, recalled, "Had I had [capital] from the beginning, I could have done it faster. I had to start small, reinvest, reinvest. The credit on my small-business loan had a very high interest rate. I had no partners, no venture capital."

Since Rubina Chaudhary had a difficult time finding start-up funds from banks, she used her own savings that she had built from her earnings. Yet even this back-up strategy came with a downside: when she approached the Small Business Administration about a potential loan, they scrutinized the source of the funds that she already had. She was taken aback: "I was the one who had earned that! The banks and the SBA all asked, 'Do you have the capacity to run a business? Where will your start-up capital come from?' I couldn't get a credit line. I had to create credit: borrow the money and pay it off." Ironically, the bank that refused to give Rubina an account in the beginning—a major nationally known bank—is today "doing *somersaults*" to get her as a client, she reported.

Entrepreneurs frequently found themselves in a Catch-22. Those starting businesses in fields that are atypical for women reported that they ran into any number of gender barriers in getting off the ground. On the other hand, women going into those fields that are *typical* for women—such as service industries—learned that the banks had no interest in investing. Credit histories—which are challenging to establish both for immigrants and for women in general—are critical for those who need start-up capital. It is not a natural advantage to be both a newcomer and a woman when you want to start a business, even as immigrants seem to give the appearance of having a better go at it than the rest of us. Therefore, both nativity and gender entered in as structural barriers that created the need to look elsewhere for start-up capital.

As a result, the needed economic capital often came via a second type of capital from Bourdieu's theory, which is social capital: these women listed a host of friends, associations, networks, husbands, sisters, parents, and colleagues who had helped them get their business started. When such individuals were able to offer informal loans, it was clearly the social capital that provided the key means of access to financial capital. Admittedly, men—and the native-born—rely on social capital for the same reasons, but they are going to be less reliant on these informal sources than foreign-born women will be. One entrepreneur borrowed money from her friends and family, and although her business is growing, she reported, "I am still paying them back."

Social capital has both come and gone for Quincy Nguyen, a young Vietnamese woman who runs her own nail salon in Los Angeles while she simultaneously manages a dental-crown lab and cares for her two small children. Since she fled Vietnam as a teenager without her family, she had to establish herself alone in the United States. She remembers how afraid she was to take the first step, without her mother to take care of things for her: when she arrived at her first job interview to work in a nail salon, she remained sitting in her car for two hours before mustering the courage to walk inside. The advantage of the nail-salon business in her eyes was that you were not required to know the language to do well at the work. When her boss noticed that she spoke English, however, she insisted on promoting her to manager—a proposal that Quincy tried to decline: "I said, 'No, no, no, I don't want it.'" Her boss convinced her, and that leap to a high level of responsibility, supervising thirty employees and managing all the finances, from early morning until late evening, became her entrée into her eventual decision to open her own shop. But that next step was also one that Quincy remembers as bringing on yet another moment of trepidation:

> I looked at the newspaper, looked around, found this one, and said, "Okay, let's open, but I'm so scared. I need staff, etcetera." . . . I bought it from another owner, but that owner took all of the employees and all the clients with her! It was tough! I didn't know what to do. . . . I don't know how they can treat people like that.

Quincy said that an American friend of hers had been trying to convince her to partner up and open a second salon, but that was another prospect that frightened Quincy; yet, when she argues with her friend, she said, "every time I use the 'scared' word, she laughs hard."

At the more formal level of social capital, women's business associations proved to be invaluable to some of these new enterprises. Among the associations that they lauded were the Orange County, California, chapter of the National Business Women's Association (NAWBO), which was a source of several contacts for this research. NAWBO offers workshops and networking meetings and places a strong emphasis on stimulating entrepreneurship. The resources of the Small Business Association were a key resource for several women interviewed here, especially in landing initial work.[17] Yet few of the women we interviewed took advantage of "set-asides"—government preference programs for contractors—or special loans to women- or minority-owned businesses. One refused to do so. She recalled, "I wanted to shine in my own light." Another reported that, in hindsight, she now wishes she had sought out these programs.

Research has demonstrated that set-asides are effective in helping to equalize opportunities. The availability of these programs at the state level has been declining, however, both as a result of public resistance to them and federal requirements that the programs must demonstrate statistically the continued existence of discrimination. At the federal level, set-asides have been ear-marked for ethnic diversity, not for gender diversity. The federal government was slow to move forward on a proposed set-aside program for women, which Congress passed in 2000. The government finally acted on this bill in 2008, but with a very restricted number of contracts and limited to only a few industries. This announcement irritated women business owners, who were vocal about their disappointment, as they represent one-third of business ownership in the United States.[18]

Surprisingly, the women we interviewed did not mention one of the most common forms of capital that immigrant entrepreneurs usually have: ethnic associations formed by members of their home nationality. Why were these not available? Two comments from the interviews shed some light: Esther reported that among Africans, there is not a large enough "critical mass" of immigrants from a common culture and language to support one another to the extent of the larger Asian communities. Even in an area such as the Washington, DC–Baltimore, Maryland, corridor, where one of the largest African-diaspora populations is concentrated (in the United States), the African immigrant population is comparatively much smaller than Asian groups and is extremely diverse. The networking activity seems to happen more informally. Esther helps other Africans get started, for example, and offers them critical advice. Might gender play a role in the likelihood of tapping into ethnic networks? The Los Angeles salon owner Pari Sayeri, for example, complained, "I didn't have time to go to all of those Iranian meetings and sit around." Between the time pressures of family commitments and struggling to earn an income, perhaps women are not finding that ethnic associations are universally filling the bill in today's world.

Two women who started their own catering business received their training through a not-for-profit venture, Mama's Hot Tamales Café in Los Angeles. Although this is not an ethnic association per se and is open to people of any nationality, it is a venture that is, for obvious reasons, popular among Latin Americans. Initiated by former community organizer and third-generation Mexican immigrant Sandi Romero, the café's mission is to help immigrants—women and men, but with an emphasis on women—move from the informal to the formal economy. Sandi opened a sunny street-level restaurant, which reflects the vibrant colors that are characteristic of Mexico, to serve tamales to the local lunch crowd and to train people to make and sell tamales as street vendors and caterers. The menu spans styles and ingredients that represent the varieties of Latin American cuisines.

Figure 6.3. Sandi Romero, Mama's Hot Tamales Café (Jerry Camarillo)

Despite the absence of support from ethnic associations in these women's lives, they reported the importance of some form of cultural capital. An example was those affiliated with Mama's, who are tapping into the resource of tradition in order to transform it into a commodity. This is one of the more standard types of immigrant entrepreneurship—taking advantage particularly of the markets that coethnics offer to serve the cuisine or other products that characterize their community. But these entrepreneurs only *started* with those ethnic markets; eventually, they innovated their products and services to allow them to reach beyond those markets. Entrepreneurship researchers note that such expansion is necessary to keep a business in a growth mode.[19] The bed-and-breakfast owner once started a food booth while living in Canada, inventing her own fast-food recipes that combined Romanian cooking with Canadian preferences. She learned that Canadians would eagerly line up at the lunch counter for these unusual morsels. Another example comes from Esther, who rarely sells her imported Ghanaian clothing to other Africans, as they can acquire the same items at lower prices on trips home. But she has attracted a clientele of African Americans who are rediscovering their heritage, and her business spikes around certain holidays, such as African Heritage Day in

February: on one Sunday during Black History Month, local churches celebrate African heritage through their attire. Firoza Diddee, with a medical-transcription business, reported, "My business knows no race or boundaries. Other immigrant businesses tend to cater to their own kind. My business and service needed access to the broader population."

In Los Angeles, the premises of Mama's Hot Tamales Café boasts an oversized wall mural of a contemporary corn goddess, named Esperanza, representing hope and empowerment for the Latino immigrant community. Sandi uses this mural, which also sports images of other corn gods and goddesses, to teach about the power and significance of corn in pre-Columbian Mesoamerican communities. Through this symbolic image, Sandi is reaching into even more ancient cultural traditions to provide sources of inspiration for Latinos, beyond the medium of food.

Entrepreneurs spoke of their own personal or spiritual resources, and we could add this as a fourth category of capital. These women seemed acutely aware of how their own personal resources contributed to their success—there was a discursive consciousness, to borrow a term from sociologist Anthony Giddens.[20] Rubina, for example, a devout Muslim, takes guidance from her religious faith in all her decisions and business dealings. Additionally, she believes that she was "blessed with an inner sense of the value of planning"—thus attributing a modicum of her success to powers beyond her own. Firoza Diddee reported, "I'm very tenacious by nature." Two women briefly and nonchalantly mentioned bouts with breast cancer that they survived while building their enterprises, and neither of them seemed to have missed a beat in their business developments. They each shrugged as they mentioned their illness. A colleague of one of these women observed, "She talks about her breast cancer like it was a *hangnail*."

### Life as a Business Owner

These business owners spoke of their challenges, the varied life circumstances that led them to their current paths, and the financial rewards that they eventually earned. Most of these businesses now provide steady incomes for their owners, as well as for a host of employees—both foreign- and native-born. The Kelly twins are proud of their growing revenues as insurance brokers and the fact that they have rarely lost a client, due to the high quality of service that they provide. As they recounted,

We always tell the employee, the client—they are always told, you know, at the beginning of each year, "If anything gets wrong with your family member, we want you calling on one of us." Because it's hard to navigate the system; it's difficult to know your options. We will do the research for you, and we'll sit down with you, . . . and you can then make an educated decision. . . . Anybody can hand you an insurance policy, but are they handing you the right ones? Are they explaining how it works? Are they helping when you go to use it?

For the Kelly twins and the other entrepreneurs, business ownership also provided broader meanings for them than financial success or prestige. Several articulated these more qualitative meanings as they reflected on their experiences. Rocio Ramirez, for example, spoke of her integration into U.S. society as she moved toward the ability to support herself independently. A recipient of Mama's Hot Tamales Café training, she moved from making and selling handicrafts to owning a tamales catering business. She had moved to the United States to be with a boyfriend, whom she later married but eventually divorced. She found herself raising two teenagers, including one who is autistic. She recalled, "Before, it was very, very difficult. It is much better now. I can drive; now I'm a citizen, and I can buy a house. My son is in a special program." Rocio proudly reported that she makes one thousand tamales per day "in twenty-five to thirty flavors." She mused that balancing her work with parenthood continues to be challenging, but she is currently applying for loans in order to reach her dream of opening her own restaurant. She depicted a life that is not only quantitatively (as measured in income) but qualitatively better.

Ana Martinez was selling tamales on the corner when she discovered Mama's through its colorful tamale carts. Ana took advantage of the training program, including the kitchen where Mama's incubates new businesses. Like several others we met, she was inspired by her mother and grandmother, who had owned their own stores, in which Ana had helped out as a child. She remembers seeing her mother with an apron full of money, and this made her determined to be her own boss and make her own money. She now has her own catering business, specializing in tamales with Honduran ingredients, and she has a set of regular clients and reports making eight hundred to one thousand tamales per day. She explained how she feels at this stage in her professional life: "I'm really happy to be my own boss [and] proud of myself." She was also proud of the tamales, which she characterized as "costing a little more, but they have great ingredients: they are *very fresh—not frozen.*" When we met her, she was in the process of buying a house. She explained that she has learned the importance for business growth of special events on the annual calendar, such as the festivals in the park and the Christmas season. Her next goal is to start a restaurant; her eyes lit up as she told the story of a Cuban immigrant who started a restaurant with five hundred dollars and now owns a chain of restaurants. But she does not plan to stop there; she also hopes to get her products into the supermarkets.

For civil engineer *Xui Li,* whose firm designs and builds bridges, business ownership gave her the opportunity to exercise both her management and her engineering skills. After receiving her engineering degree from an American university, she began her career as an employee for a large firm. She began to realize that there was no future for her in her company, even though she felt that the quality of her work was higher than that of her supervisors. She reflected on her own abilities to learn: "I am a hard worker; I pick up fast." Once she went into business for herself, she was able to live up to her own potential. As she remembered, "I did it on my own, though I had a partner at first, who was the one pushing me. I got one bridge design project, so I started with that. I then started to get federal water projects. I didn't want to do one bad job." *Xui Li* developed another skill as she and her husband raised three children while her company grew: balancing business ownership with family demands. Yet she feels that she successfully did both. She is currently juggling five federal contracts, has seven permanent staff members, and hires a steady number of temporary contractors in the field.

Rubina Chaudhary, who is originally from the Punjab region of India and who also runs an engineering firm, MARRS Services, was the entrepreneur who opened her enterprise on a dare from her trainees. She also spoke about her eventual path as one that has a broader meaning than simply bringing home a steady paycheck. She recalled that when she was earning her MBA, one of her professors admonished her to "figure out what's your reason for being." After earning her degree, Rubina had fallen into a career track as a motivational trainer, and when a trainee dared her to put her own words into action, she took him up on it. Today, Rubina's office buzzes with activity—employees walking in and out, stopping for a coffee in the break room. With success has come that sense of purpose to which Rubina's business professor had alluded: "It was the sheer joy of seeing an opportunity and going after it." With nearly thirty-seven employees across three offices,

Rubina spoke proudly of her firm as a place to build opportunities for other people: "I help people grow, then my company grows. I have encouraged valuable employees to go elsewhere to further their careers. Yet we have an excellent return rate. I look at my clients as my employees, and vice versa, and work to meet their needs as best I can." MARRS continues to expand and win awards.

Another award winner is Yolanda Voss, president of her own fashion-design studio and showroom in Columbia, Maryland, who migrated from Ecuador in 1962 with the dream of becoming a fashion designer. She immediately began taking courses in her field and establishing apprenticeships with mentors whom she admired. Her big break, which encouraged her to continue pursuing her career path, was the day that First Lady Betty Ford took notice of one of Yolanda's coat designs and purchased it for herself. At the beginning of building her business, however, Yolanda simultaneously endeavored to pass on the trade to younger generations by holding classes for students in the basement of her home. Thus, the pursuit of her own dream was, from the beginning, tied up with helping others to achieve their dreams. In the mid-1980s, Yolanda opened her own showroom for her haute-couture designs in New York City, and eventually she moved her business back to Maryland, where she had started her career. Today, she is a highly regarded member of her community.

Shirley Nathan-Pulliam decided to open group day-care facilities for the elderly and disabled after observing the conditions of facilities where her patients resided when she was working as a nurse. She had also desired more autonomy in her work. She wanted to open a place that people could come to and enjoy their surroundings. She envisioned a bright, cheerful environment where the elderly and disabled were truly cared for and comforted. Today, her two businesses, Nathan Networks and Extended Family Adult Day Care, bring in half a million dollars per year, with the capacity and growth potential of over one million annually. Shirley spoke of that internal drive that she continues to feel and that keeps her motivated: "So it's just that inner passion and drive that you want to see people happy, and when I walk in my center—whether you're Alzheimer's, whether you had a stroke, whether you have dementia, whatever your problem is—I come alive when I walk in and hear the patients talking."

Sheela Murthy echoed the "passion" motive, as she chose her law career out of a passion to advance social justice. After completing her degree at Harvard and working for a large law firm, she made the decision to go out on her own. She reflected,

Always for me was a driving passion and a burning passion to change the world, and I think in the world of immigration law when we help clients, a lot of them even, if they work with companies or with families ultimately, it's individual lives we're changing. . . . And many of them send money back to their home countries, so now you're helping the world economy, you know, people.[21]

Maria Sobrino began her entrepreneurial life in the travel business in Mexico; after expanding the business to Los Angeles, however, with the collapse of the Mexican peso (as mentioned earlier), she was uncertain whether she could revive her Mexican business. She looked around her in the United States and noticed the absence of a particular comfort food that Mexican children enjoyed three times a day: flavored gelatins, or *gelatinas*. Maria began experimenting with some samples, and her friends encouraged her to start producing them and to name the business Lulu, which is her nickname. She remembered, "Whatever you do, you need to love it. . . . Do you know how many people laughed at my idea of having *gelatinas* and selling them with a little jar three hundred cups a day that I was doing? Today we sell about fifty million cups a year of gelatin, and we distribute to supermarkets."[22]

Firoza Diddee, owner of a medical-transcription company, reported, "I didn't know what passion was until now. It is anything connected to *service*." *Elisabeta*, Romanian owner of a bed-and-breakfast, wants to create an environment for people where they feel that they are in a home away from home. She has chosen furnishings to create this atmosphere, and she decorates the walls with her own paintings. She serves full breakfasts at a meticulously decorated table, with the freshest ingredients and every possible desired condiment provided. She reported that her newfound business venture, one in a series that she has taken up across her adult life, fits with her nature: "I love people, work with people, their stories, from all over the world. I'm in my own environment, relaxed in my mind, have time to paint."

A young Thai woman, Luck Pongsamart, got her business off the ground almost overnight, with few roadblocks. She happened to notice that a Chinese restaurant in a local shopping center was about to go out of business. Luck took her savings and bought the restaurant. She moved quickly. She closed the facilities down for one week, did some basic renovations, practiced cooking a set of Thai recipes, and immediately opened her new place. Her Thai restaurant, set in a convenient corner of a shopping center and decorated with original art from her second business as an art dealer, has grown weekly since. She recounted with a spark of enthusiasm and energy all the roles that she is currently juggling: she delivers mail for the postal service full-time, raises her children, runs her restaurant, and collaborates with her husband to run the art-collection business, all while working on her bachelor's degree part-time.

Other entrepreneurs spoke of intangible contributions of their business to their community. Pari, from Iran, owns her own hair salon, which she built through years of hard work while also raising a family. Today, the hair salon has a family feel to it: Iranian immigrants, among others, form a steady, loyal clientele. A glass case that displays decorative objects from Iran adorns the shop, giving it an unusual feel for a salon. Pari describes it as a "warm place": "Everybody comes here, has a coffee, a cookie, they say they love me. It keeps me busy." She explained that she never wanted to be famous; she reflected, "I find an easy way to live, a clean way to live." Despite ups and downs, she stated that she enjoys the business even more than before. She explained, "I *love* this shop." The pride of doing clean, "honest" work is also what *Lucia* recounted as the reason that she continues to run her own cleaning business (in partnership with her husband) year in and year out despite no free time for vacations—even when it comes to family wedding invitations in Mexico. She offered, "I'm proud of myself. For me, it's good. A lot of people want to do it. It's a good, honest job." Repeatedly, the women spoke of their pride in inspiring and training other women to own their own business. Denise, for example, now has a grown daughter who has opened her own firm.

## *"The First Two Years Were Hell"*

None of these enterprises has grown without challenges—and many quite serious. The responses to those challenges offer interesting insights into the agency-structure relationship. A particularly engaging story came from Pari, the salon owner in Los Angeles. Her first shop was located in the popular Century City shopping complex. For years, she successfully ran her salon, and her popularity grew. One day, however, Pari suddenly learned that she was being booted out. The shopping complex was renovating, updating, and upscaling. As she put it, "It was the rich people versus the normal people." Pari fought to try to keep her space in the complex, but she lost her battle. True to her entrepreneurial spirit, she did not give up. Out of spite, she simply reopened her salon directly across the boulevard from the original complex, but she kept the same name: Century City Hair Design, with bold signage facing directly across the boulevard—meant for the eyes of the shopping-complex owners. Pari expected a lawsuit, but one never came. She proudly kept the name and is still operating today.

Repeatedly, the entrepreneurs we interviewed reported how tough their initial years in the business start-ups had been: "There were more downs than ups"; "The first five years were very, very hard"; "We grew our own business on our mistakes, not our successes. It was a huge pain. The first two years were *hell*."

Challenges did not end after the business was off the ground. Judith, who runs the home-based child-care center, fights with inspectors and regulators and finds herself frequently frustrated by contradictions within the rules. She is reminded of similar constraints in a former food-stand business that she ran; after investing a large amount of money in what she understood to be the proper, legally required equipment, the authorities closed her down, citing "improper equipment." She lost her entire investment. Ana Martinez reported that she also had to "get a lot of permission from a lot of people" to start the tamale business and that rent is very high in the Los Angeles area.

Often, these business owners ran into obstacles that were clearly related to their race, nativity, and/or gender. Since each of these individuals would not have gotten where they are without a personality characterized by positive attitudes and hope, it is significant to note how adamant they were when they enumerated the structural constraints behind those challenges: "There is always the problem of racism. Even if it is subtle, it is always there"; "I'm just a number"; "Few women have big empires. Men still have the lion's share." This last comment is confirmed by statistics. The loan programs available for women- and minority-owned businesses are primarily for companies that need less than fifty thousand dollars in start-up funds.[23] Additionally, among all the start-up capital that is invested in the United States, only a sliver is invested in women's enterprises; in 2006, only 3 percent of all venture-capital dollars went to women-owned businesses. Erin Abrams, writing in the online publication *The Glass Hammer*—a reference to the "glass ceiling," the barrier to women's rise to top positions in business—has asked why stereotypes of the typical recipients of venture capital continue to be male.[24] Rubina Chaudhary gave a firsthand account of those stereotypes: "The other biggest barrier is people questioning the fact that you're a woman. It ended when I put 'MBA' on my business card and saw people's reactions."

Shirley Nathan-Pulliam became increasingly aware of the challenges she faced as a woman, an immigrant, and a person of African descent in a society where racism still constrains people. This knowledge added to the understanding of the great risk she was taking in attempting to start a business. Nevertheless, she was determined to stand up to the challenge. She keeps a framed sign in her office that reads, "We women must close our eyes and walk in the dark."

A vivid example of the presence of gender and nativity stereotypes was offered by the attorney Sheela Murthy, owner of a highly successful law firm and not one to whine about problems. One day she invited a broker to her office to consult with him about investing her company's profits. As they met, this broker repeatedly asked her, "Who really *owns* this company?" to which Sheela replied, "*I* do." The broker kept asking, however, "No, who *really* owns this company?" And Sheela kept insisting, "*I* do." As both parties repeated themselves with incredulity, Sheela's name was clearly visible: "Murthy Law Firm" was etched prominently across the glass windows and doors of the office where they met as they carried out this circular exchange of misfiring words.

The intersection of gender and nativity (or race) had an initial inhibiting effect on attempts to secure contracts for Rita Kalwani of KAL Architects. A colleague of hers observed, "She looks Indian, and government buyers who are looking for architects/engineers are not usually looking for Indian women for the job. She's had to really struggle and burn the midnight oil, but it has paid off—tenacity and patience hand in hand—and she's landed some whoppers."

## Structures as Enablement

Anthony Giddens, in *The Constitution of Society,* has emphasized that societal structures not only constrain; they can also help enable individuals to act. And in contrast to the structural constraints of some of the home societies of these entrepreneurs, many of them found this more positive role to be the case in their new home—despite the myriad of challenges mentioned earlier. One remembers watching with delight as her business blossomed: "The American dream was happening right before my eyes." Another stated, "The opportunities are there everywhere. You have to focus on doing something better every day." And immigration attorney Sheela Murthy said, "In Asia and Africa, you have to bribe someone for a business license. This is a great country to open a business in." *Elisabeta* observed, "Women are strong, very intelligent. They need to free themselves. . . . You can get all the help you need to make it [as a business owner]." Through these women's interpretations of the access to opportunity that they found, there were audible echoes of the American myth of autonomous individualism, although this was not the only identifiable strain in their reports.

Theories of immigrant entrepreneurship have taken note of the enablement of entrepreneurial activity that emerges from the constraints of structures—such as a hostile or exclusive work environment—and from the opportunities of structures, such as the support and markets provided by coethnic networks. The middleman-minority theory, for example, emphasizes the role of the entrepreneur as mediator between the hostile, native-born, ruling elite and less-privileged minority groups. The market-niche approach suggests that the entrepreneur can offer specific products and services that his or her own ethnic group tends to need. We found several examples of this among the women we interviewed, though for many of them, their markets expanded beyond such groups. Combining insights from these two approaches, the enclave-economy theory states that the economic structures that contribute to entrepreneurial opportunity interact with the cultural context of the ethnic community, where the entrepreneur can find the social capital and solidarity needed for the business to get off the ground. Alejandro Portes and Leif Jensen, for example, found that ethnic enclaves were significantly important among Cuban migrants to South Florida.[25] And as other scholars have also documented, the eventual businesses that are formed become important for the broader community of immigrants and their integration into the society.[26]

Intersectionality theory might predict that the more social locations in which an individual is situated in the less advantaged status (lower class, female, foreign-born, etc.), the higher the likelihood of oppression and discrimination. The preceding pages have provided a host of examples from the interviews to illustrate this dynamic. Yet one entrepreneur, Sheela Murthy—whose business gives immigration legal advice—took a dramatically different angle on her set of social locations, describing her comparative disadvantage as an advantage in her service profession: "People say I have three strikes against me. But those three are my strengths. As a woman, I have more empathy for clients; as an immigrant, I am more sensitive than the native-born to immigrants' needs; and I understand what it feels like to be a minority, so I can empathize with other minorities." Sheela did acknowledge the roadblocks that her "triple minority" social location has placed in the path of her progress and that of other immigrant women. This realization helps to explain Sheela's forays into immigration rights activism. Nevertheless, her argument was that she highly values her social locations and that her strength as a business owner is rooted precisely in this intersection. Sheela's approach is a reminder of the elasticity of human agency: the reinterpretation of one's relative social disadvantage as a social advantage.

*Lucia,* who owns a housecleaning business in Houston, resisted the tendency to categorize such social locations into an advantage/disadvantage dichotomy. As she explained, "I am not really advantaged or disadvantaged. I want to think of myself as a bilingual person. One thing I noticed: if you don't speak English with them [the clients], they see you as a lower-grade person. I'm always talking straight with them. I can communicate. I haven't found any problem with it. For me, it's working great."

The enablement that these structural constraints engendered among these entrepreneurs included creative innovations to get around the roadblocks. Nail-salon owner Quincy, for example, would attract clients from the customers eating at the Thai restaurant next door. She also learned that linking up with a local charity would help get her salon some name recognition if she is listed as a donor. Denise, who sells capacity-building services to businesses, reported, "I almost went under" during the dot-com bust of the 1990s; her firm had to downsize dramatically, sell its building, and move into a rented office. But she decided not to give up and moved out of marketing her services to the private sector and into the not-for-profit market. This strategy worked: "The skills we had fit so well with nonprofits: they were nicer people and were not trying to compete with you. We believed in what they were trying to do."

Firoza Diddee remembered trying to start her business in the midst of a recession, even though she said, "This country offers so much hope." She and her husband worked part-time jobs around the clock. They were able to find Americans to sponsor their visas, and by 1997 they started a computer-software company together. The struggles did not end, as they had to face another historical challenge: the widespread fear that computers (and all the systems that they support) would crash on January 1, 2000 (the Y2K issue), due to the potential confusion of the new date of 2000 within those systems. Firoza and her husband weathered this storm but continued to struggle, until she "reinvented" herself and started a medical-transcription service. Today, Firoza employs more than one hundred people, including transcribers in India, to transcribe digitally recorded tapes into text and deliver them to clients quickly.

## The Roles of Men

Men played various roles in these women's careers and lives. Several entrepreneurs were inspired and encouraged by their fathers; one remembers her father teaching her that education is better than wealth, because, as he insisted, "as you give it away, it increases." Others owed their passage to the

United States to fathers. And the women's stories often contradicted Western stereotypes of men in more traditional societies: a number of these entrepreneurs spoke of fathers who encouraged their business development and success. Many spoke of their husbands' moral support for their enterprises, as well as their assistance with particular tasks, such as heavy lifting. Pari's husband helped her start her business by footing the bill for the rent at the Century City shopping center. She reported that his support was critical in less economically tangible ways as well: "I worked daytime, and at night my husband worked. He watched the kids while I worked. . . . Me and my husband, we work together."

Notably, none of these women said anything like "My husband gave me all the capital." This point needs to be emphasized for two reasons: it illustrates that the women are looking for resources on their own, and it counters the assumption that female-owned enterprises are simply companies run by husbands with the wife's name on the letterhead in order to qualify for targeted loans or set-asides.

The number of stories of supportive men surrounding these women vastly outnumbered stories of unsupportive men. But, as mentioned earlier, one story repeated itself more than once: that of escaping an abusive husband. This came in two patterns: The first and most common was the context of exit from the home country. The second pattern was escape from abuse after arriving and living in the United States. We ran into a repeatedly expressed belief among many of these women that business ownership can help one escape domestic abuse. This unsolicited passionate belief that business ownership is a key to escaping abuse came up on occasion across several locations. One Baltimore entrepreneur reported that she does not suffer from abuse personally, but she sees it all around her in her community. She wants to see women start their own businesses so they can have the economic independence to escape.

### Structural Consequences

If, as agents in society, according to social theorists such as Anthony Giddens and Pierre Bourdieu, one of the results of our activity is that we produce and reproduce societal structures, how is all this entrepreneurial energy affecting the economy—and the society? It is near impossible to calculate a total monetary gain from business start-ups, called a "multiplier effect," including jobs created, tax revenues generated, consumer activity, homes purchased, interest paid, tuition money paid into higher education for children, phil-anthropic giving, or contribution to the business stability of neighborhoods. Until recently, the regularly administered national Economic Census did not ask respondents to indicate their nativity on the survey, resulting in the absence of hard, specific numbers of how much business revenue immigrant women generate and how many job they create.[27] From the reports of the entrepreneurs we interviewed, however, we can glean that the women have contributed a range of broad and varied economic benefits.

For example, the immigration attorney Sheela Murthy has built a firm that generates four to five million dollars per year, employs more than seventy individuals in her Baltimore office, most of whom are native-born, and has opened a branch office in India with seven additional employees. She elaborated on the spinoff economic activity that her firm has created: "I hire contractors to clean my offices, and at lunch, my employees go across the street and shop at the mall. I have used clerks as interns from the Baltimore Law School."

In the late 1990s, the *Baltimore Business Journal* named Sheela's firm as one of the top-twenty-five women-owned businesses in the area. As mentioned in chapter 1, for three years in a row, from 2007 to 2009, Sheela received the accolade of a Maryland "Super Lawyer" by *Super Lawyers* magazine. Rubina Chaudhary is managing several multimillion-dollar public contracts and consults with other large public and private clients. Maria de Lourdes Sobrino, owner of Lulu's Desserts, now runs a $9.2 million business, operates a factory where the desserts are produced, and hires teams of employees to manage the orders, marketing, sales, and delivery of her products. She has also written a book highlighting the stories of Latina entrepreneurs in order to help other aspiring business owners to succeed. Angela Chan moved from working in a company with just over twenty employees to running a business with twenty-five hundred employees since it opened in 2001; the company makes two million wheels in the United States and manages five manufacturing plants in China. Trang Nguyen, owner of the restaurant Saigon Remembered, proudly reported that she trains her employees to open their own restaurants. Others have trained their children in entrepreneurship, passing on the wisdom and inspiration.

On June 11, 2008, the National Archives in Washington, DC, brought three of these entrepreneurs together for a public panel discussion on immigrant women in business ownership. Shirley Nathan-Pulliam, Maria de Lourdes Sobrino, and Sheela Murthy were joined by Yolanda Maria Welch of Baltimore, founder of a home health-care business. At that time, this group of four women employed 224 individuals across their firms, illustrating that, collectively, the multiplier effect as measured by job creation could be calculated as "times fifty-six."

These entrepreneurs, with the exception of those in the early stages of business development, are intensively involved in philanthropy. Sheela, for example, set up a foundation to support children's education in India and donates her company's used computers to public schools in Baltimore. Rubina has begun to mentor inner-city youth in Los Angeles and is establishing a not-for-profit organization to expand her work. Ecuadorian fashion designer Yolanda Voss hosts regular fashion shows to benefit a medical clinic. Every year, she provides twelve internships in design and merchandising, which have totaled more than two hundred over her career. She insisted that she "give back" to her adopted home country, a place that she dubs her "passion." Salon owner Pari sends "a lot" of money to Iran for poor children and for local schools. Thai restaurant owner Luck sends funds to Thailand to provide services for children who are mentally disabled and have been abandoned by their mothers. Angela Chan personally gives to a Taiwanese foundation that helps people victimized by earthquakes and other disasters; she and her employees give volunteer hours to a free health clinic in Los Angeles County, and they give food to a homeless shelter. Such efforts mirror trends that have been documented nationally: women and immigrants are known for higher levels (per capita) of giving to their communities than are men and the native-born. More than half of high-net-worth women business owners (both native- and foreign-born) contribute more than twenty-five thousand dollars annually to charity; 19 percent give one million dollars or more.[28]

Shirley Nathan-Pulliam straddles the worlds of business and politics even more directly. A native of Jamaica who has lived in Maryland since 1960 and is the founder of two health-care businesses, she began to contribute to Black-empowerment initiatives in the 1970s. One of those was a local organization attempting to keep Black-created wealth in the community, on the realization that "the dollar stays in our community only overnight." Shirley served on this organization's board and, after a few years, decided to run for state-level political office. After one defeat, she ran as a state assembly representative from a newly created district, won the election, and has been reelected ever since. Today, she is among the most passionate defenders of immigrant rights in the Maryland State Assembly.

### Reflections and Policy Recommendations

Economists pay attention to entrepreneurship trends because history has shown us that new start-ups are critical to a society's economic development. In the United States, for example, many entrepreneurial ventures eventually become the small- and medium-sized businesses that employ most Americans; this fact alone indicates that such businesses form a bedrock for the U.S. economy. More specifically, economists report that a steady stream of new business start-ups is good for economic flows because the newer and smaller businesses have more growth potential than those that are older and established. Among other advantages to new business start-ups are their tendency to draw on local resources and to serve the local community. Given the mounting anxieties over the vast—and rising—number of jobs and services that are "outsourced" to other countries, leaving whole communities with sudden downward plunges in employment rates, locally based enterprises may—potentially—offer some hope for a countertrend. The full picture is much more complicated, of course, as some of those new businesses—including those run by immigrant women—are finding the need to outsource their work in order to remain competitive. Those with employees in other countries often frame this arrangement as contributing to those countries' economies.

How might more public visibility of these women's economic contributions counter the "invisibility" that these women reported when they went to banks for a loan? Maureen Bunyan, a leading Washington, DC–area broadcast news anchor, who moderated the "Citizens by Choice" panel on which three of these women participated in 2008, admitted to her own recent learning curve on how active immigrant women are in business ownership. As she stated publicly,

> I was surprised to read your writing[29] and the fact that immigrant women business owners are growing. The numbers are growing, but nobody seems to know about them. We, in the media, certainly have done a lot of stories, and many of the stories focus on day laborers. And I have done stories like that. And you see the reporter standing in front of this long line of men who are usually Latinos, and they're waiting for jobs. And there's political controversy.

The women we interviewed were adamantly forthcoming with advice and suggestions to assist immigrant women in their business development. Among the most frequently cited challenges to these women's business start-ups was the early phase—from obtaining the needed capital to bureaucratic and other hurdles that made the process difficult. Repeatedly, these women emphasized entrepreneurs' need for good information. Several women have requested good details about regulations, as these can be confusing; additionally, there is a panoply of local, state, and federal laws to learn.

The integration of more immigrant women into decision-making bodies related to start-ups, set-asides, venture capital, and business associations would help raise awareness of the continued challenges and needs that are specific to immigrant women. Since discrimination and workplace equity issues force some of these women out of the conventional labor market, it is clear that the established business world is in need of further progress on these issues. The fact that these structural barriers ended up creating the need for these women to establish their own enterprises does not mean that those barriers do not warrant continued critique.

Commonly, these women spoke of their struggle to combine business ownership with the pressing demands of family life. *Xui Li* reported that she has watched women drop their family responsibilities to focus on their business because they are so overwhelmed. But she believes that the kids will start to have problems later. She joked, "They will come back and get you. They are alive!" This advice is a reminder that the business world as a whole has yet to settle into new patterns of structuring work to allow women and men to attend to their personal lives without jeopardizing their business success. In fact, business ownership does not necessarily translate into a renegotiation of gendered constraints that women face in family relationships. It should not be viewed as a panacea for barriers either in the conventional labor market or at home for the goal of expanded, full opportunities for immigrant women.

# 7

# "There Is Still Work to Do"

## *Immigrant Women in Gender-*
## *Atypical Occupations*

Sitting in a café near the Park Slope area of Brooklyn, New York, Femi Agana explains how she became a carpenter. When she arrived in this country from England in 1983, she was originally pursuing a career in fashion. She had a fair amount of success, working first as a designer's assistant and then on her own.

> One thing about going to a new place where I didn't know the rules is that I could break them and get away with it. I would make the clothes, take them to stores, show them to salespeople, who would get me an appointment with the manager and buyer. . . . It was easy, before I had children. I thought, "Oh, America is a great place to do business. It's like a game." Over time I found out how to do it right, making appointments with buyers and making collections a season ahead.

When she had children, she shifted to creating children's clothes and experienced continued success. About the time her third child was born, her visa expired, and she was unable to renew it. Being a newly undocumented immigrant hampered her business, as she had difficulty securing a bank loan for financing. She was able to continue designing and creating clothes, but she no longer enjoyed the work. "It became a job, a numbers thing, killing my creativity." Then, an injury derailed her. Unable to work and with mounting medical bills, she realized she needed a change of careers: "It was a rude awakening. I needed work with benefits, medical insurance. My kids needed medical coverage. . . . And I wanted to do something different. I wanted something with attractive wages and to do something challenging." She came across a flyer advertising an organization called NEW (Nontraditional Employment for Women), for women who wanted to learn trades. She signed up for a three-month training course. Her training offered a broad introduction to many trades, including electrical work, plumbing, and maintenance, but she chose to focus on carpentry. It might seem like a drastic shift from fashion design and sewing to carpentry, but she does not see it that way. "It didn't seem outlandish to me, because it [carpentry] is taking things, putting them together, and measuring," like creating clothing. Now, she belongs to a union, is a shop steward, and works in the construction of high-rise buildings in New York City.

Halfway across the country, the windows in *Dama's* large corner office afford views of the streets and buildings on this large, urban university campus. She sits at a large round table in the middle of the room. The table and her desk are both piled high with papers and books, and many more books crowd the shelves lining the walls. In this setting, she tells of how she became an engineering professor. As a child in India, *Dama* had always been drawn to math and science, and she excelled at both. In college, she started as a physics major and saw it as a natural transition to move from that to engineering. She completed her bachelor's and master's degrees in India, before coming to the United States for graduate school. Her desire to move to the States had its roots in early childhood memories. As *Dama* and her sister were growing up, their father often told them about his experiences at an American engineering graduate school in the late 1940s. This was around the time of India's independence, and, as she explains, with the British leaving, a degree from abroad was highly valued. Her father's experience in the United States had a profound effect on him: "He came here before India was independent, and he had told my sister and I a lot of times that for the first time he realized what it is to be in a free country. He was treated a lot better here than he was in India." Given this experience, her parents encouraged the two sisters to pursue their graduate education in the United States, though her mother did worry that they might be getting "too qualified to get married." Since *Dama* earned her Ph.D., her engineering career has included working in government and academia, where she now works as a department head. Her current job involves research and administration, with a minimal level of teaching.

*Dama* and Femi may not seem to have much in common. *Dama's* desk in her corner office is very different from the construction sites where Femi works. Femi's demanding training included having to prove that she could carry a sixty-pound bucket around a city block, while *Dama* needed to complete research on complex engineering problems to begin her career. *Dama* needed to show she was able to secure prestigious grants, while Femi had

Figure 7.1. Femi Agana (Photo by Audra O'Donovan)

to demonstrate proficiency with a wide range of tools and carpentry skills. Femi belongs to a union, while *Dama* belongs to a professional organization.

What *Dama* and Femi do have in common, beyond being immigrant women, is that they work in gender-atypical occupations: engineering and carpentry. In this chapter, we examine the experiences of immigrant women in such occupations, exploring the common issues that arise for them. Women working in such fields can be thought of as "gender pioneers." Rather than new geographic territories, their "frontiers" are predominantly male workplaces. How do immigrant women experience these fields? Part of this exploration includes considering the barriers such women face. Although many of them mentioned such obstacles, they all, by definition, had surmounted at least some of them and had many positive things to say about their work. That is an important part of their stories as well. The title of this chapter, quoted from a woman we interviewed, can be read two ways: there is still work to do to make these workplaces more welcoming to women, but also these occupations show that even in a shaky economy there is still work to do, in that there are employment opportunities in these fields, many of which can provide well-paid, stable, and important work for women moving into them.

In discussions of women in the workforce, it is important to underscore the point that large numbers of women of color, poor women, and immigrant women have long worked outside the home. More women outside these groups have joined them, and women as a whole are now more likely to work outside the home than ever before. Consequently, women are making up a larger percentage—about half—of the workforce.[1] Although women are now more numerous, they remain concentrated in service-related jobs[2] and, even in professional jobs, are highly likely to be working in what are traditionally considered women's occupations, such as dieticians, librarians, nurses, and elementary-school teachers.[3] These fields are often referred to as "pink-collar occupations" or "pink ghettos."[4] Not surprisingly, many jobs that are traditionally female occupations are poorly paid. The fact that there are many such occupations is a testament to the extent of gender segregation of the workforce. This segregation is important because, as noted by Barbara Reskin and Irene Padavic, "[j]ob segregation is the linchpin in workplace inequality because the relegation of different groups to different kinds of work both facilitates and legitimates unequal treatment."[5]

According to the U.S. Department of Labor Women's Bureau, occupations where 25 percent or less of the workforce is female are "nontraditional occupations."[6] We refer to these as "gender-atypical" occupations. These include blue-collar jobs such as carpenters, electricians, and construction laborers, in which the labor force is below 5 percent female, as well as professional ones such as engineers, CEOs, and clergy. Women make up between 6 percent and 24 percent of the workforce in professions such as these. Nina Toren draws an analogy between women in such fields and immigrants, arguing that both groups are "*strangers* in a country that is not their homeland."[7] She notes that, just as immigrants cross borders between countries, these women "cross the boundaries separating the genders in the spheres of work."[8] If we accept this analogy, foreign-born women in gender-atypical fields are, in a sense, twice immigrants. This could lead to them experiencing more difficulty, or it is possible that their experience as true immigrants helps them better negotiate the "border crossing" between "male" and "female" work.

Women's increasing presence in the workforce, as well as their presence in these gender-atypical fields, is due to many factors, including feminist activism. The fact that there are any women at all in some of these "male" fields is testament to the hard work of earlier gender pioneers. In fact, many occupations that once would have been considered gender atypical for women, such as law and medicine, are no longer on that list. As earlier gender pioneers helped establish a place for women in those fields, gender pioneers such as Femi and *Dama* are currently doing likewise in their respective fields.

Designating fields as "gender atypical" using statistical cutoffs is a moving target, as the gender makeup of jobs has changed and will continue to change dramatically. For example, the construction field is one that has experienced concerted efforts to encourage women's participation. Presidential Executive Order 11246 of 1978 established goals and timetables to expand the role of women in nontraditional industries such as construction. This has had some success, as the rate of business ownership by women in this area increased 36 percent between 1997 and 2002.[9] There now exist local and national organizations to help women move into construction trades as well. Despite such efforts, these trades still remain overwhelmingly male, a fact which activists in these organizations continue to attempt to change.

Not all gender-atypical occupations pay well, but many pay better than typically female jobs that require similar education and skill levels. This is one argument made for more women to enter such fields. A report from the Institute for Women's Policy Research shows that "placement in nontraditional jobs could increase women's hourly wages by as much as one-third."[10] Cornell University's Institute for Women and Work notes that many gender-atypical, or nontraditional, occupations offer not only higher pay but also good benefits, job security, and opportunities for training.[11] On the other hand, the institute notes that there are deterrents to women's entering gender-atypical occupations such as construction, including "discrimination, cultural constraints, sexual harassment, and the lack of training and hiring programs"[12] that specifically target women. It is possible that these obstacles particularly affect immigrant women, who might face discrimination on the basis of racism or nativism, as well as sexism. In addition, some of the gender-atypical occupations, such as firefighter or police officer, have language and educational requirements that some immigrant women may have difficulty meeting.

But immigrant women such as *Dama* and Femi *have* entered gender-atypical occupations. What have been their experiences? Have they experienced the benefits or the obstacles? Women are scarce in these occupations, and immigrant women are even scarcer. If we are interested in the agency of immigrant women, these atypical occupations are a good site for study. Given the hurdles for women in these occupations, women do not just happen to find themselves in them. How do these women exercise their agency to enter, and often excel in, jobs that until recently had been almost exclusively male? In some cases, such as *Dama*'s, the women immigrated in order to work in these fields; in others, such as Femi's, they worked their way into these fields once in the United States.

## Choosing an Atypical Occupation

For some women, the choice of an atypical occupation was made long before immigration, and they may have immigrated because of the field, such as *Dama*'s immigration to pursue an American graduate education in engineering.[13] For others, such as Femi, the choice of an atypical occupation happened long after the initial immigration. Whichever is the case, it is still useful to examine what drew women to these fields, despite their knowledge that they would likely face obstacles due to their gender.

In the account in the preceding section, *Dama* noted a "natural transition" from being a physics major to being an engineer. She noted, though, that neither physics nor engineering was her first choice of field of study when she applied to college. Drawn to science and, particularly, math, she initially wanted to be a math major: "And then, my father was a civil engineer, and he said, 'Civil engineering is a rough place for women, so why don't you be an architect?' So he had put that in my head. So right after high school I applied to architecture schools." There were very limited spots for architecture students, however, and some were reserved for students from "scheduled castes" (formerly known as "untouchables"). She did not get in and so moved to studying physics. At many universities, physics classes would be filled with more men than women. This had not been the situation at *Dama*'s all-women's college in India. She also completed her master's in engineering in India. Although her graduate class in engineering was decidedly more male (she said there were two hundred men and sixteen women), her preconceived notions of liberation for women in the United States led her to expect more gender equality in her doctoral engineering education. Upon arrival at her American graduate school, she was surprised to see even fewer women in her classes. Similarly, another immigrant, *Matilda*, who works in the male-dominated oil industry in Texas, noted that in her home country of England, there were very few women in her geometry and finance university classes. *Betty*, an immigrant from China, also noted a gender imbalance in her math, science, and engineering classes, both in her native China and in higher education in the United States. Although the skewed gender composition of some university classes clearly did not prevent any of these women from pursuing their intended field, being in male-dominated classes sent messages to these women, their male classmates, and other students about whether these fields are indeed appropriate for women. The demographics of these classes might prevent some women from similarly choosing gender-atypical occupations such as engineering, if they do not relate to their male role models or do not find the level of mentoring that they need, for example.

Interestingly, more than one of these women reported stories of encouragement by men in their lives to pursue these gender-atypical jobs. As in *Dama*'s story, *Betty*'s father was important to her choice of a field of study. *Betty*, from a young age, had interests in the arts. Her father discouraged such pursuits, seeing them as dangerous in Communist China, and so encouraged the more practical pursuits of math and science. "He had told me, if you're technically competent, anyone would always want you. They would always need your help. And he would say, about me being an artist, you could always get your neck chopped off! And it happened!"[14] Because of such messages, she was pushed toward engineering, and she immigrated to the United States to pursue her engineering education.

Unlike *Dama* and *Betty*, whose migrations were specifically tied to their gender-atypical career aspirations, *Femi*'s immigration had nothing to do with an atypical occupation. Indeed, as noted earlier, she came to pursue a career in fashion and sewing. Although many of the best-known fashion designers are men (such as Calvin Klein and Ralph Lauren), clothing and sewing are certainly seen as "appropriate" traditional female endeavors. *Femi*'s later decision to enter into an atypical occupation was decidedly practical: a search for better pay and benefits. And, unlike *Dama's* and *Betty's* experiences, Femi's entrée into an atypical occupation, through the classes she took, was a direct result of the work of an advocacy group encouraging women to pursue work in the trades. Whereas *Dama* and *Betty* were educated at research universities to enter their gender-atypical professions, Femi underwent a three-month training program run by the advocacy organization. She described the training program this way: "I got an overall introduction to electrical work, plumbing, maintenance, and fitness training. You had to pick up a compound bucket, which weighs sixty pounds, and walk it around the block by the end of the training. . . . Tradeswomen came in and talked about their experiences." The experience had such a profound effect on her that she now teaches and mentors other women in the program, while her day-to-day work involves building high-rise office buildings and condos in Manhattan and Brooklyn.

### Experiences as Women in Male-Dominated Fields

Having made the decision to enter male-dominated fields, how do these immigrant women characterize their experiences? *Matilda,* the British immigrant working in the oil field, felt comfortable in a male-dominated environment, noting that she is "not a girly-girl." And *Natalia,* a young Colombian immigrant working in a neuroscience lab, finds her gender an advantage in her field: "You know, I'm lucky that I've picked a field where I'm a minority. I'm a double minority: I'm a woman, and I'm Hispanic." She was referring to attempts by universities and other institutions to diversify her field, drawing in more women and more racial and ethnic minorities. She noted that, in her lab, there is much more of a gender mix among the graduate students and postdoctoral researchers, whereas the principal investigators (often associate or full professors) are almost all men. On the one hand, she seems to see this as a sign that soon the field will be more equal (on the assumption that the graduate students and postdocs will primarily move into the ranks of tenured professors). On the other hand, while she remains optimistic about her own future, she did note that there are elements of being a scientific researcher that may be more difficult for women.

Some women claimed that, far from being inferior in these male-dominated fields, women are actually better than men at them. Interestingly, these comments came from blue-collar workers. Christina, a Mexican immigrant woman who owns her own landscaping business, stated, "I like that people like my design. I'm a little one. I'm a woman. Women do a hundred-percent better job in gardening than men." And Femi, the carpenter, argued,

Companies are learning that women *can* do the work and *like* to do the work. We're more reliable than the guys. Many of the guys don't like the job, just the paycheck. Women *like* the work, so companies are realizing that now. We try to make it *fun*. We set goals for how quickly we can work. You don't have to be miserable.

Some of the women found that the experience of being a woman in an atypical field could be very different depending on the setting of employment. *Dama,* who is currently an academic, has done quite well in that field, as a department head.[15] She conveys having encountered more resistance as a woman engineer in academia than during a previous career working for the federal government and the military, which she found very inclusive. She found a lot of acceptance and positive mentoring, which she sometimes finds lacking in academia. Although she said that the academic environment is not hostile, she said, "The expectations are less. Always. And it still takes me aback after so many years when I see it." She continued, "Somehow whatever you say isn't taken as seriously as when a male says it. I still see that, as head of my department." She believes she is seen as "half a head," and she said that she gets positive feedback from her male colleagues when she is agreeing with them, "and then they're taken aback when I say something they weren't expecting me to say." The sociologist Nina Toren finds this type of experience common in academic scientific fields, based on her research in Israel. "Women . . . have to convince the committee that they are indeed worthy and overcome the primitive, primordial attitude that they are strangers who do not really belong because they are not suited to do creative work in the realm of science and scholarship."[16]

*Dama*'s experience is interesting because engineering is a field in which there are currently programs and funding sources—both public and private— to encourage the success of women in the field. Although this can be seen as a positive development overall, *Dama* notes that it has led her male colleagues to devalue women's accomplishments in engineering. For example, if a woman receives a prestigious grant, it is assumed that she won it because of her gender, rather than because of her abilities. Femi says that some of her male co-workers resent her presence, and, though there is education to raise awareness about sexual harassment, "still the guys try it": "I don't take it personally or invest emotion in it. I nip it in the bud. I'm very business-like. For me it's the best way. Not to say I don't laugh at jokes, but you have to set the boundaries." She often gets the sense that the men would prefer that she not be there. "There are times you'll feel they don't want you to be there. For example, women have to have their own bathroom. Some general contractors don't like it. If it's a small job and the bathroom is clean, I will use the guys' bathroom. But if another woman comes, I will ask for one." Thus, Femi's method of handling sexist issues is to stay calm and not be too demanding but, at the same time, to stand up for herself and other women when she feels it necessary.

*Betty*'s experience in the field of engineering was different and very negative. Working in a Fortune 500 company, she did not feel unwanted due to her gender. Where she felt some resentment was with regard to her work habits. As she describes it, she worked too hard and therefore was not seen as a "team player." She feels that she could have used better mentoring. Although she does not specify that this lack of mentoring was attributable to her gender, in the absence of mentoring, the books she turned to were ones with names such as *Games Your Mother Never Taught You How to Play* and *Dress for Success,* which were targeted at helping women in corporate environments. She continued to find the work environment extremely stressful and eventually developed a stress-related illness and resigned. Although this ultimately turned out to be a positive development for her, as it led to her successful career in the arts, which she had always loved, it is hard not to speculate that, had she experienced more positive mentoring, she may have flourished as an engineer. On the one hand, it may seem odd to include her story here, as she is no longer in a gender-atypical field, having left engineering. On the other hand, in trying to understand what it is like to be an immigrant woman in a gender-atypical occupation, it seems that we miss something if we focus only on the success stories. In addition, part of the reason there are so few women in these fields is not just that few enter them but also that many are leaving these occupations, seeking more hospitable climates.

Much of what defines the experience of a woman in a male-dominated field is simply being the only woman, or one of very few women, at her workplace. This experience can be exacerbated if one is also the only person of one's race or ethnicity present as well. *Shanice,* a Trinidadian immigrant, is an accountant, which is not itself a gender-atypical occupation. In her case, it is her industry—the oil industry—rather than her occupation that is male dominated, as well as predominantly white. She remembers first walking into a roomful of accountants at work. "I realized they all were white men. I almost cried. I thought that here's an area where they could have some diversity, and they don't. . . . I can clearly see when I walk into a room and there is one color and one gender in the room, I can tell something is wrong." As with the undergraduate and graduate classes with few women, such an environment sends a message about who truly belongs in these fields.

## Obstacles to Immigrant Women in Atypical Occupations

So why are the rooms full of men? With all the gains of the women's movement, why are these occupations so male dominated? What do our interviews tell us about the barriers experienced by immigrant women in fields such as engineering, carpentry, landscaping, and the oil industry? The explanations these women gave include the socialization and education of boys and girls, the physical demands of the jobs, the actions of co-workers and bosses, and concerns about work-family balance, to which they generally believe women are more susceptible.

*Dama,* when asked about why there are so few women in engineering, replied, "Well, it's not even just male dominated anymore. It's starting to be a disaster, actually." She traces this back to elementary school. From the time she spent volunteering to teach math in her son's classroom, she noted, "I would see from third or fourth grade that the girls would start getting intimidated," whereas prior to that, "they were perfectly okay, confident calling out their answers and so on." In her current position she endeavors to recruit more young women into engineering, but she feels more needs to be done to turn young girls on to math and science as early as possible. Her explanation of the dearth of women in her field hinged solely on socialization and education.

*Matilda* turned to biology, rather than environment, for an explanation. She clearly stated her belief that, "in general, men are stronger than women." She explained that this held women back in the oil and gas industry, saying that there is a lot of work outdoors in a "very, very rough environment, with heavy irons." She argued that with technological advances the field should become more open to women and that countries such as Norway were doing more to recognize "the value women could bring to the workplace." Interestingly, another comment about the physicality of the work came not from Femi or Christina, who, as the carpenter/construction worker and landscaper, probably had the most arduous physical jobs, but from *Natalia,* who works in a science lab. She argued that being on your feet a lot in the lab could discourage women. She focused specifically on pregnancy, noting that "men can't get pregnant," suggesting that being on one's feet all day would be more difficult for a pregnant woman. *Natalia* also argued that it is crucial to time childbearing right if one wants to do scientific research and lamented the fact that if a woman applies for postdoctoral research, the assumption is that she plans to get pregnant during that time (i.e., prior to applying for a tenure-track appointment). And *Matilda* noted that family demands could hold one back in the oil and gas industry and that such responsibilities are often borne more by women. "I have to say I can't be there at six a.m."

Nina Toren notes that these very assumptions are used to hold women back in academic fields, as those doing the hiring and promotion tend to assume women's domestic plans or responsibilities mean that they are less committed to their scientific careers than are men.

> In academic science these assumptions have served to justify discrimination against women in terms of hiring, salary, tenure, promotion, and inclusion in men's informal collegial networks. . . . Male professors are reluctant to serve as mentors to women Ph.D. candidates because they think they are unstable workers ("She'll get pregnant and leave").[17]

Interestingly, the women we interviewed, who are in these fields, are themselves hinting at these explanations. In a sense, we see the very women whose lives contradict such stereotypes seeming almost to endorse them. Their comments are less expressions of their own assumptions about women as less desirable workers than reflections on the realities of limitations that may be placed on women because of the physicality of some of the work and the conflict between family responsibilities and demanding hours. Toren goes on to cite numerous studies that demonstrate that familial responsibilities do not reduce the productivity of women in academia. Clearly, nonetheless, such stereotypes remain strongly held.

*Shelly*, who also works in the oil and gas industry, recounted what many people would consider a hostile work environment, with male co-workers consuming pornography in the workplace. Her response indicates that not all women would report such conditions but may instead have other ways of handling such issues. "The guys get embarrassed when I walk in and they're showing porn. I would just say, 'I've seen that one.'" Femi also noted letting sexist jokes pass, rather than getting upset about them. Despite the fact that women such as *Shelly* and Femi find ways to handle these issues, this type of joking creates a hostile environment, marking the organizational culture of the workplace as fundamentally male. Like the predominantly male engineering classrooms, this sends a signal to both men and the few women in these workplaces that women are the intruders and that men are the ones who truly belong in these settings. Just as these women, in their experiences as immigrants, had to figure out whether they would assimilate to American culture or hold on to the cultural practices of their home country, as women in predominantly male workplaces they "are confronted with the dilemma of whether or not to be like the dominant majority, that is, to give up their identity and accept the prevailing values, norms, and modes of conduct of the new environment."[18] In this case, instead of baseball and apple pie representing the new culture, it is sexist jokes and pornography.

Femi stated that women in construction get treated differently than men. "They tend to give women the mundane jobs and also put women by themselves." She said that such segregation of the workplace makes it more difficult for women to learn from more senior and skilled male workers. "So how do you learn? In spite of it all, we learn stuff. We use the schools more than the guys do. We buy books. If they were evenhanded with the training, they'd have quite a workforce on their hands." This comment demonstrates an important theme in the women's discussions of obstacles. These women are the ones who are in these male-dominated fields; therefore, though obstacles may have frustrated them, they have surmounted or are surmounting them. The women who found such obstacles insurmountable would not show up in our sample. They may have never entered these fields or, like *Betty*, may have left after encountering frustration. Many of the women we spoke to pointed out that those who try to hold women back in these fields are the ones who will miss out on having talented workers and colleagues.

In the women's discussion of obstacles in their fields, rarely did immigration status come up. Instead, gender was the main focus. Did they really face more obstacles due to their gender than their nativity? This is difficult to disentangle. Just as it is difficult to sort out the effects of race, class, and gender discrimination, so too would it be difficult to determine exactly which slight is due to gender and which to nativity. Additionally, it is possible that a co-worker who feels hostile to an immigrant woman co-worker because of her nativity may voice that hostility through sexist jokes, for example, consciously or subconsciously reasoning that that is the most effective way to make her feel uncomfortable.[19]

Another factor is that while these immigrant women are often the only woman, or one of very few women, in their workplace, they are likely not the only immigrants. If we focus specifically on *Dama's* and Femi's fields, engineering and construction, both are known as fields with many immigrants. Mark Erlich and Jeff Grabelsky note that the construction trades are increasingly turning to immigrants to fill jobs,[20] particularly nonunion jobs. Erlich and Grabelsky argue that these jobs may no longer be as lucrative as they once were. As a variety of factors have weakened unions, wages and benefits have decreased, and, particularly in the South and Southwest regions of the country, nonunion labor is increasingly relied on in building projects, resulting in even lower wages. Erlich and Grabelsky note that, in such a climate, immigrant labor, including that of undocumented immigrants, has become an increasingly important source of labor.

This change in the workforce may point to how immigrant women's experiences in at least some of the gender-atypical occupations differ from those of native-born women. They are in the interesting position of being one of few women, but many immigrants, in their field. Since being one of few women is one of the difficulties of their work, it might be assumed that being one of many immigrants is an asset or comfort, drawing strength in numbers. We speculate that it might not be so simple. First, the strength-in-numbers argument presumes solidarity among immigrants. Although this may be the case among immigrants of the same nationality (though certainly not always), it should not be assumed among diverse groups of immigrants. So while Femi is unlikely to be the only immigrant at her workplaces, her immigrant co-workers may not share much in common with the British immigrant of both African and Caribbean ancestry. Latino immigrants, for example, would not necessarily feel a sense of solidarity with her simply on the basis of being an immigrant, just as native white and black co-workers would not be assumed to see each other as allies simply on the basis of being native-born Americans.[21] In addition, as an immigrant from Great Britain, Femi argues that her accent is often an asset. "People find the English accent interesting. It may actually have *helped* me. It sure helps on the phone, trying to get a job." It is unlikely that a Latino immigrant's accent would be received as favorably. Femi also notes that, having heard her accent, employers are often surprised when she shows up and is black. She did not note having lost any jobs due to her race though.

With regard to the way nonimmigrant, male co-workers perceive an immigrant woman in their workplace, their reactions to her gender and nativity may have similarities. Particularly since many of the immigrants being hired in, for example, the building trades are preferred by employers because they are not union members, it would be easy for a native-born male in a union to see immigrants as undermining his own job prospects and/or wages.[22] Additionally, while women, by definition, are in short supply in gender-atypical fields, the more the occupation is associated with masculinity—as are many of the jobs requiring physical labor—the more women may be resented for infringing on male territory. Thus, being "one of many" as an immigrant and "one of few" as a woman in a gender-atypical occupation, an immigrant woman may be resented doubly—both for being a woman and for being an immigrant.

## Surmounting Obstacles

*Dama* notes that, despite parental encouragement, she got other messages about her capabilities as a girl and young woman growing up. "A lot of times my aunts would say, 'It's so sad that you're a girl and good in studies. You'll never be able to do anything with school!'" *Dama* laughed before continuing: "It was good, actually, because it's so overt. You know, you have to either fight it or give in to it." Clearly she, Femi, and other immigrant women in gender-atypical fields have chosen to fight such sexism. Given that the voices we have heard in this chapter are of those immigrant women working in gender-atypical occupations, we in some sense hear the success stories. The very fact that these women are so scarce, and in some cases (particularly the trades) were so hard to find, suggests that there are many more women out there who could have been, but are not, in these occupations. One immigrant woman we know has told us of wishing to work in construction because of the good pay. When she phoned a construction company to inquire about such work, she was told flat out, "We don't hire women." That was enough to discourage her from further attempts in that field. And *Dama* spoke of the countless girls who get the message very early on that they should not pursue studies in math or science and so do not see engineering as a viable career. This leads us to ask what is being done to encourage more women to enter gender-atypical fields. Are there ways particularly to reach immigrant women in such attempts?

Earlier in this chapter, Femi referred to NEW, the organization that helped her train to be a carpenter. This organization's approach is one example of how to draw more women into these gender-atypical careers. On Saturdays, Femi now teaches carpentry to other women at the organization's employment-training center in Manhattan. The leaders of NEW hope to diversify the construction field as they simultaneously pave the way for women to earn higher wages by securing jobs in the construction trades—a sector in which only 3 percent of the jobs go to women. The organization's website implores, "Become a NEW Woman."

Organizations such as NEW stress that trades can help pull women out of poverty. They also note that jobs such as carpentry, plumbing, electrical work, and construction tend to pay well, have good benefits, and are often in demand. Such arguments are behind this organization's work to bring women into these fields. And Femi senses that such efforts have helped in the field of construction. "It's a good time for women. There are more opportunities now. . . . There were women who paved the way. They had it a lot harder. There is still work to do, but it is better."

No doubt things are better now for women in gender-atypical jobs such as construction and engineering, but as Femi notes, there is still work to do. Engineering is facing a severe shortage of qualified people to fill jobs in this country. This is one reason for a heavy reliance on immigrants to fill the jobs. Another way to deal with this shortage, as well as to promote equality, is to encourage more women to enter the field. *Dama* explained that her department and university are encouraging more women to enter the STEM (science, technology, engineering, and math) disciplines, and she noted that some grants are targeted at women. Amy Sue Bix argues that pioneering women engineers have worked to increase the acceptance of women in the field.[23] *Dama* was proud to note that the number of women faculty in her department had increased under her tenure as chair. She noted, however, that much of the change had to happen earlier on in women's lives, in the way science and math are presented to young girls, so that when they arrive at college they are able to pursue fields such as engineering. From her experience, as well as that of *Betty*, we see that parents, in their cases fathers, can have a huge role to play in encouraging girls to enter such scientific fields as well.

For *Dama* and *Betty*, this parental encouragement happened in India and China. This begs the question of whether girls elsewhere in the world are being more encouraged to pursue these fields than are girls in the United States, and if so, will the large numbers of immigrants in engineering morph into larger numbers of immigrant women in such fields, making such fields less heavily male? Occupations that might in the United States be gender atypical for women could in other countries be considered more typical for women. For example, during the Soviet era, it was far more likely for women to work as scientists and medical doctors in the Soviet Union than in the United States, and currently there is evidence that women are more visible in the construction trades in parts of Asia than in the United States. Thus, immigration from such areas could help even out the gender balance in such jobs.

## Discussion

Many endeavors have been labeled "masculine" and "feminine" historically, particularly paid employment, and such labels are tied to the deeper gender divide. Such labels do not always remain: clerks and teachers used to be almost exclusively male and now are predominantly female. But the careers discussed here, particularly engineering and carpentry/construction, have been historically and are currently very much seen as male endeavors, and we see this both in the education/training leading up to these careers and in the actual workplaces.

Modern societies, including the educational and occupational sectors, are structured largely along gendered lines. Globalization and the concomitant immigration are processes that muddy these binary distinctions in interesting ways. These immigrant women, by their very presence in their fields, are making these occupations less male dominated, and some of their efforts may increasingly challenge the gendered nature of their work. In addition, immigrant women's aspirations, as well as their survival needs, have pushed and pulled them not only to the United States but also into these gender-atypical occupations. Women immigrating from societies with more rigid gender roles now move outside those boundaries (literally and figuratively), which may make them more open to challenging the norms that dictate that certain jobs are for men and others are for women. This allows women such as *Dama* to actualize their dream to enter the masculine world of engineering. Here, the change is deeper, at the level of ideology and acceptance and, perhaps, of the altered role of women. As Nina Toren notes, "Women are limited in their performance of certain tasks by our perceptions and expectations, and the structural arrangements built around them."[24] Thus, the task is to change these perceptions, expectations, and structural arrangements.

Governments are too often not aware enough of the pool of proficiencies that immigrants, particularly immigrant women, bring with them. Policies and initiatives should be attuned to the broad array of possibilities immigrant women bring to the job market, so that they are not pushed to the domestic realm or to the service sector or the like because of a segmented labor market. If women are coming with atypical labor-market experience, it needs to be identified and enhanced, especially in those fields, such as engineering, in which this country faces shortages. If immigrant women aspire to such atypical areas, those fields of practice need to be made available at the level of subsidized training and education. And perhaps, where immigrant women may not aspire to these occupations due to lack of knowledge or awareness that there is a place for a woman in them, organizations such as NEW (with additional government funding) can do more outreach to immigrant communities, to try to draw in such women.

# 8

# "Always in Life, We Are Ripping"

*Culture Work*

It is a balmy June evening in Miami, Florida. The monthly art walk offers the occasion for art enthusiasts to stroll leisurely from gallery to gallery, touring the latest works of Miami-area artists as they sip glasses of complimentary wine. On this evening's self-guided tour but slightly off the beaten path is the GIL Gallery, where Cuban-born artist Lilian Fernandez, dressed fully in white, crouches in the gallery's display window and carries out a silent, studied performance-art piece with her back to her sidewalk audience. Lilian explained later,

> I was rubbing charcoal on the wall. The other artist and I were writing things we think heritage means for him and me. We were writing. But when the performance started, I didn't feel I needed to write. I started to do flowers: the same ones my mother painted. I was expressing heritage. The flower is like an icon for me. The other artist is angry about personal heritage. I feel it's a special set of tools for life. Heritage is like a tool you can use at different times. That's the treasure. I think you rip and reconstruct with these tools.

*The Flowers That My Mother Painted* was the title of a large painting that Lilian had completed years earlier in homage to her mother, who first taught her to paint—and *ripping* is literally what Lilian did with it. In a previous performance piece, Lilian had positioned herself on the street in front of the local convention center in Miami Beach and publicly ripped this treasured painting into envelope-sized squares. Incensed that she had not been selected to exhibit in the art exposition taking place inside the center, Lilian voiced her protest by doling out individual pieces of her painting to startled passersby on the street. Although she had no way to know how the judges made the final choices for the show, this performance was Lilian's way of asserting her presence, as a literal outsider artist—in the mode of the street artist's defiance of the confining and exclusive walls of museums.

> I did it as a cleansing, sending the work out into the world sort of like a message in a bottle that people toss into the ocean, dreaming of a response in the future. . . . My hope was that this year I would have the opportunity to exhibit my work during the fair and that the people I gave the pieces to would remember my performance.[1]

Later, Lilian scattered flyers all over Miami requesting the return of those ripped pieces. To her pleasure and surprise, six of the art fragments made their way back to her, for which Lilian exchanged six of her artworks. In an artistic "recycling," she featured the six floral remnants in a new composition that hung in her gallery exhibit the evening of the art walk. A metaphor for life—and apropos of the life of a transplanted Cuban—Lilian reflected, "I think that always in life we are ripping. It needs to be ripped and reconstructed again."

## Mirrors and Windows

Why do we include a chapter on culture work? First, culture work carries a distinctively gendered dimension. As Janet Mancini Billson has illustrated in her interviews with Canadian women across a range of ethnicities, women have historically been "keepers of the culture."[2] They bear tradition on their shoulders—including the reproducing of the particular culture's cuisine, textile patterns, home-based religious objects or shrines, aphorisms, language, habits, and morals.[3] Second, growing numbers of immigrant women are making substantial contributions to cultural production in the United States in the early twenty-first century, from novel writing and storytelling to music and dance to the visual arts. Some draw from their imported cultural traditions to keep these forms alive in the diaspora, educating the broader community in the process. Others are breaking new artistic ground with more avant-garde ideas and technologies. Still others offer a blend of both, creating a dialogue between tradition and their new home, from which something completely new emerges. Despite this growing contribution, according to a *New York Times* news piece in 2006, "immigrant art is often overlooked."[4]

Third, the arts (and humanities) offer a hermeneutic window into the world of the individual immigrant woman—her memories, struggles, conflicts, and triumphs. They open up the deeper, complex meanings of immi-

Figure 8.1. Lilian Fernandez (Photo by Gilberto Perez)

gration as subjectively experienced. The art created is thus both a window into the immigrant's experience and a mirror that she turns to face the host society. The artist presents this mirror-window (from her perspective) for the viewer's consumption as a window-mirror (from the viewer's perspective). A Polish immigrant woman penned the introduction to a 2007 exhibit, "In Your Face," at the Bernice Steinbaum Gallery in Miami, which featured several immigrant artists' works. She phrased the art-consumption moment this way:

> These works stare right back at the viewer as if to say, "Here I am. Look at me! Am I making you think?" . . . Their work suggests that the images we are viewing reflect fragments of our own experience, postulating that this exhibit is not apart from us, but rather part of us. We are asked to recognize that our own identity within this culture is inextricably linked to those who surround us.[5]

In the case of the United States, where this exhibit was displayed, allegiance to ethnicity and heritage has been both glorified and feared throughout the history of our political culture, and this contradiction was a prominent theme in the exhibit. When race is added to the equation, this approach-avoidance attitude toward immigrants incorporates yet another critical dimension.

The artists in this chapter are working today, and the products of their imagination are lenses into the experiences of contemporary immigration. By interviewing culture workers and observing their works, we are responding to a call by sociologists of the arts to expand our sociological analyses to incorporate the important societal role that the autonomous artist plays, in addition to analyzing the institutions through which the arts are incorporated into society.[6] Many artists will reflect publicly on the intentions behind their creations, but others prefer observers to take an individual meaning from their interaction with the works—since they hope to engage the listener/observer in a meaning-making experience that will differ from one audience member to another based on his or her biography. In this chapter, we have the opportunity to hear from those artists, through interviews, to supplement that direct observation of their work with more knowledge of their intentions.

### Leaving Home ("There/Then")

The women in this chapter represent a variety of cultural genres, including painting, mixed media, storytelling, photography, radio production, writing, film acting, film directing, installations, poetry, playwriting, dance, and music. Although aesthetics represent only one branch of the broader phenomenon of culture, we are encompassing a large range of aesthetic genres here, including mass media and new communications media, as well as visual and performing arts. The contexts of immigration departure and reception for these artists range widely: from those who were in search of a new place for their artistic venues, training, or freedom of expression to dramatic stories of refugees and asylum seekers escaping perils of oppressive regimes. Atlanta artist Roya Pazooki, for example, was jailed in Iran for four years as a political prisoner, and she witnessed the torture of other women in her prison. Some of these artists arrived with very little or nothing. The Vietnamese actress Kieu Chinh recalls that she landed in North America (Canada, initially) with a few dollars in her pocket. When Saigon fell, she had been at the peak of her career as an actress in Vietnam. She had both acted in and produced movies in her country and throughout the region; she had also hosted a television talk show on which she regularly interviewed Hollywood actors visiting the region.

The 1979 Iranian revolution was the backdrop and context of exit for several of these artists. Some had been active in the revolution before the Shah was deposed, and many were hopeful that the new regime would bring broader reforms for women. As the new government quickly turned authoritarian and required the veiling of women, not only were several of these female artists restricted by gender constraints on their lives, but their own livelihoods were threatened. As the Iranian poet *Golnaz* explained, "Guards attacked my house; they did not arrest me, but . . . as a woman, I was under lots of persecution, in a different way. I didn't want to go into all the details, but I lost . . . one job in television because a few hairs showed [from under her headscarf] and I had sandals." *Golnaz* left behind a difficult marriage in Iran, along with the political circumstances that she encountered after the revolution. She took her thirteen-year-old son with her to France, and after two months she was able to get to the United States to be with her sister, who lived here. She found herself in a much less densely populated urban environment in the United States than the ones in which she had always lived, and this was quite an adjustment for her. She recalled, "It was unbearable to see the streets empty—to me, empty. And I wanted to connect with people. I was full of energy for connections. I wanted to start a new life. I said that's my rebirth, . . . and I wanted to write all the things that were hidden inside me. And I was happy." Thus, the craft of fiction writing simultaneously enlivened the experience of life as an immigrant, offered emotional healing, and was fed by the unique experiential confrontation between the old and new home. *Golnaz* also had to adjust to living on the wages of a babysitter while trying to support her son—quite a status adjustment for the daughter of a medical doctor. It was her avocation as a writer that allowed her to infuse meaning into her new existence.

Prior to Neri Torres's arrival in the United States, the Cuban-born dancer and choreographer had been practicing her craft in Italy, a country to which she had fled. In 1991, she explained, she had "a traumatic experience": "I was kidnapped by the Cuban KGB. They just didn't allow people to leave the country." With assistance from a foundation, she was able to free herself and move to Miami, Florida, where she received refugee status and began to establish herself in the dance profession with an emphasis on Cuban-inspired dance forms. Neri had felt the need to leave her home country because, she said, "I wanted freedom. Everything was very hard in my country. I wanted a better life." Her family was not in the inner political circles, she explained: "They were opposed to communism. In Cuba you were either with or against the revolution." In Miami, she found that the Cuban community "really nurtures you, and then later, you can make it on your own."

Another Miami resident, Liliane Nérette Louis, had been a teacher in her native Haiti during its rule by the dictator "Papa Doc" Duvalier. Fearful for her family's safety, she surreptitiously left Haiti for New York, where she found herself laboring in jobs that she characterized as "menial," until she landed a position with a hospital and trained herself in the medical-records field. After marrying and bearing three children, Lilian moved to Miami with her family and worked her way up in various hospital administrative positions. On the side, however, she loved telling Haitian folk tales, a passion that led her onto a path of storytelling and writing.

### Why Pursue the Arts?

What was it in the backgrounds of these women that led them to choose to do art? The women we interviewed often portrayed the inception of their identities as artists as a blend of natural ability with particular—and usually, constraining—circumstances in their lives. Many trace their beginnings to early childhood. For example, one had grown up with nine siblings, and she sought solace by escaping into a room and doing artwork. Some stumbled on their vocations more accidentally. As Taiwanese *Xia-Hwa* recalled, "When I was younger, they thought I had a learning disability. . . . What it turned out to be is that I have dyslexia. I couldn't do math. And in Asia, especially in Taiwan when I was growing up, you don't have a future if you're not good with science." It was not until *Xia-Hwa* immigrated that she realized her artistic calling—and again it arose out of another situation of educational constraint, but this one was related to being a transplant: the language barrier.

> When I first came, . . . I signed up to be in the telecommunications program. And then when I arrived and started taking classes, I realized I can't understand a word when people are talking. So I showed up one day, and they were doing a quiz, and I couldn't do it. I couldn't bear the thought of going back to Taiwan without a diploma, so I switched my major to art. I figured in art I don't have to talk. I just have to draw!

*Xia-Hwa* is now a successful filmmaker, whose films play the festivals in both the West and the East.

*Betty* can trace her artistic beginnings to the pleasure of play during her childhood:

I remember when I was four or five years old, when we were still in China, I remember my [maternal] grandmother. I would take the sheets and pretend like I'm a Peking opera star. And I loved dancing. . . . I think there was a shift, maybe about fourth grade or so, I start drawing and writing poetry, and I joined a dancing group. And my dad found out—it was like absolutely forbidden. Oh, I cried and cried. Because the teacher actually picked me as the leader of the group. I was just like, "I love it," but "Nope, you can't do it." So, I'd say all along there was that part of me that wanted to express, wanted to create.

Vietnamese-born actress Kieu Chinh tells a story of serendipity that helps fuel the prototypical Hollywood "discovery" myth. As a young newlywed, she was walking to the post office one day in her home city when she was approached by a Hollywood filmmaker, who happened to be in Vietnam filming on location. The filmmaker asked if she spoke English and French and told her that she had the "perfect height" that they needed for a female part in the film. Kieu Chinh was invited to a film test, but she was disappointed that she had to turn it down because her in-laws were opposed to the idea that their daughter-in-law would be an actress and felt uncomfortable with her portrayal in romantic scenes. Being a performer was not widely accepted in the culture at that time. She took a small role in the movie instead. At the reception for the actors, however, a Vietnamese filmmaker approached her with an opportunity for a part in another film. This role met her family's approval: she would play a Buddhist nun in the film *The Bells of Thien Mu Temple*. Kieu's career blossomed from there. She became an actress, producer, and talk-show host in Vietnam and also landed roles in American films while still in her home country. About this unexpected turn of events, she said, "Though there were obstacles, being an actress was my fate."

Trinidadian native Karen Walrond similarly wandered accidentally into the world of producing photography-based blogging. Trained in both engineering and law, she was in the throes of a successful corporate law career when she created a website with photos of her daughter to share with far-flung friends and family. To her surprise, she found strangers gravitating to her website and responding positively to her work. She decided to post a daily blog entry and photograph, directed toward her larger, growing world of virtual friends, and to invite guest comments. Her intimate characterizations of motherhood and family life eventually caught the attention of talk-show host Oprah Winfrey, and Karen unexpectedly found herself interviewed for the program in 2009. Although when we interviewed Karen, she said that she viewed photography as an avocation rather than a vocation, by 2010, she had moved out of her law practice, had displayed her photographs in a local Houston gallery, and had written a book featuring her photographs and writing.

Dancer Neri Torres characterizes her introduction into her artistic trade almost as a family heirloom passed down through generations—although under circumstances that were less than free in several regards. Her great-grandfather had been enslaved and was famous on his plantation for his dancing. Neri began her training at around age twelve under Ballet Africa in Cuba and eventually became interested in modern dance, before she reached back into her own heritage and took to Afro-Cuban forms.

Repeated across the biographies of these cultural workers was a revelatory moment or a period in their lives when they realized that they have to do art. They insist that they cannot *not* do art: it is the pivotal means by which they can express themselves. That passion sometimes constituted the motive to leave home: if expression was not an available option in their own native country, they had to leave. The Cuban-born Lilian Fernandez recalled, "Always in my mind were my dreams as an artist. I worked to buy my first canvas. I want to develop my art, my ideas. Because I think in art. I can't be free and quiet and normal. These things attack me."

This drive that Lilian describes helps explain why a number of these women pursued their art while living in places where artistic expression was dangerous. Cuban dancer Neri Torres came from a family that opposed communism. Susie Thang was trained as a pharmacist in her native Vietnam before needing to leave her country. She landed in Houston, Texas, where she integrated into a growing Vietnamese community. After establishing herself professionally, however, she looked around and noticed that despite living in a relatively calm and resourced society, her compatriots were not getting the information they required to meet some basic needs. She also realized that her community was dispersed across the metropolitan area and needed a communications hub to draw it together toward common interests and concerns. Her brainchild was the first Vietnamese-language radio station in Houston. Susie set up a studio in a set of rooms in the office where her husband practiced dentistry. She and her husband continue to fund the downtown-Houston station as well as a host of musical education events and concerts for the community.

# Memory

Artists are visionaries. They look ahead and are credited with helping to move societies forward in the direction to which they point. Despite this future orientation, the art form also incorporates a backward gaze: memory is a potent source for artistic materials. Immigrant memory, however, carries additional dimensions that native-born individuals' memory cannot know in quite the same way. Memory for immigrants is deeply associated with a distant place and distant people. This means that "then" is more likely to be associated with "there" than with "here." These cultural workers engage their memories in their innovations, but those memories often have a presentism or futurism to their purpose. They educate, question, or help to transform.

Natasha Duwin created a series of pieces that she entitled *Remembered I*, interweaving her family's personal memory with public history. A reference to Argentina's "Dirty War" that began in 1976, during which thousands of Argentineans mysteriously disappeared, these pieces feature a line of individuals standing (or lying) in a row, silently posed in outline form, decked in white gauze that might evoke burial shrouds. The figures represent members of Natasha's own family and provide a reminder that it was at the family level that the war was lived.

Iranian artist Roya Pazooki offers visitors black handmade blindfolds at the doorway to a small three-room exhibit in Atlanta, Georgia. She leads the blindfolded down a dark corridor lined with floor-to-ceiling black fabric hung to demarcate simulated prison cells. Sounds of tiles breaking beneath the visitors' feet accompany the otherwise silent walk down the corridor and around the corner to the other "cells." After removing the blindfold, Roya reveals the prison scene that she has re-created, based on her memories across four years of imprisonment in postrevolutionary Iran. Painted outlines of feet on the floor tiles peak out from the curtained rooms: executed prisoners, perhaps? Finally, the visitors reach the room that simulates solitary confinement in all its stark, lonely darkness.

In 2007, Roya produced "Blindfold: A Simple Truth" as her graduate art-school thesis project in a prominent Atlanta gallery location, crafted from her memory of her stint in an Iranian prison. She dedicated the exhibit "to the memories of all those who had died dedicating their lives to the human rights." The work both chronicled the artist's personal memory as an exposé of the regime's brutality and commemorated the resistance movement's martyrs. Among the martyrs were her friends; Roya knows that she narrowly escaped the same fate. Printed across the exhibit floor was this recollection from her prison days:

Mother received the clothes and said to the prison guard: "For seven years I came from my home in another town to visit my daughter. Anytime I asked you when my daughter is going to be released you said pretty soon. Now, you are just giving me her clothes without telling me the location of her grave. I am going to hang her clothes on the sill of our home so we could never forget what you did to us."

One indirect, more metaphorical aspect of the exhibit was also represented by the blindfolds, which Roya had handsewn. Referencing more universal human experiences to deal with pain and discomfort, Roya explained, "In life, we make our own blindfolds." Both Roya and Natasha (in her *Remembered I* piece) are making their memory of the there-and-then available to those in their new homeland who are far away from those experiences.

Memory takes a second form in these artists' works, which is that of homeland heritage as a resource of personal artistic expression and as a body of community identification. We saw the former in the work of Lilian Fernandez, who viewed heritage as a set of personal tools. Since the memory that formed several of her pieces was of her mother's art, this particular instance of heritage was more individualistic. The artist Hung Liu grew up during the Cultural Revolution in mainland China and remembers singing the communist anthem, "The Internationale." Although keenly aware of the constraints that the communist system placed on her art and her life more broadly, Hung reproduces memories from that era in her work, and she credits the revolution with the ideals that she learned, celebrating the labor and sincerity of the common worker. As an artist and professor in the United States, Hung paints images of peasants, laborers, and children in humble surroundings. She stated,

> History is not a static image or a frozen story. It is not a noun. Even if its images and stories are very old, it is always flowing forward. History is a verb. The new paintings are my way of painting life back into my memories of a propaganda film that, over time, has become a document of the revolutionary sincerity that permeated my childhood. Even the actors in the film believed in their roles. When they walked into the river, carrying their dead and wounded, they were going home.[7]

Childhood memories also fuel the creativity of Liliane Nérette Louis, who developed her Haitian storytelling skills into public performances after living most of her adult life in the United States. In the beginning, Liliane told her stories informally to friends, but word of her storytelling quickly spread throughout her community. She began to receive invitations to recite stories in various venues around Miami. Her engaging, animated style, which incorporates humor, captures children's imaginations in particular. As her reputation as a storyteller grew, Liliane put pen to paper, and one result has been her popular book of stories, *When Night Falls, Kric! Krac!* These stories that remind her of her childhood were unfamiliar to young children born to Haitian families in the United States. Therefore, Liliane's work developed into an educational mission to help keep this heritage alive by passing on the stories.

Vietnamese radio-station manager Susie Thang is nostalgic for her country and wants to remember her culture and promote the continuation of its music and language. She uses the medium of radio both to provide information and to keep cultural memory alive. The station offers a packed schedule between the hours of 2:00 p.m. and 8:00 p.m. each day, which includes call-in talk shows on issues such as women's health. Now that Houston's Vietnamese community is well established and includes a whole generation of bilingual young people, the radio provides an outlet for introducing the second and third generations to their culture. Yet Susie incorporates the young tastes into programming as well. She said, "I ask my children to help get hot, up-to-date music." Again, cultural fusion enlivens the artistic production and bridges two worlds both temporally and spatially.

Both Susie and her husband are lifelong, passionate supporters of the arts. Entering the small office adjacent to the room where Susie's husband treats his dental patients, one is struck by the display not of dentist tools but of the accoutrements of a music studio. Lining the walls are keyboards, guitars, a well-stocked shelf of music CDs, and a host of music memorabilia. The offices display posters of performances that the couple has sponsored. Both Susie and her husband cannot stop talking about their favorite performers, concerts, and musical communities in which they are involved. They have underwritten and organized classical-music education for children across the years.

For Argentinean writer *Victoria,* the concept of homeland heritage is particularly complex. Her novel begins with an account of her family's story of fleeing genocide and multiple dislocations and migrations across continents. "So I grew up in a very . . . long line of immigrants, for us, and that's part of the novel: never staying put. . . . Basically it's about people being forced to move, and relocate, and start over." *Victoria*'s family memory is a clear example of one where the story "dropped" on her. Her story is a reminder that the artist's representation of *mixed* heritage can be also present—in addition to more solo forms of ethnic cultural memory—and is no less rich for its mixtures. *Victoria* has added yet another culture to her biographical mix by marrying a Jewish American man. The consistent theme across her works is not that of one particular ethnic heritage but the memory of her home city. She said, "Buenos Aires fits in; it's always more or less in my work."

For actress Kieu Chinh, the theme of her Vietnamese background is occasionally present in her work, but this theme cannot infuse her full oeuvre because of her need to play Asian roles in a wide range of films. There are so few parts for Asians in Hollywood that Kieu finds herself competing with many actresses. Thus, she has portrayed a variety of Asian ethnicities in her films. In the 1993 movie *The Joy Luck Club,* for example, based on the novel by Amy Tan, she played a Chinese woman named Suyuan. The story of four Chinese-born women and their relationships with their U.S.-born daughters gave American filmgoers a glimpse into the boundary-straddling challenges of immigrant women whose migration also represented a leap from bounded traditions to modernity. But the 2005 film *Journey from the Fall,* about a family's life following the 1975 fall of Saigon, not only drew Kieu into a story of her own homeland but touched on her personal biography as well, since this was an event that dramatically affected her life and permanently separated her from her father. In the film, Kieu portrays Ba Noi, a matronly grandmother who makes it to the United States smuggled below board in a small boat. This is a family drama, in which mundane events such as kite flying play out on the grander stages of war, cruel reeducation camps, postwar landmines, piracy, and the cultural clashes of the immigrant experience. The theme of betrayal also spans the personal and grander narratives, from a woman's exposure of a runaway that leads to his death to blunt politicized statements that Americans betrayed the country by pulling out their military forces too soon.

By beginning with a story about genocide, the writer *Victoria* also mines the painful memories of the past for her aesthetic material in a critical engagement with memory that has some parallels both to *Journey from the Fall* and to Roya's exhibit "Blindfold: A Simple Truth." For all three, the personal and familial memories are simultaneously the memories of the ethnic and communal.

Several of these artists use their craft to document the past in part because, eventually, human memories fade. This can be especially true when people live at such a distance from familiar sights, smells, and sounds that continue to stimulate those personal memories. Thus, documentation is an important task for many of these artists, whether that documentation serves the purpose of making a political statement or preserving the beauty of cultural heritage.

## Gendered Meanings

Gender asserted its presence as a theme across quite a few of these artists' cultural products. This is not surprising in several instances, since constraints on their options as women or their political involvement with women's issues were the context of departure for several of the artists. The film, novel, painting, dance, and performance pieces are tableaux on which these artists express their reflections on living as women and as diasporic women. Although we did not select the women to interview based on this criterion, it was striking how many came to their art as women's rights activists or view their art as a venue for exploring gender-related themes. The Cuban-born dancer and choreographer Neri Torres offered her reflection on her contributions through dance: "We need a little bit of the female energy in the world. There's too much male energy, too much testosterone." Gender also arose in our conversation with *Betty*, who reflected on how it felt to step onto an American university campus in the 1970s, where she no longer felt the gendered restrictions that she had known at home; this had a major impact on her immigrant experience: "I felt very at home, very welcomed. I felt being a Chinese woman, a Chinese girl, was a plus. It wasn't like, 'How dare you be a woman. We don't need you.'"

To an extent, these women's cultural products are intended to challenge certain aspects of cultural memory, such as older societal expectations for women. Miami artist Natasha Duwin, an Argentinean of Italian and Russian parentage, for example, wants to challenge conventional images of womanhood that continue to persist. She said of her home country, "One of the biggest companies in Argentina says that the Bible says women can't wear trousers. Argentina has the highest rate of psychiatrists and plastic surgeons in the world. There are high rates of anorexia. The women are all gorgeous. My work is about how to be a woman different from the one I was raised to be." Natasha reported that she is broadening her mission to infuse a more universal message: "I explore the construction of the female identity and the interactions between the historical baggage that continues to be handed down to girls everywhere, the impact of the social, cultural, and economic revolutions of the twentieth century, and women's own stories and journeys."

Natasha is confronting tradition head-on through her work, but in the process she does not abandon the symbols, products, work, and journeys that defined women before this revolution. She uses her own body fluids in her work, including some she kept from giving birth to her child. She explores the meanings of women's bodies and the experience of mothering. And she incorporates materials and processes that were traditionally used by women to make functional objects: embroidery and weaving, for example. In this way, she calls attention to the work of the female, which has not traditionally enjoyed much visibility. For example, the products of difficult and time-consuming textile work are not labeled with the signature of the artist the way that a painting would be. By drawing from materials and themes with traditional and practical functions, Natasha makes aesthetic objects without practical functionality, in a celebration of the significance of practical art. As she explained,

> Much like birthing, weaving, embroidery, needlework, tapestry, quilting, lace, textiles in general, and traditional women's work have long been relegated to the worlds of labor and craft, and they are usually described as weak, ineffectual, feminized mediums. I use all of the abovementioned mediums to produce representations of the essence of women: strong, fragile, forceful, pliant, rigid, aggressive, inviting.

Natasha's personal experience permeates her work: "I can't help it: exploring gender and immigration themes. I wish I could." She expounded on one of her three-dimensional mixed-media art pieces, which resembles a bird's nest; it has thorns on the outside, but the inside is soft and feathery. Her intention was to represent the dichotomous feeling of being a woman: soft and delicate inside but hard on the outside. As it turns out, her piece had more universal appeal than she had anticipated; after viewing it, several men remarked to her, "That's exactly how I feel as well."

Chinese-born artist Hung Liu wants to combine the documentary power of material forms with the creativity of aesthetics to aid the memory process. She explained, "As a painter, I am interested in subjecting the documentary authority of historical photographs to the more reflective process of painting." She layers many of her paintings with additional washes and drips superimposed over the more representative image. She believes that this opens the viewing process "to a slower kind of looking." Many of the subjects in her paintings are derived from old photographs of Chinese women and men that were taken by foreigners. Those photographs frame the subjects through a Western, often male, gaze that "orientalizes" them.[8] Hung's literal "washing" is also a figurative statement; she said that she intends to "wash [her] subjects of their exotic 'otherness' and reveal them as dignified, even mythic figures on the grander scale of history painting"[9]— and the subjects to which she gives special attention are women. The Asian woman has taken on a particular exoticism and fetishism in the Western male gaze, and exposing this tendency critically is one of Hung's missions. In this sense, neither the work of Hung nor the Vietnam War film *Journey from the Fall* shy away from direct confrontations with the themes of imperialism and colonialism that characterized the history of these immigrants' new host society.

Hung Liu uses art to bring visibility to the historical work of women from her country who suffered from disrespect and invisibility. In one of her projects, she displays, in large, 36-inch-by-36-inch confrontational formats, portraits of Chinese "comfort women." Starting from wallet-sized, historic photographs of sex workers taken by foreigners, she produced a series of large-scale oil paintings with the artistic magnitude usually reserved for the portrayal of emperors. On an even larger canvas (80 by 160 inches), Hung reproduced an image of Chinese women filed into a line, including some who appear to be just out of puberty, waiting together with furrowed brows and downcast eyes. She entitled the piece *Strange Fruit: Comfort Women*. Although Hung is rescuing these women from obscurity and restoring the dignity that was robbed from them through both the orientalized images and their commodified use as "fruit," the women in the paintings look anything but comfortable. Hung's paintings preserve the signs of emotional scarring that the women's faces emit.

*Xia-Hwa* uses filmmaking to explore a variety of themes arising from her relationship with memory, heritage, and gender. *Xia-Hwa* is a Taiwanese with feminist politics, and several of her films have critiqued the Chinese preference for boy children to carry on the family name, which made *Xia-Hwa* feel unwanted in her family. She also felt constrained by the education available to her as a girl in Taiwan, which was confined to the "domestic arts." Her personal and artistic development has been nurtured by forgetting as well as by remembering. She explained, "I work with themes. The themes are—it's about how I believe that all beings seek for better life. All beings desire happiness. And it's human nature to seek a better life."

*Xia-Hwa*'s work excavates the private knowledge of the dark secrets of human family and business relationships: sexual abuse and human trafficking, for example. *Xia-Hwa* culls memories of sexual abuse from her childhood as an artistic source. She takes up "any issue about seeking a better life: for example, immigration issues." Her commitment to social change means taking on heritage and memory by putting them front and center.

## On Immigration and the American Experience

Lilian Fernandez's statement about the process of ripping as a metaphor for life is one to which immigrants, in particular, can relate. What do we learn from these women's artworks about the worlds of immigration and about the American society in which they are living? The introductory text for the 2007 exhibition at the Bernice Steinbaum Gallery text explained,

> The diversity of the artists in the exhibition reminds us that America the "melting pot" is a cliché, punctuating that we are not diluted within the proverbial stew. Rather, the artists comprise a patchwork quilt whose individuality remains intact. Like unique pieces of fabric, symbolically woven together, they convey their stories and personalities, and more fundamentally, their American experience.[10]

If not the intention of every artist in the exhibit, it was clear that, collectively, the pieces worked to convey this sociocultural mirror as viewed by artists such as Hung Liu from China. The artists' distinct biographies and the ideas and images that represent their own ethnic histories infused each of their works. As the exhibit text implies, this fact does not make these individuals any less "American."

*Victoria*'s novel chronicles an immigration story that is not personally her own, but because she grew up with her parents' stories of leaving Turkey, she is mining her life for inspirational material for her book:

> Because growing up, both of my parents would tell me their stories. And my father was five years old when he had to walk—he was in the marches that the Turks had the Armenians do. And it meant a lot of people died along the way. So he always talked about all that. . . . So a lot of that ended up in my writing, because I grew up hearing all these stories in Buenos Aires. . . . For me, growing up there, my life was so far away from all that.

The writing process may have helped *Victoria* sort through the complexities of immigration and the way that it can play with the notion of an individual's sense of heritage: "When people left Turkey, they went to all different places, depending on where they got in. So some went to Romania, some went to France, some went to Venezuela—wherever they got in. Some of them went to Greece. And then many of them came here. It is really very complicated. That's why I wrote the book." *Victoria*'s individuality was a result of this unique ethnic blend and the experience of ethnic commonalities across a diaspora.

One lesson from these women's cultural productions squares with a central theme of this book: the less-recognized gendered component of immigration—or the history of women as agents in immigration. One of Hung Liu's attempts to restore acclaim to those who history forgot is her portrayal of the Chinese immigrant woman Lalu Nathoy, who is represented through Hung's large-scale portraiture techniques with the washes and drips. Lalu, whose story began chapter 2, eventually took the name Polly Bemis and was nicknamed "China Polly."[11] Hung Liu's painting of Polly is 66 by 70 inches. Portrayed in her older years, in simple Western clothing and leading a horse, Polly appears to have a guardian angel floating above who is regal and youthful but full of certainty and adorned in the rich decorative elements of Chinese tradition. By introducing audiences to this woman through portraiture, Hung hopes to reveal publicly the integral role that Chinese women played in settling the American West. She exposes how certain women have transcended even the most drastic form of migration—that of pure physical force—have found independence, and have become social contributors. The film *Journey from the Fall* also underscores the strong-willed determination of women to immigrate with and without male partners, despite the many types of vulnerability that they face on the high seas.

## Boundary Transgressions

Even as these artists reflectively reproduce the ethnic and gender cultures that they value, many are simultaneously challenging boundaries between ethnicities, between nationalities, and between genders. In fact, the arts provide an arena for exploring contrasts across boundaries and for transgressing boundaries of all types. And the experience of migration compounds that transgression. That cross-border move was a turning point of these women's lives that brought them to where they are today: the temporal "then" is connected to the spatial "there"; the temporal "now" is connected to the spatial "here." These associations must permeate the immigrant's thoughts and actions at various levels of awareness. In 1990, sociologist Anthony Giddens referred to the increasing availability of faster transportation and communication as "distanciation,"[12] an experience that changes the realities of social relationships, since people can maintain ties across distances. This affects immigrants particularly, as researchers have documented that more immigrants are living transnationally—returning "home" when they can, staying in telephone and e-mail contact with family—keeping an ongoing bridge across the boundary between "here" and "there."

Even the self-definition of *home* changes to one that straddles geographic boundaries in this era of transnational living. As Yen Le Espiritu has observed, "Given that immigrants are multiply located and placed, . . . home is both an *imagined* and an *actual* geography; or more specifically, it is about how home is both connected to and disconnected from the physical space in which one lives."[13] Le Espiritu dubs this experience of an individual's transnational life the "space between."[14] This near-erasure of the spatial boundary complicates the situation even further, and we could describe this transnational experience as one in which "now" might be both "here" and "there." Although not interviewed by us for this book, the Iranian American writer Azar Nafisi has asserted that "genuine home is when it allows you to feel both at home and at the same time it allows you to transcend boundaries,"[15] a statement that affirms this transborder mentality as an asset, even a comfort.

The arena of the arts—visual, tactile, theatrical, musical—is an ideal place for playing with contrasts across boundaries. These include the imagined borders between light and dark, male and female, order and chaos, change and continuity, material and ideal, tradition and modernity, freedom and imprisonment, and memory and forgetting, to name but a few. Poststructuralist thinkers depict the prevalence of "binaries" (either-ors) as traps of our modern and postmodern condition. Through the arts, we can explore the blurring, fluidity, and erasability of boundaries between the binaries, as well as the choices one makes when there is a need to be on one side of the border versus the other. It is well known in the field of music that one of the most fruitful sources of creative innovation is in the meeting point between cultures through their distinct rhythms, tones, melodies, harmonies, and themes. Border crossing offers raw material for new creations by transforming one cultural sound into endless possibilities of innovative variations on that sound, as a creolization between the creative sources takes place.

Filmmaker *Xia-Hwa* is one of these artists who has discovered that making a work more personal gives it broader, cross-border appeal. Her own culture appears in some of her films, such as her inclusion of Taiwanese pop music that her audience recognizes. But her primary approach is to make films with universal appeal. She explained, "In most of the work I encourage the students to do, they need to be personal in order to be universal. And they need to be very specific in order to be global." This echoes the sentiment expressed by American poet Lorraine Hansberry in her play *A Raisin in the Sun*: "I believe that one of the most sound ideas in dramatic writing is that in order to create the universal, you must pay very great attention to the specific. Universality, I think, emerges from truthful identity of what is."[16] Like the timeless and universal appeal of Shakespeare's plays, the making of art that illuminates the vagaries of human relationships at the levels of power, envy, love, grief, and joy results in universally relevant works.

Trinidadian photographer/writer Karen Walrond came to this same conclusion in her experimental blog creations that captured the attention of people around the globe. Her posts of simple stories of daily events, accompanied by brightly colored professional-quality photographs, found a grateful audience. She remembered, "I realized I had a voice different from people in the United States and Trinidad; but people all over the world responded to it and found some part of themselves in it." People write in to offer their own corresponding personal hopes, quirks, pet peeves, and learning moments in response to Karen's own personal description of herself and her day, and they also respond to one another.

While Neri Torres works to keep her Afro-Cuban dance traditions alive in the diaspora, she intentionally tries to build bridges across the boundaries that separate the native-born of African descent from those from her homeland. Having had subtle and less subtle encounters with racism directed toward her after she migrated, she shares common experiences with the native-born. She has invited the acclaimed African American choreographer Katherine Dunham to work with her troupe and has collaborated with an African American ensemble to bring diverse communities together both as dancers and as audiences. Neri stated that she wants to "get people who have the same roots across our uniqueness to celebrate our origins": "I try to unite them through music, and then other people can come together." In fact, she insisted, "Afro-Cubans have changed the face of American music"—contributing their cultural distinctiveness at the same time that they transform diasporic music into something that is boundary blurring in its end product. Neri feels that this Cuban influence has not been sufficiently recognized; its very incorporation into the music outside its boundaries ironically makes it invisible to the world. She takes her company on the road, in part, to help reverse this impression and "spread the word about Cuban dance and the role of Cubans in the world."

When Lilian Fernandez ripped her painting outside the art exposition, she erased the boundary between the inside and outside of the show, and she remarked that this act made her feel like she was *in* the show. The artist can (agentially) create a situation in which she becomes part of the exhibit or performance, even if the insiders do not recognize her to be so. Lilian has expanded the boundaries of the exposition, while simultaneously critiquing the inside/outside boundary.

How do these immigrant women self-identify in their own geographical boundary crossings as migrants? There is not one consistent pattern in this regard. Trinidadian Karen Walrond finds that she easily blends in and is mistaken for African American, but she said, "I can never be an American; I'll always be a Trini." On her website, she says that she loves all things "Trini," with the exception of certain, very ethnic-specific foods, which she presents as a puzzle. These identity questions are far from static and clearly change with historical circumstances. Natasha Duwin—Argentinean with Russian and Italian parentage—always considered herself to be "a citizen of the world." Then 9/11 happened. She recalls that this event moved her closer to identifying with the United States, because of a new feeling: "'This is my country. You did this to *my* country.' I changed my loyalty at that point." Simultaneously, she bemoans the feeling of exile: "I'm an immigrant, and my kid will never have the experience of kneading dough with his grandmother ten thousand miles away."

*Betty* creates through adapting an ancient Chinese art form of paper marbling, which involves painting images on water or fluid and transferring the images to paper. In China, the genre only used the colors of black and white; *Betty* incorporates color. There was more than the fusion of two aesthetic cultures in this innovation, however. The new cultural context contributed to the form and meaning of her art. As she insisted, "In this country, you can be *free.*" Since, in her estimation, American culture fosters innovation, rebellion, and creativity, *Betty* felt permission to break from tradition. Through her art, she attempts to blur and fuse more than one set of boundaries between binaries simultaneously. She is bridging East and West, as well as science and art—as she transitioned to her avocation from a science field. *Betty*'s assessment of immigrant art is that such boundary crossing gives immigrants an advantage in the art scene: "Immigrant artists tend to do bolder, more creative work." And although it is the American cultural context that offers the opportunity, there are diverse forms of expression to which immigrants have unique access, allowing them to escape the tendencies within the arts to be "simply derivative." Among the effects that *Betty* hopes to achieve through her work is to communicate the beauty of science, as the observer examines one of her pieces of paper marbling.

## Art and Social Change

These culture workers also breech the boundary between the aesthetic and the political. As the descriptions of their cultural products make clear, many of these artists are visionaries who see themselves as potential change agents: their works are platforms for making political statements, whether directly or indirectly. This sometimes began before they left their homeland. Lilian Fernandez, for example, recalls a performance piece that she did in a Cuban gallery. She lay on the floor, asleep, covered in a blanket made from hair donated by friends. She called the piece *Sleeping Conscience*. Her point was that "in Cuba, the conscience is asleep." To her disappointment, and perhaps reinforcing her point, "I think many people didn't understand." How does Neri Torres's native Cuba regard this emigrant's flourishing career? "They appreciate what I do. It keeps tradition alive outside of the country. . . . I don't do it for political reasons, but personal, to expose people to our tradition." There is an irony to this effect that her work has, if indeed it results in raising the profile of Cuba to a more positive level in the United States—in light of Neri's disagreement with the current system there. Quite a number of the women we interviewed combine such activism through the aesthetic form with other projects or positions that they have taken in which they strive to change social conditions. Natasha Duwin, for example, works in a Miami facility for senior citizens and helps run a battered-women's shelter.

Film star Kieu Chinh spent her first years in Canada and the United States helping Vietnamese refugees get resettled, before returning to her own career with help from her sponsor, actress Tippi Hedren. After Kieu had made a name and career for herself in Hollywood, she was invited to be one of the readers of names engraved on the Vietnam Veterans Monument ("The Wall") in Washington, DC, for a ceremony marking an anniversary of its dedication. As she read each of the names aloud, Kieu began to cry. She realized that she wanted to do something to honor and remember the families and children who had also died in the Vietnam War and whose names were not engraved on The Wall. She teamed up with Vietnam War veteran Lewis B. Puller Jr. and journalist Terry Anderson (who had been held hostage in Lebanon for almost seven years), and they decided to make this gesture by supporting education in Vietnam. They founded a charity called the Vietnam Children's Fund. Kieu explained that the purpose of the charity is to "build a network of elementary schools in Vietnam dedicated to over two million lives lost in the war." Together with a group of friends, they pooled many donors. In 1995 they opened the first school, in Quang Tri Province in the old demilitarized zone. They continue their efforts today and still plan to meet their ambitious goal. As Kieu reported, "We founded more than forty schools all over Vietnam, north to south, with enough room for thirty thousand children. Our goal is to build sixty-one schools in sixty-one provinces throughout the country, to accommodate fifty-eight thousand children. We want to match the fifty-eight thousand names on The Wall."

Radio producer Susie Thang also hopes to effect change in Vietnam and "the world arrangement." She said, "I regret that with the 1989 fall of the Berlin Wall, a lot of countries changed, but Vietnam didn't take that chance." She broadcasts her radio programming over the Internet, but the Vietnamese government has blocked her programs from listeners within Vietnam with a firewall. Susie has discovered, however, that "talented young people" have been able to hack through the wall and gain access. She receives e-mails from these listeners, and she reads these on the air. The Vietnamese government is able to hear her station's broadcasts, but she stated, "I am not afraid, because I never say something that is not real. I say just the truth." Now that the Vietnamese community in Houston is more stable and integrated, and no longer has the more emergent needs that it once had, the radio programming is somewhat less essential locally. But Susie wants to persist, shifting her agenda to an extent, in the hope of helping her home country's people. She said, "I could retire the radio right now if Vietnam becomes a democracy. I feel we have an obligation to raise the Vietnamese voices."

Artist Roya Pazooki, who left a life of activism in Iran, moved into the arts after she arrived in the States. Although the arts may seem to some people as if they are at a distance from direct, more practical activity toward social change, Roya reported, "After a while, I realized, 'I'm a painter, I *can* do something with my art.'" Out of this realization grew her ambitious exhibit in an Atlanta art center that reproduced a prison.

The arts also provide a means for many of these women to heal from the trauma that they escaped. In addition to the change-oriented cultural work in which women such as Susie Thang engage, directed toward their communities, art production has become change-oriented action toward the artists themselves. Several artists spoke about their personal transformation that emerged through engaging with art. *Betty*, for example, contracted fibromyalgia in the midst of a stressful employment experience in the corporate world. After enrolling in art classes in which she studied "Sumi-e" painting, flower arrangements, and tea ceremony, *Betty* began to heal. She became obsessed with teaching herself the technique of paper marbling.

Hung Liu has created a series of self-portraits that chronicles her own transformation from "Proletarian" to "Immigrant" to "Citizen." Each portrait is derived from the photograph on her official identification cards in those three epochs of her life, and she preserves the images of those ID cards by reproducing each one in the corner of its respective painting. Notably, each of these portrait images also exemplifies traditional Chinese naming practices, in which the name is derived from an attribute of an individual or the circumstances of her or his birth or existence. The final effect is a chronicle of Hung's transformation across time, culminating in the face of a proud, wise, free, and independent adult.

After the tragedy of 9/11, Hung Liu offered a public work of art as a gift to her new homeland, to effect change at a more personal, emotional level. As one enters the San Francisco airport terminal, for example, one can view an installation that she created, which is 160 feet long, painted on glass imported from a longstanding family-owned German glass studio. Bringing Asian culture into this piece, Hung reported that she incorporated the image of a bird—clearly imaging the experience of flight—but the choice is that of a particular bird: the crane, which represents fortune, longevity, and "all blessings" in China, Korea, and Japan. Hung explained that the crane looks heavenly: it can survive in very few regions in the world. She elaborated that since 9/11, flying is physically and psychologically inconvenient for Americans (and all nationalities). She reflected, "It's not the same anymore. We need some blessings. We all need to know we are blessed to be on our destination through the sky and come back safely." As she described the painting, she explained,

> We all want to come home: whatever it means—to a person, place, etcetera. So there are two layers: eighty prints. On the second layer of glass is an aerial weather map of the Bay Area, July 4, 2006: American Independence Day. You are going away to your gate, ascending farther away from the earth, land, going through wind, going the opposite direction. Light comes through the little gap windows facing west. When the setting sun glows through the glass, there is a golden light. I was taken away. Sometimes your work is much bigger than yourself in public space. I get letters from people about this.

Hung is one of the immigrants who views her role as one of contributing to the post-9/11 healing process. In this work, Hung has linked two sets of meanings—Asian aspirations for hopeful futures with American political dreams of independence—in a viewer's temporary suspension from the troubled and uncertain realities on the ground. Hung has blurred the boundaries between her Asian and her new homeland and has made a cultural offering, with Asian roots, to her adoptive community.

### Culture and Agency

These artists are creative agents with tactile methods of pulling both history and future visions into the present through their creations. Sociologists Mustafa Emirbayer and Anne Mische have explained that individuals "are always living simultaneously in the past, future, and present, and adjusting the various temporalities of their empirical existence to one another (and to their empirical circumstances) in more or less imaginative or reflective ways."[17] These scholars are describing the realities of human agency, which incorporates these multiple dimensions, making agency a varied and distinct practice across different contexts. This description is particularly relevant to the immigrant culture workers that we have met in this chapter. As Emirbayer and Mische explain, "They continuously engage patterns and repertoires from the past, project hypothetical pathways forward in time, and adjust their actions to the exigencies of emerging situations."[18]

*Betty*'s account of her experience helps illustrate this dynamic. She decided to succumb to family pressure to study engineering rather than the less valued or financially stable terrain of the arts. She managed to get a scholarship to study fluid mechanics, which ties into the artwork that she does now. She studied aerodynamics, "the study of the air, and air is a form of fluid, just like water": "So then doing my research work I was taking a lot of photographs of the smoke moving in a wind tunnel, and we'd put dye in the water, to study the flow patterns like viscosity and surface tension. So it was a visual study; we call it visualization, fluid visualization." When she decided to take the leap and follow her personal yearning for artistry, *Betty* was able to take this training and relay it into inventive productions in the medium of fiber art. The seemingly disparate worlds of science and aesthetics were actually cross-fertilized in *Betty*'s hands.

The works and personal reflections of these artists uncover a second level of the insights of Emirbayer and Mische. While human agency does manifest this varied temporal dimension, the movement across various spatial dimensions intersects with those temporal movements—especially in the lives of immigrants. The quite complex mixtures of the "there-then" with the "here-now," and the addition of the "there-now" for those immigrants who also live transnationally, stimulate the inventiveness, the social messages, and the multilayered aspects of immigrant artwork. Hung Liu's layered paintings with faded, ghostly Chinese imagery juxtaposed with themes and formats representing more contemporary concerns come to mind. Thus, in addition to Emirbayer and Mische's observation that people live simultaneously in past, present, and future, immigrants are living simultaneously in two or more places, whether virtually or actually.

## Reflections and Policy Recommendations

Many of the artists portrayed in this chapter are intentionally engaged in pursuing the theme of freedom—an underlying ideological axiom that lies at the heart of art production. In contrast to Iran, Vietnam, mainland China, and Cuba, the artists are grateful that the American galleries and educational institutions provide uncensored outlets of freedom. These particular artists continue to push the theme of freedom to new limits, however, as they confront the lack of freedoms in their new home country. They are living in an age when imprisonment is the current fate of foreign-born women, men, and children awaiting asylum, deportation decisions, or terrorism trials—in their new host country. The artists are holding a mirror to past restrictions on freedom: the feet-bound Chinese women enslaved in their arranged marriages, for example.

These are artists who are now successfully pursuing their artistic visions: they are exhibiting in galleries, publishing, performing in public venues, and teaching in the academy. Nevertheless, policy issues are still relevant. The arts, entertainment, and sports guest visa (P series) is one possible "regular" means of entry for the artist, and it can be renewed annually for up to ten years. And while here, the artist can petition to be a lawful permanent resident. Since 9/11, however, the processing time for guest artists—regardless of ethnic origin—increased from a maximum of forty-five days to unpredictable waiting periods, ranging from forty-five days to six months. Not-for-profit organizations have complained that they cannot afford the "premium" processing fee of one thousand dollars that can override these waiting periods. Advocates have worked to change these waiting periods and have proposed a congressional bill, the Arts Require Timely Service (ARTS) Act. Although the bill received strong bipartisan support, by 2010 the bill had not been passed. In addition, across the 2001–2010 period, professional arts organizations reported that opportunities were being missed to expose the American public to international artistry. Furthermore, the paucity of art exhibitions and events hurt employment opportunities for both the native-born and foreign-born who were working in support services for these events.

For those attempting to immigrate permanently, visas such as the P visa, though useful, are only a starting point. Several of the women we interviewed started in this country on the typical "starving artist" track, where they found plenty of company among the native-born. Yet, in contrast to the native-born, their day jobs often pay substantially less and offer few if any benefits, and one day job is rarely enough. At least one of the women discussed in this chapter works cleaning houses to support her art. This draws us back to the discussion of the need for practical income-earning work that artists inevitably must confront. A wealthy woman in the Washington, DC, area was surprised to realize that the woman cleaning her house was actually an artist, and she immediately got busy trying to find an outlet for this artist's work. There is a hidden quality to domestic work that is in stark contrast to the public visibility of art. Thus, greater enforcement of wage- and hiring-equality laws across the board would boost the productivity of the arts. The poet and professor *Golnaz,* in fact, warns her American students about the struggle of the artist's life: "I tell them that, okay, writing is great, but you have to have another profession—if you wanted to teach, try to get that certificate to teach in high school, or learn computer, or anything, because it's difficult."

American higher education provided training, resources, nurturing, and artistic outlets for many of these artists. Two of them now teach in such institutions. Academic freedom is a proud feature of the American system. Yet this system could also be pushed to further heights. Instead of the system's encouraging more non-U.S. students to study here, one of our respondents has noticed the opposite trend: American universities are establishing branches in other countries to teach technical subjects in which those countries already excel. In objection to this trend, she mused, "Liberal arts teach you to be educated, to think." Additionally, how many budding artists are left out due to the lowering of caps on foreign-born student admissions or entrance restrictions on children of undocumented immigrants? And how many academic departments of fine and performing arts could benefit from greater faculty diversity (ethnic and gender) to reflect our current population and the range of artistic forms and ideas from around the globe? The same applies to age diversity. There is a strong chance that a foreign-born academic will move into her academic career at an older age, if she has spent some years in prison, was underemployed in the United States while getting retrained, or took longer to finish her training due to language studies, family obligations, visa complications, or other barriers related to nativism or sexism.

Through our analysis of the messages of these artists, we have illustrated a few ways in which immigrant women contribute to the aesthetic fabric of the United States: through their exploration of ethnic-specific and globally fused themes and materials and through their challenges to binaries and boundaries. These women both produce works of beauty and potentially raise the level of consciousness of aesthetic consumers about personal feelings, political contradictions, and ethnic and gender identity. We now move to the stories from our final set of interviews, with women who are organizing to make change happen directly: the activists.

# IV

## Where They Are Going

# 9

# "Misbehaving Women"

## *The Agency of Activism*

Haitian-born Marleine Bastien sits behind a desk in her busy Miami office of the organization Fanm Ayisyen Nan Miyami/Haitian Women of Miami (FANM), which she founded and directs. She has just finished an interview with a newspaper journalist, and her assistant reminds her of an upcoming meeting—signs of the many demands on her schedule. Posted behind her on the wall is a bumper sticker that states, "Well-behaved women rarely make history."[1] In the previous chapter, we met artists who are simultaneously engaged as political and social activists. Marleine is an individual whose "master status" across her adult professional life has been that of an activist—advocating most centrally for the rights of Haitian and other immigrants—yet she has been known to draw on the power of the arts when the need arises. For example, she opened her talk at a September 2002 conference on women and immigration at the Woodrow Wilson International Center for Scholars in Washington, DC, with an original poem. The poem began with the following lines:

*Who are we?*
Who are we?
We are the women of the world
Lost in a foreign land
Shamed, denied, violated, arrested,
tortured, lapidated, maimed, intimidated
crushed, victimized, abused
by those in power in the countries
that gave us birth
we are the wives, fiancées, sisters
daughters, mothers forced to leave
our motherland in conditions
not fit for human beings . . .

Marleine Bastien's lifework found its grounding in the conditions of this poem. The scenarios to which the poem alludes continue to be familiar ones—especially to women (and men) who have come from Haiti. Long among the most disparaged stepchildren in American immigration and refugee policy, Haitians have faced uphill battles pushing their way to American shores. Later in the poem, Marleine uses the words "sweet arms of mother liberty" in an ironic tone, mirroring that same hope that Lithuanian-born activist Emma Goldman had romanticized almost a century earlier:

> The dream of being comforted
> By the sweet arms of mother liberty
> Kept us going, hoping
> Then reality sinks in
> Our dreams are shattered
> Steel sounds of shackles
> Hug our ankles
> Leave scars deep in our flesh
> Scars that last a lifetime

## Activism and Women

Throughout history, activist movements have been dependent on the work and leadership of women. Yet historical records rarely acknowledge that dependence, and societies may only recognize it in retrospect—if they recognize it at all. In the early twenty-first century, for example, new scholarship has revealed the breadth of women's activities that galvanized and supported the American civil rights movement of the 1960s[2] and the Polish Solidarity movement of the 1980s.[3] And although Dolores Huerta cofounded the National Farm Workers Association in the United States with acclaimed labor organizer César Chávez, it is Chávez's name that has become the more recognizable one. The reasons for women's involvement as activists are myriad, ranging from the significance of the causes for their lives and those of their families to their already existing civic community roles, to discrimination and particular needs related to being female, to the logistical need for women to take over activist tasks while the male activists were jailed. As this book is being written, an immigration rights movement has gained momentum across the United States with the integral leadership and support of foreign-born women. Observers are noticing that the critical female factor in the movement has largely escaped public comment—underscoring

Figure 9.1. Marleine Bastien (Photo by Nick Decius, Nick Quality Photo Studio)

the ongoing erasure of women's visibility in public discourse over activism and social change. The media, in fact, have profiled the basses and tenors but rarely the altos and sopranos. Yet the movers and shakers in the immigration rights movement are as likely to be female as male. They are behind the scenes and behind the desks; to remain true to the metaphor, they are conducting, accompanying, stage managing, and inhabiting the front and back rows of the chorus.

Further, these are not new parts for them. Long before they had the right to vote, women were leading the charge when it came to causes that affected them as immigrants and as women. Historically, immigrant women have been behind a range of movements for change in the United States. In addition to "Queen of the Platform" Ernestine Rose, the suffragist mentioned in chapter 2, another eastern European Jewish activist with a substantial social-justice footprint was Dorothy Jacobs (later known as Dorothy Jacobs-Bellanca). Arriving as a child from Lithuania during the early twentieth century, Dorothy was one of the prototypical garment workers of her era in a Baltimore, Maryland, buttonhole factory, suffering long hours and harsh conditions. As a young teen, her refusal to endure this life led her to organize her fellow workers to strike against their employers. She went on to become the first full-time organizer for the Amalgamated Clothing Workers of America.[4] Preceding Dorothy in garment-manufacturing work was the legendary Mary Harris Jones, or "Mother Jones." This Irish immigrant became a tireless labor organizer in Chicago, Pittsburgh, and other cities, on behalf of miners, steel workers, child textile workers, and others. She was nicknamed the "Miner's Angel."[5] This nickname ironically contrasted with her own self-branding, as she reportedly corrected an academician's description of her: "Get it right. I'm not a humanitarian. I'm a hell-raiser."[6]

We have been speaking throughout this book about human agency and its relationship to social structures. In this chapter, our analysis centers around a specific form of agency, which is the work of individuals who resist and attempt to transform the structures. Significantly, those efforts are not single, isolated efforts. The women in this chapter are figures of "charismatic authority," as the sociologist Max Weber labeled the phenomenon of exceptional heroic individuals—the visionaries who inspire populations to look toward a radically revised future. For Weber, charismatic leadership is a key, promising component in social movements and has the potential to challenge traditional authority and norms.[7] We are focusing on the work of several activists who represent the various regions of the United States where we conducted interviews. First, we continue with the story of Marleine Bastien.

## Marleine

In Marleine's early years growing up in Haiti, she had dreamed of becoming a doctor. Her hope was that she would someday be able to remedy the scenes that she witnessed daily: impoverished people who could not get adequate hospital care for their needs, many desperately carrying their sick family and friends on makeshift beds to the nearest medical facility. Marleine learned to clean wounds and pull nails out of people's feet as a child, since her family home served as an unofficial refuge for members of the local community with health-care crises. Later, she began her studies in Port-au-Prince to forward her dream of entering the medical profession. At that time, her country was under the dictatorship of "Papa Doc" Duvalier, and there was a city communiqué that restricted people from studying because of the scarcity of lighting. As a result, Marleine would study for her courses under the streetlamps in the local park. She never made it to medical school in Haiti; her family, she explained, had a history of contentious relations with the government, which placed a "mark" on her.

Following the communiqué, Marleine rallied three classmates and orchestrated a series of protests. A well-known journalist, Konpe Filo, interviewed the foursome at the famed Radio Haiti Inter. After the interview, Marleine and her friends feared that they were being followed by security forces. When Marleine's father, who at that time lived in Belle Glade, Florida, learned of her political activism, he feared for her. He advised her to leave Haiti immediately, to come to the United States, and to seek political asylum. When she arrived in Miami in 1981, however, her image of the country changed immediately. She started volunteering at the Haitian Refugee Center two days after arriving in the United States and accompanied HRC lawyers to Krome Detention Camp, where Haitian asylum seekers were held to await deportation. Behind its gates, she viewed women and men housed together, pregnant women, people kept in isolation because they did not speak English or because they had not obeyed orders they did not understand, and one case after another of physical and mental abuse. As stated in her poem, quoted earlier, she was baffled by the scene of noncriminals put in circumstances reserved for the hardest of criminals. She thought, "The U.S. is a signatory to the U.N. Declaration of Human Rights. Something is wrong." When Marleine arrived, in fact, the United States was still using the Guantánamo Bay Naval Base to house Cuban and Haitian "boat people" captured at sea. In 1993, a U.S. district court judge ruled that that camp was unconstitutional—supporting Marleine's position about the detention centers.[8]

As soon as Marleine arrived in the United States, she began working to help her compatriots who were refugees. Her father had arrived one year earlier and had a position with the state of Florida helping refugees and immigrants adjust to life in the Belle Glade area. He assisted them with forms for schools, work, and other benefits. Like Marleine, he organized "chita kozes"— informal workshops to help understand the system. Marleine started her work in the United States as a paralegal to help the detained asylum seekers with their claims. She recalls spending many a day waiting for her requested meetings with the detained and ending the day without gaining access to see one detainee. She remembered, "These were people whose only hope was to see us. I see them hanging, grabbing the gate, saying 'Help us! Help us!'" As she reflected on those days, she took account of the practices that have remained unchanged, even though it is now easier to access detainees. In the first decade of the twenty-first century, asylum seekers were continuing to be housed in harsh institutions such as south Miami's Krome Detention Center, as discussed in chapter 4.[9] Marleine offered her own commentary on these scenes unfolding before her: "We treat animals better than we treat humans."

The contrast between the American receptivity toward Haitians and that toward Cubans was stark—and their coexistence in the same city brought that starkness into particularly sharp relief. Marleine remembered, "Every day, something negative was written about Haitians as masses of 'black, unskilled people.' The Cubans coming at the same time were getting the red carpet." Recipients of Cold War policy preferences for refugees from communist regimes, most Cubans got welcome receptions and moved into a dynamically expanding economic community, benefiting from the "wet-foot/dry-foot" practice: if a Cuban national arrived in the United States, he or she received asylum. Although Haitians were escaping political persecutions as well, they were labeled as economic rather than political refugees, and the policy, in contrast, has been to repatriate them without due process. The evolution of Miami's "Little Havana" took a path that "Little Haiti" could not, given the contrast in resources and reception by the host society.

With persistence over time, Marleine was eventually able to gain access to the detainees' stories and became known in the community for her ability to chronicle these stories. And she emerged as the spokesperson for the problems that women faced. She traced her own response as an organizer to traditions from her home country:

> I always saw women working all the time. In the market in Port-au-Prince, I saw women going home with big loads on their heads, children at their

side. My image of women is that they are always working, multitasking. So when you see a problem, you organize people in your surroundings. . . . I gathered the women and said, "*We have to do something about it*." I started putting activities and information forums together. I met with members of the university, anybody who would listen.

The organization Fanm Ayisyen Nan Miyami (in Creole), grew out of those efforts. With donated space from Barry University, Marleine organized FANM in 1991. She began training people in matters related to immigrant and refugee rights, such as situations in which people were victimized by certain family laws, as well as landlord-tenant relationships. She realized that the U.S. governmental and legal systems needed to be educated about Haitian culture: "to get them to understand our values." For nine years, Marleine ran FANM as a volunteer group, with no funding, as she simultaneously made her living as a medical social worker at Jackson Memorial Hospital. At the end of 1999, she recalled, "there was a miracle":

A group of funders came to town. . . . The funders heard about my work and came to study underserved communities in Miami. There were fifty people representing different funders who came to my office. They were laughing: they were in this hot room, sweating. I presented my budget, which was five thousand raised from flea markets and candy sales. They were flabbergasted.

This group was so impressed with the work that FANM was able to accomplish on a shoestring that requests for funding proposals began to trickle into her office soon after the meeting. Higher levels of grant funding then followed, and Marleine hired her first part-time employee. By 2002, Marleine's expanding operation to forward her vision of rights for Haitians had caught the attention of the New York–based Ford Foundation, which honored Marleine with a prestigious community leadership award from its Leadership for a Changing World program, funding her work for two years.

Today, FANM has a full-time staff of twelve and an additional seven part-time staff. Under Marleine's leadership, the organization combines advocacy and services for the local and broader Haitian community that include promoting the need for affordable housing, fighting gentrification, reforming refugee policy, and—among one of its foremost goals—teaching leadership skills. Marleine proudly remembered the 1998 mass demonstration in Washington that drew thirty thousand protesters: "Afterwards, we *cleaned*. Police officers shook our hands. They had never seen that at a protest. This gave us leadership experience and confidence that we could do that: common people taking a cause into their own hands." When Marleine lists FANM's key achievements, the theme of leadership is prominent:

> We were able to change that belief that you have to have special talent to be a leader. Anybody can impact change. We're bringing sensitivity to the conditions of the poor. Unlike the views that the poor are lazy and can't do anything for themselves, we demonstrate they *can* better themselves. Most people want to contribute and not be dependent on the welfare system.

Today, FANM is used as a role model worldwide. Marleine regularly receives visitors from countries as far away as China. Such visits particularly excite her, since her dream is to work on women's development at the global level. In fact, Marleine advocates on behalf of causes to bring relief to the country of Haiti, and FANM stepped in immediately after the 2010 Haitian earthquake to fundraise for victims. Despite this success and her growing local and international profile, Marleine reported that it is still very difficult to find adequate funding.

### Reyna

In chapter 5, we met Honduran native Reyna, who swam the Rio Grande and eventually made her way to Miami, Florida, on her own. We pick up her story here. Once in Miami, she was able to find janitorial work with a cleaning company to support herself, but in order to make ends meet, she held down three jobs simultaneously. She cleaned buildings from 5:00 p.m. to 2:00 a.m., then slept for two hours, got up and went to a local bank, where she cleaned from 5:00 to 7:30 a.m., after which she went to her factory job from 9:00 a.m. to 4:00 p.m.—and an hour later started the daily cycle over again. Her exposure to chemicals through her job resulted in serious illnesses and propelled her into the world of activism in Miami. Today, Reyna makes her living as an organizer, although her earnings remain modest and her mobility and activity have been severely limited by the toxic chemicals to which she had been exposed.

Like Marleine Bastien, Reyna was taken by surprise at the absence of protection of her rights—but in this case, it involved employment rather than immigration authorities. "I didn't know my rights. I had a different image of what the U.S. was. I always thought that the U.S. defended human rights elsewhere and within the United States. The company was allowed to use chemicals that were harmful to us." One day, after using the cleaning chemicals for six hours straight, Reyna's rubber gloves began to melt. She started feeling sick. Around this time, union representatives appeared on the scene to educate the workers about their rights. In the beginning, Reyna resisted meeting with the union. In Honduras, she recalled, the unions "meant nothing"; in the United States, Reyna assumed that joining a union would jeopardize her safety, since she was undocumented. Further, her employer threatened her. "The company started to scare me a lot. They said if I accepted the union I would die because they wouldn't take care of me." The company management warned that they were seeking a restraining order against the union.

In the midst of this union-management drama, Reyna's illness landed her in the emergency room. As she lay in the hospital breathing with the help of an oxygen tank, she awoke to see two people standing over her: her boss and the union representative. Her boss gave her an ultimatum: "Do you want to go with the union or with me?" She recalls being unable to speak at that time; her boss took her from the hospital, put her in his car, drove her around for one day, delivered her to a different medical facility, and then returned her to her home at midnight.

Although Reyna's company agreed to keep her on salary, she decided to join her co-workers, who went on strike for two and a half months, and their actions included a seventeen-day hunger strike. Reyna's life became a ricochet between the strikes and the hospital for her health. She was proud that the strikers won and that the media took up her cause. But she remained nervous about going public:

We went to Tallahassee. . . . But I was afraid because of the dangerous situation in my country. It was dangerous for my family in my country. So I wanted to remain anonymous. My co-workers and the union gave me the strength, because I used to be a coward. One day, I put my name and picture out there. My daughter called me [from Guatemala]: "Mommy, do you know what you're doing?" I said, "Yes, I know."

Reyna had found her courage by attaching herself to this new cause. Weighing her odds against the more certain risks that she escaped, Reyna chose her current battle. Her daughter argued, "But they're going to deport you." She explained, "I have to choose between losing my life in Honduras or fighting for a good cause in the States. So if I end up getting killed, I will know I did something good here." The union's victory, which resulted in the company's agreement to stop using the toxic chemicals, inspired Reyna to move into other battles: in particular, the rights of immigrants. She eventually earned a paid position with the union. One day, she found herself standing, unafraid, in front of an immigration rally in Tallahassee. At that point she looked around her and thought, "I have no papers. If I can do this, why can't we all get together?"

Symbolically, it could be noted that cleaning positions are doubly about invisibility: women and men work behind the scenes, after hours, rendering their efforts invisible to the building's occupants. Also, cleaning is about erasure; successful work is the appearance of nothingness. In contrast, activists such as Reyna make it their business to *expose*, rendering visibility to the people whom no one sees. Eventually, she was able to get her asylum papers, and today she is able to work legally. She feels fortunate that she has health-care coverage through her new position with the union—but this only underscores her desire to help other immigrants so they can have the same. In addition to lung impairment, the chemicals from her former job damaged her blood and liver. She must frequent the doctor's office. She muses, "How would it be if I didn't have that [insurance]? The bills would be exorbitant." She is determined to keep her illness from stopping her.

> I think I will get better, but I have to fight. It's not fair. God give me the virtue to fight more. I am going to keep doing it as an immigrant woman. They don't realize immigrants are suffering because they give us bad jobs, paying us whatever they want, getting us sick. . . . They don't realize we are cleaning their offices, their buildings. *They are taking our soul.*

She returned to her admonition to the citizenry and government of her new homeland: "I thought that this country really fights for human rights. . . . So I say, 'You want to punish my country for its violation of human rights, why don't you punish yourself? You go to war for human rights elsewhere but don't care about rights of people here.'" Like Marleine, Reyna wants to see even broader change beyond her world in the southeast corner of the country. She has sights on the larger system—and the culture that sustains it: "We're fighting against the system—the government—because according to them we're stripping them of their jobs. They don't realize the vegetables that they're eating have the taste of tears. They get them for cheap because we work for cheap. If it weren't for us, this country wouldn't have the money they do." Although Reyna's words amount to what could be viewed as a tall order, she is not deterred: "It's not an easy struggle, but we can fight for it."

## Maria

A few states away—in Texas—yet another Central American is involved in grass-roots organizing for social justice for janitors. In a busy Houston restaurant on a summer afternoon, Maria Xiquin excitedly explains how she got into a career of activism, literally and figuratively sandwiching an interview into a busy workday schedule. Maria immigrated to the United States from Guatemala.

After high school graduation, Maria started her higher education at the University of Houston, with an interest in studying architecture. She had to interrupt her studies for financial reasons and because she was about to give birth to her first child. A key issue in this interruption was that she was inhibited by the rules of the educational structures: she was not eligible for certain college scholarships because she was a refugee. Six months later, she reentered the workplace, and after weighing several job possibilities, she chose one with the Service Employees International Union, rather than a drafting job, which would have been in her originally chosen field. Her personal biography was part of the motivation: "There is a lot of discrimination in my country. . . . There were no unions there. So this job caught my attention. It was about wages and fair labor practices." Although her father had been a teacher in Guatemala and her mother had work experience, their credentials did not transfer to their new home in the United States, so Maria's father went into restaurant work and her mother into babysitting. Maria's desire to help low-wage workers was directly related to years of watching her own parents toil away in these exploitative corners of the economy. Maria was also inspired by her parents' example as political organizers. Her family is Mayan, from the Quecchian region, and her parents had been involved in indigenous rights movements at home in Guatemala.

Maria started her organizing activities by going directly to the building sites where people were working to uncover situations of abuse. She would approach the janitors and ask them simply, "How do you feel?" She expounded on the uphill battle of convincing the workers to come forward with their complaints: "The company that we fought was a private one. At the beginning the workers were scared of retaliation. Nobody knew what a union was. They didn't have it in their culture. We did a lot of house and building visits. It was hard for them to understand. They know that some union organizers get killed." Maria reflected on the fact that despite legal protections that are in place for employees, "most of the community is not educated about their rights." When she began organizing, Houston workers were not yet mobilized. But she was inspired by progress elsewhere. She asked herself, "How do we stick with the process so to make it possible? People from other cities have seen it happening there. Enough is enough." As they continued their efforts to mobilize the workers to complain, Maria had a moment of realization that is reminiscent of Reyna back in Miami: "They decided not to be invisible anymore. One month, we had a lot of actions. The janitors did civil actions and got arrested."

The Service Employees International Union is a nationwide organization that uses the unionizing model that has become familiar in the manufacturing sector to mobilize service workers to protect their employment rights. Since service employment has replaced factory labor as the base of the American economy, SEIU has become the fastest-growing labor union in the country. Yet the union dates back to 1921, when it was formed primarily by immigrants who were laboring as janitors, as suggested by its original name: Building Service Employees International Union. Although labor unions have experienced a steep decline in recent decades, SEIU has seen the opposite, with a membership growth from 625,000 in 1980 to more than two million currently.[10] Given the fear and hesitation that both Reyna and Maria articulated, these numbers illustrate that the union's message is finding a receptive audience.

In Houston, the janitors went on strike to raise the wages from $5.15 to $6.25 per hour and for health-care protection. Maria expressed how upset she was when she encountered a worker with breast cancer who had no health insurance. Further, comparisons across cities were eye opening—and due to differences not between companies or industries but within them. Maria recalled, "The same companies were paying $12.00 to $13.00 per hour in Chicago, $20.00 per hour in New York, but in Houston, $5.15 per hour, with no insurance." Through organizing campaigns, collaborative projects with other organizations, and supporting sympathetic politicians, Maria has seen change. Nevertheless, she perceives the battle as far from won. She observed incredulously, "They can work twenty years and still make the minimum wage." In Houston, in fact, according to Maria, janitorial jobs tend to be part-time, offering no benefits. Maria loves her job, in large part because she feels that she is making a difference for her own community: "Because I'm educated, I feel happy working at something that's not just a job. I am educating the community. They don't know things can be different."

## Ingrid

It is a cool summer evening under the stars on the patio at the Los Angeles Museum of Contemporary Art. The occasion is a special exhibit/performance by the artist Suzanne Lacy, who is chronicling women's stories about their work.[11] The organizers have put together a meticulously orchestrated potluck dinner, complete with blankets to distribute to shivering guests. Inside, the museum hosts a full retrospective of international feminist art from the 1960s to the 1980s. The outdoor performance consists of individually rendered short testimonials from women who work across the spectrum of occupations, with an emphasis on the struggles of work. When the appointed time comes, Mexican-born *Ingrid* rises and describes her experience as an exploited domestic worker, using the word "slavery."

Back in her office where she works as an organizer for domestic workers, *Ingrid* elaborated further on her work and the conditions of slavery to which she alluded. Hanging above her desk is a poster with the words "Justicia para Trabajadoras de Casa" (Justice for Household Workers). It features a drawing of a woman with six arms, each of which is devoted to a different task, including holding a crying baby, cooking, ironing, dusting, and washing dishes. *Ingrid*'s activism started at home in Mexico, where she was a teacher and active in a teacher's union. Her union-organizing work there had resulted in death threats. She explained her goals in organizing household workers in her new home country: "We are dealing first of all with abuse. The salaries are so low, and we are exploited. Our work hours are more than everyone; there is a lot of fraud, and also there is physical, psychological, and verbal abuse." *Ingrid* spends her days circulating through the city streets educating household workers. She distributes "know your rights" brochures to every worker she meets, offering the assistance of her organization's lawyers. She detailed the organization's approach:

> *Prevention* is our main goal. We can't give them anything [brochures] with extensive writing. They're always in a rush. We have to talk to them while they're working. It lists their rights and contact information. It says, "Educate yourself." Also it says, "This is not just an individual problem, but society-wide. We need to get together to change it." Also there's a square [on the brochure] where they can document what's happening to them while they're working.

*Ingrid* reported that people are often afraid to take the brochures, especially women who receive work through agencies. Her organization makes the brochures pocket-sized so that the women can quickly tuck them into their pocketbooks.

*Ingrid*'s passion for her work and her in-depth understanding of the problem came from her own firsthand experience as a domestic worker, which is the work that she found after she immigrated. She believes that this background contributes to her success in mobilizing workers, who know that she identifies with them. She said, "I don't have a strong educational background. I worked in very bad conditions. But I made the effort to join groups to make changes. So they can see that I had a similar experience as theirs." And like other activists we met, *Ingrid* drew inspiration from her family's courage against unjust systems in her home country. "My mom was an autonomous indigenous woman who was exploited. She *fought.* She taught us to fight and be smart. My grandfather was a community leader. He lived only into his early fifties. He gave jobs to people. He was a business owner. He gave clothing away. He taught me."

*Ingrid* gave an account of how the system of household-worker recruitment operates. According to surveys in her area, approximately 60 percent of household workers find their jobs through agencies, and 40 percent through friends and other networks. New immigrants are lured by attractive classified ads in the newspaper that ask, "Do you want to earn $300, $500 a week? You don't need legal status." Although the ads indicate that this is a free service, applicants show up at the employment agency and find themselves charged sixty or a hundred dollars for a one-page application. The fee, however, does not guarantee that the applicant will get the job; those who do land a position may find that the agencies also charge them an additional fee that is deducted from their new wages. *Ingrid* remembered,

> I have gone to the agencies and looked at the applications. I try not to sign something in a language I don't know. The application says, "Funds are not refundable; there is no guarantee you'll find something." You can wait months. I see people filling out applications. One worker said, "I'm not paying until you find me a job." Then the clerks say, "Get out!"

The agencies that *Ingrid* referenced are locally based, not national chains; in fact, she has not run across any national chains, such as Merry Maids. Agency staff does threaten to call immigration on the workers, but *Ingrid* does not worry that this is a strong possibility. She said, "They need us just as much as we need them—sort of like slave traders: selling us, giving us away. We don't know where we're going to go. They keep saying, 'We'll get you something.' We wait months with no work." According to *Ingrid*, these agencies do not have legal permits to operate, do not pay taxes, and do not give receipts: "It's like a mafia, like a black market. . . . When we protest against one agency, other agencies come together, and others come to protect them and help them change their names." *Ingrid* and her colleagues distribute a newsletter about employer trends to illuminate the practices for unsuspecting employees. Whereas the existence of such shady businesses might deter some individuals from speaking against them, *Ingrid* echoes the sentiment that Reyna expressed: she is willing to die for this cause.

In addition to educating workers, *Ingrid* and her colleagues also advocate for changes to state and federal policy and law. They wrote a new bill to protect workers' wages, which made it through the California legislature. Although severely scaled down through the politics of compromise, it nevertheless met a veto when it reached the governor's desk. Despite such setbacks, *Ingrid* is proud of their accomplishments: "I've come to learn that as an organizer, even those hard to reach, for those we have success stories. We're doing something credible. We help them change their lives and see them as leaders. Over time, we helped them realize their own leadership skills."

## Ola

The Polish native Alexandra Lissowska (nicknamed "Ola") serves and advocates for immigrant and refugee women through her professional position with the organization Tapestri, Inc., in Atlanta, Georgia. Tapestri grew out of a coalition of groups and organizations working to meet the needs of immigrants and refugees in the Atlanta area; these groups had begun to recognize the need for a set of services for women from a cross-section of cultural backgrounds and had decided to join forces; Tapestri, Inc., was born. This organization is dedicated to serving women who find themselves in situations of domestic violence, sexual assault, or human trafficking.

On the day we met Ola, she was sporting a full-term pregnancy. Although her baby was due to be born the following day, Ola's attachment to her work kept her in the office until the last minute—but seemingly with no regret. While in Poland, she had been active in the human rights organization Amnesty International; this experience led her to realize that she wanted to pursue a profession that involved social or psychological matters. After migrating to the Atlanta area, she began to volunteer with Tapestri and persistently pushed until she received a work permit and could join the staff. Ola's morning commute takes more than one hour, a fact that she proudly offered as evidence of her excitement about this work.

Ola and her co-workers provide case management for clients whose backgrounds span fourteen languages and forty-six countries. These numbers illustrate the vast internationalization that has occurred in the demographics of Atlanta in recent years. The staff offers a hotline for domestic-violence calls and another dedicated line for trafficking calls. Tapestri is one of twenty-five organizations across the country that compose the Freedom Network, a group that advocates on behalf of survivors of trafficking, provides services, and educates the general public. Primarily, Tapestri meets women caught up in labor trafficking rather than sex trafficking—even though it is the sex trafficking that draws the media and public attention. Ola and her co-workers point out that there is a fine line between labor trafficking and labor exploitation; they have noticed repeatedly that if a worker is not getting paid and the employer threatens deportation, the situation can easily tip over into one that is closer to the trafficking definition, an example of which we met in chapter 4. Since the U.S. government began offering a special visa (the T visa) to victims of trafficking, a number of trafficking survivors have stepped forward, but not the crowds that were expected, with an estimated fourteen thousand to seventeen thousand trafficked into the United States per year. Ola and her colleagues at Tapestri are not convinced that these low numbers represent the full scale of the problem, for at least two reasons. First, the T visa requires cooperation with law enforcement in identifying and prosecuting the trafficker; many trafficking survivors are daunted by such a proposition, especially since traffickers regularly threaten to hurt their family members back home if they fall out of line. Second, some of them prefer to apply for relief under a different visa, such as a green card offered through the Violence Against Women Act.

Ola believes that many Atlanta trafficking victims remain in hiding and that approximately 50 percent of trafficked women are in domestic work. Among the challenges that Ola and her co-workers have faced is the diplomatic immunity that protects foreign diplomats who work in Atlanta consulates from jurisdiction in the United States. When those diplomats virtually enslave their household labor, prosecution is not possible—a problem that also faces antitrafficking activists in the Washington, DC, area, where diplomats who work in the embassies and international organizations such as the World Bank enjoy the same immunity, as discussed in chapter 5. Further, Atlanta does not have shelter beds specifically for trafficking survivors; this means that the women go to shelters set up for domestic-violence problems, such as the International Women's House. Although this house is not set up with programs specifically for trafficked women, it does offer the possibility of transitional housing in a safe place for as long as two years.

Addressing intimate-partner abuse carries its challenges as well. Tapestri's programs include classes for batterers to address their problems, in addition to services for the survivors. One mechanism of control that batterers use is to threaten women with deportation or separation from their children. Batterers also frighten their partners about the situation "outside": Ola has noticed that since 9/11, some Arab husbands warn their wives that they cannot go out because of the dangers they will face from the anti-Arab climate in the United States. Underemployment plays a role in the mix, when men see their wives as less valuable if they cannot find the same level of work that they had in their home country. Among the difficulties that immigrant women face when they are in a situation of abuse is their vulnerability if they were to escape. For many, this entails leaving the family's main breadwinner, trying to survive with minimal English-language skills, or falling into an uncertain legal status. The women's ability to exercise agency may become constrained: if they try to better their skills, such as by taking classes in English for speakers of other languages, and to further their independence, some husbands have been known to say, "You're behaving like an American woman."

Despite such challenges, Ola and the staff of Tapestri reported their success stories:

> One of our clients escaped domestic violence. Today, she has her driver's license, owns her own car, and has a place to live. She took the GRE and is opening her own business importing textiles. Another was a domestic-servitude case. After working for years, she had been paid two months' wages. The Department of Labor got involved in investigating. She may get years of back wages. Another was a sex-trafficking case. She got out; she owns her own housecleaning business and now has her own car.

The success narratives that Ola recounted echo a familiar theme that we encountered in interviews with entrepreneurs, as noted in chapter 6, which is that a number of women are finding business ownership to be an avenue of independence that helps them escape either partner abuse or trafficking.

### Nadia

In another major U.S. city, *Nadia* described her work for a not-for-profit organization that addresses the same issues as those that Ola tackles at Tapestri. We met *Nadia* in chapter 3, where we related her arduous journey across Turkey following her escape from Iran. When she applied to work at a domestic-violence shelter in the United States, she learned that her language facility with Farsi, spoken in her native Iran, was in demand for the

Iranian and Afghani women who were shelter clients. Shelter directors also valued her familiarity with Islam and the particular application of Shar'ia law in Iran, which shaped some clients' understanding of the law.

*Nadia* has seen the shelter grow in order to house women for longer periods of time and to add transitional housing. As the enterprise developed, *Nadia's* responsibilities increased. She reflected,

> I think that, for our women, that come from other countries, ninety days is not enough, because shelter is for three months or four months. And I talk about that: I don't think that is enough, because they have language problems, they have to go to some training if they want to get the job, many things that—immigration, divorce papers, many things that they have a problem—that it's not easy for them for just ninety days to handle it.

Her opinion is that shelters should be available for one to two years for a woman escaping abuse, but this is a major challenge, given government cuts in funding for shelters. Some shelters have had to close.

Like Maria, *Nadia's* path into activism had family roots. Her father died when she was young, resulting in loss of income and a low social status in comparison with other relatives, since hers was generally a well-educated family. This gave *Nadia* a strong awareness of social class differences. She was inspired when she learned about the activities of a man who was unpopular with the Shah, and she started reading books, which fostered her political consciousness. She was imprisoned in Iran, however, and came to the United States as a political refugee. Her activism around women's issues in Iran translated into similar activities after immigrating. Her choice to work with women who are escaping violence dovetailed with her moral passions.

She recalled the first case that she had, on her first day working at the shelter:

> I can remember that one Iranian woman that came to the shelter, suddenly when I say "Salaam"—it means "hi" in Farsi—when I say "Salaam," she start to cry. Cry. For half an hour she cried. And from her cry I start to cry. And she said, "Finally someone's in front of me, and you speak Farsi with me." So I have many experiences like that, even with Afghani women: one came, and she didn't know that I can speak Farsi. And suddenly I start to speak Farsi with her, and she was so excited; she was kissing me, hugging me, crying.

And two days before our interview, an Iranian in need reached out to the shelter:

She was Iranian woman, and her voice was very narrow and shaky. . . . Looks like the Iranian guy went to Iran, married her, and brought her to the United States. And just after six months, he said that "I don't want to live with you anymore." She doesn't speak English yet. She speaks a little; she's going to ESL class. . . . It was very important to her that she suddenly heard my voice, an Iranian woman talking with her. And she can talk about her problems, everything, which is not easy for her to talk with anybody.

The clients come from a range of world regions beyond Iran and Afghanistan; *Nadia* has assisted women from China and Ethiopia, for example. *Nadia* puts a great deal of emphasis on the act of mentoring:

A good thing is, I just want to give them this mission that you have to believe yourself. You have to have job. You have to survive by yourself. You can live with somebody else. You can even, if you love somebody, marry with that person, but not because for survival. And I can see that they got that point from me. And many times when they have opened a store, or they did something, they want to show me that they got my message, and that really makes me happy.

*Nadia* explained how she copes with the stress of such a position:

Most of the Saturday I go by the beach, I stay over there, and I said to myself, thinking about hundred, two hundred years ago, that they didn't have anything like that. The history of domestic violence [advocacy and services] and those issues is almost thirty-five, less than forty years. . . . And I said that, okay, appreciate it, it is hard, everything is not good, but this is wonderful, that after thirty-seven years, we have many shelters. And we have to have all those countries, we have to have a shelter.

Despite the stress, *Nadia* related an excitement with her work that recalls the sentiment that Ola expressed: "This job is so unbelievable, how much I enjoy my job."

## Marga

Marga Fripp immigrated to the United States with her husband and children from her native country of Romania, to seek medical treatment for her young son. She brought with her a passion to help immigrant women empower themselves economically, and she was particularly committed to helping women in the creative fields. She and her family settled in the Washington, DC, area—a region that was bursting with diversity, as it had become the fourth-largest gateway for immigrants in the United States. The cost of living in the DC area was also quite high, and Marga knew that artists face major challenges trying to support themselves through their art. She began to envision an organization that would train, support, and promote immigrant women's artistic endeavors so they could become economically self-sufficient.

Out of Marga's entrepreneurial vision, Empowered Women International (EWI) was born. With a small amount of start-up funds, Marga took the risk to open A Woman's Story Gallery in the Old Town district of Alexandria, Virginia—a combined office and gallery exhibition space where she could highlight the women in her program. Once word got out about this positive, inspiring venture, individuals volunteered to be board members, crowds gathered for gallery openings, and local businesses began to offer financial support. Women across nationalities signed up for workshops with EWI that offered training to turn their artistic ventures into businesses. Painters, jewelers, dancers, singers, sculptors, and textile artists began knocking on Marga's door. Some were seeking to expand a profession in which they were already working; others were looking to turn a skill or hobby into paid work. Today, Marga's organization views its work as supporting women's individual agency with the larger goal of community change:

> We believe the arts and immigrant women's cultural heritages are extraordinary assets and means for helping them integrate in a new culture, develop leadership and entrepreneurial skills, and establish a foothold in their new community and the labor market. Art has an inherent capacity to bring people together and act as a platform for dialogue, tolerance building and multicultural understanding. Art has a demonstrated multiplier effect that engages people in community building, education and cross-cultural dialogue about local and global issues.[12]

One day, EWI's brand of activism through economic empowerment unintentionally found the organization face to face with another critical issue, which brought them into the sphere of activism in which Ola and *Nadia* work. One of the EWI artists was beginning to enjoy a modicum of success with her jewelry making when she was found murdered. This artist's husband, an immigrant from a different country who was struggling with maintaining employment, was arrested for her murder. Marga Fripp had both mentored and befriended this artist, whose death left behind three young children. Immediately, EWI embarked on a campaign to raise awareness and funds to address domestic violence. This story tempers the accounts of other women who found that business ownership helped them escape abuse; as this story illustrates, the entrepreneurship avenue is not necessarily a guarantee.

Marga integrates gallery events and performances with politics and activist campaigns. Event titles have included "Across All Borders Dance Concert" and "Jewels of Hope and Power." Marga reflected on her choice to focus on the arts: "It works at the spiritual and mental level of people. Maybe they can find a viable way to be active and be somebody." Although the organization is relatively young, Marga has already seen visible progress for the EWI clients. She mused, "I hear the women's stories. They have really changed. They are better engaged in their homes and communities." Even though a show or opening may draw only fifty to a hundred people, Marga believes that audiences are learning to appreciate the diversity of the United States. EWI was fortunate to earn the listing in the 2007–2008 "Catalogue for Philanthropy" as "one of the best small charities in the Greater Washington region."

## Marta and Valeria

*Marta* and *Valeria* are young employees at a local grass-roots immigrant organization in a major city which is a one of the country's largest immigrant hubs. Their agency is housed in a building at the end of a block peppered with abandoned buildings and empty lots; the billboards in the area are all in the Spanish language. The airy, light, windowed building where *Marta* and *Valeria* work contrasts with its surrounds; its charmingly exposed brick walls and homey atmosphere are strikingly cheery. Framed posters from the organization's summer arts festivals from years past decorate the walls.

*Marta* and *Valeria* originated from two different regions of Mexico that are across the country from one another. Both came with their family to pursue economic and educational opportunities but found themselves constrained by their status in an undocumented family. Through the battles they waged to get entrance and funding for their own college degrees, these young women became acquainted with the need for policy change. Non-U.S.-born children with undocumented parents are currently constrained when it comes to higher education. Although they have the right to public education all the way through twelfth grade in every state, once they graduate from high school, they are often barred from higher education. In some states, they cannot enroll in any institution of higher learning. In others, they may enroll but are charged out-of-state tuition, even if they have lived in that state since immigrating to the country.

Some state governments are beginning to recognize that these barriers come at a cost not only to the immigrant children but to the state. They are finding high rates of high school dropouts among students who cannot envision a future past high school if they have no access to college. Ten states have allowed undocumented students who graduated from high school in the state and meet other requirements to receive in-state tuition rates. These include the states with the highest numbers of students in this situation, such as New York, Texas, and California. Building on these gains at the state level, activists have been working to pass a piece of legislation known as the DREAM (Development, Relief and Education for Alien Minors) Act at the federal level. The DREAM Act would extend this right to students across states, as well as make federal financial aid available—a benefit that undocumented students do not currently enjoy, regardless of the state where they reside. This act came to a vote in the U.S. Congress in 2007 but was defeated. It was in the process of reintroduction in 2010.

*Marta* and *Valeria* have become passionate activists for the DREAM Act, and their organization offers a range of educational services for youth in the area where their organization is located. The theme that *Marta* and *Valeria* insist is critical to progress is the word *network*. The organization provides educational scholarships for both documented and undocumented immigrants. In exchange, the scholarship recipients work for the organization for a set number of hours; many of those recipients then go on to get involved with the organization's activist efforts, and some land positions with the organization. *Marta* started out as a student volunteer. Originally, she was not involved with organizations. Since she was undocumented, she said, "I felt like I'd get a degree but not be able to get a job." But when someone told her about the organization's scholarship, she decided to try it; she gave eighty hours of community service to the organization, during her junior and senior years. As a result, she reflected, "It opened my eyes to issues—education and civil rights. I felt like I could make a difference through sharing and building alliances."

Since *Marta* joined the staff, she has helped organize a university round-table, involving twelve area universities, community colleges, and trade schools. She has built relationships with administrators, professors, community centers, and student volunteer organizations, and she networks these people with one another. The roundtable meets about four times a year, and *Marta* hopes that it will begin to meet more often. *Marta* also helps organize an education summit for families, to help parents understand the system and plan for their children's educational needs early in game. She said, "Predominantly in immigrant communities, parents come here for education, have to work two and three jobs, and don't have time to go into high school. There's also a language barrier and time constraints. Parents send the kids off, but the students just get lost."

*Valeria* works part-time to advance the civil rights of immigrants. She has helped organize citizenship workshops at different schools and churches, as well as voter registration. She participated on a taskforce to raise awareness in the African American and white communities about the realities of immigrants, to counter the assumptions that immigrants "take away jobs." *Valeria* relates immigrants' stories to these citizen communities. One of those stories came from her babysitter: "The government has the right to say, 'This is not your country.' The kids—what about them? Can't say, 'This is not your country.'" Yet *Valeria* has found that it is not only citizens who project restrictionist attitudes toward the undocumented. She has also heard the same words, "this is not your country," from Mexicans who immigrated legally. To this, she responded, "I'm especially saddened when I hear this from immigrants who just came." She works to raise awareness among these immigrants as well. *Marta* reported that she has seen success using this approach: "They change their minds when they hear testimony."

In regard to *Marta*'s own progress, she reports that she has learned how to channel anger and keep working. She is majoring in accounting and finance full-time at an area university while she is also employed full-time. She said, "Hard work has made me a stronger woman." *Valeria,* echoing her colleague, stated, "I agree with *Marta*. Struggle has made me more strong, more humble. I have my feet on the ground. I try to help with social services, organizing, being a better role model for my daughter." This self-described strength is reflected in *Valeria*'s current personal biography. Due to an experience with domestic violence, she had to move to a more remote location in the city, but her determination to help continues; she still returns to the community, with her daughter in tow, to volunteer.

*Marta's* advice to other immigrants is grounded in her own life experience as well as her style of activism: "Tell your story. Network—you never know who you'll run into. I was lucky. I found educational sponsors, scholarships, waivers; I didn't pay a penny, and my B.A. cost one hundred thousand dollars." She insists that students need to meet others. She met a high school sophomore student who was depressed because she could not go to college, but *Marta* explained, "She found out my story and is now interested in college. Knowing a story can make a difference." Despite *Valeria's* own personal life difficulties, she remains optimistic. She said, "I'd say to not give up. There is always a way, even if it is a struggle. Don't give up. Opportunities come up—volunteer, join organizations."

## The Activist Awakening

What compelled these women to take their respective activist paths? Among the nine women we have just met, six found their activist voices and channeled their own personal agency through confronting and escaping the exploitation in which they found themselves after immigrating. Several bluntly confronted a perceived disconnect between the ideals—those sweet arms of Mother Liberty or the Declaration of Human Rights—and the tangible, tactile realities: the shackles, the gloves melting on their hands. As they observed it firsthand in their own lives, they also began to notice a systemic pattern across the experiences of immigrants whose fate they shared. Reyna's gut feeling that she was watching her daughter sinking in the Rio Grande was an emotional bridge between her life and that of the teenage stranger in front of her.

As the lure of the United States as a beacon on a hill lost its halo in their eyes, these women discovered bright lights in other corners of the society—among activists, fellow immigrants, the not-for-profit sector, and the arts. The opportunities that they uncovered in their various individual journeys seemed to infuse them with a purpose orientation that made it possible for them to find a home and a community—where they can work to change the society to become closer to the one that once existed in their dreams.

Listening to the political rhetoric that these activists employ to argue for their causes, several appeal to a shared moral reference—such as that of human rights. These activists follow Martin Luther King Jr.'s chosen approach to frame the civil rights movement by quoting from the shared values inscribed in such documents as the Constitution and the Declaration of Independence and using those foundations as an imminent critique of our democracy. It was often these women's amazement over the lack of human rights protection that fueled their activism. For many of them, there was a moment of awakening about the contradictions of the American system, an awakening that was based existentially—in some cases even physically—in their own personal experiences and those of their compatriots around them.

Specifically, several of these awakenings were built on personal revelations of how the intersecting social locations of gender and nativity place constraints on immigrant women's rights and opportunities. Yet this intersectional characteristic also inspired a resistant style of agency among these activists that was, in turn, built on that intersection. One activist, for example, characterized her multiple identities as a source of her strength: "I'm a nurse. I'm a Filipino. I'm a feminist. I'm an activist. I was marching in Manila: 'Down with the dictatorship.' . . . I challenge all women: organize yourself. Only [we] can fight our battles and win, and nobody else."[13]

But for these women, that awakening was only the first stage of engaging their agency toward a risky endeavor—whether the risk is physical, political, or economic. What motivated them to take the leap? First, for many of them, politicized agency was modeled for them. Just as a number of the entrepreneurs told of the individuals in their lives who modeled business ownership, several of these women had watched parents or other family members stand up to even more daunting political powers in their home country. Often, those models were women. Marleine Bastien carries around an image in her memory of women working, actively solving problems. Although these activists tend to discuss those activist role models using the language of "inspiration," that modeling also takes on an educational form—activism is clearly learned behavior, passed from one generation to the next. Significantly, several women were activists in their home country before arriving in the United States, and their preimmigrant passions found new—or similar—targets after they arrived.

Second, we heard several instances of these women making rational calculations of the steps they were about to take and realizing that an activist path was the more reasonable choice. But there was variation in the actual substance of the choices before them. For Maria, who works with the SEIU in Houston, the choice was between a professional position built on her specific technical training and one in which she could have an impact on the lives of others. Unfortunately, some, such as Reyna and *Ingrid,* felt they were choosing between death on one side of the border and death on the other: which one, they mused, would be the more valorous death? There were likely social class differences here, as the women whose activism grew out of the more low-wage exploitative jobs were those who viewed their activism as potentially inviting some level of danger. There were ways in which these women's politicized agency—across the social class differences—contributed to a certain savvy about negotiating the system in their new community. A repeated theme was an emphasis on immigrants' need to educate themselves and one another. Sociologist of immigration Alejandro Portes has observed that "immigrants learn the ropes of the system through their involvement in politics."[14] Although this is an unintended outcome of activism, it underscores the benefits of such activity after it gains momentum; several of these women commented in similar terms on noticeable changes in their communities.

Third, we heard repeated stories of women who dipped a toe into activism before pouring themselves into it. Although resistant at first, for example, Reyna gradually began involving herself in union activities and tried to stay publicly anonymous, and then eventually she built up courage to go public and become a full-time organizer. Thus, the development of agency has an unfolding quality to it, with one experience building on another to create a full-fledged activist persona. Stories such as Reyna's, and the snowball effect that the women's political activism takes after those initial trials, illustrate the significance of the *networking* aspects of their work; these women are charismatic leaders in a social context of supporters and other leaders. It would be tempting, in fact, to insert these women's stories, like the entrepreneurs' stories, into a familiar Horatio Alger–style American-immigrant "bootstraps" chronicle. But doing so would ignore the messages of their work and the larger groups and movements within which they struggle to reverse the conditions of immigrants from the bottom up—including ethnic cultural networks.

In fact, the agency of these women was infused with cultural pride and community bonds; a cornerstone of Marleine's activities is her effort to teach native-born decision-makers and service providers to respect and understand Haitian culture. Literary scholar Ylce Irizarry has observed that late twentieth-century Latina fiction writing in the United States placed more emphasis on empowerment within the Latina woman's own cultural community than on integration into mainstream American culture.[15] Further, it is notable that several of the activists discussed here were also involved in cross-border political activism, mirroring the transnational living situation of today's immigrants. They were simultaneously working to effect societal change in their home country as they do the same in their adopted home. Some were continuing the social-change work that they had begun before migrating.

In 1998, the social theorist Alain Touraine called for a "return of the actor" in social theory and suggested that studying social movements offers a lens into understanding individuals' subjective activity and intentions. In 2005, he observed that "the subject is coming back"—perhaps resulting from his earlier admonition—and that "subjectivization can be collective as well as personal."[16] The stories of the immigrant women activists profiled in this chapter illustrate both the personal and collective moods of subjectivization. The women were both representing and dependent on networks of other individuals—many of which they built themselves. They were also building networks of networks—such as the antitrafficking Freedom Network and the new National Coalition on Immigrant Women's Rights—formed by organizations such as the National Latina Institute for Reproductive Health, the National Asian Pacific American Women's Forum, and Legal Momentum of the National Organization of Women.[17]

Political scientist Robert Putnam warned in his book *Bowling Alone* that the democratic American tradition of community involvement may be gradually slipping away, resulting in the loss of social capital—those valuable networks that support the health of individuals and societies. The stories of the women in this chapter offer counterexamples to that trend. Like other immigrant women, they had very little economic, political, and social capital when they arrived in the United States. Instead, they built their social capital from the ground up—drawing from their coethnic networks, cross-ethnic networks of women, and beyond. It is that social capital that served as the basic resource that they are mobilizing, but their activities represent a broader change in social organizing. Today, much social-change work exists in a post-charity milieu. Rather than distributing resources to the disadvantaged, for example, organizations are offering tools and starter loans for people to grow those resources and create lives that are not dependent on charities or government subsidies, as Empowered Women International's name suggests.

These women's moral entrepreneurship does represent a new phenomenon that few of their immigration foremothers had available to them: the possibility of making a livelihood through the activist profession. The growth of the third (not-for-profit) sector, with activist organizations in every corner of the country—whether focused on the local, national, or global—is a recent phenomenon that offers viable employment, even if it is not always predictable, lucrative, or easy. Moreover, as the stories of these women illustrate, some moved into these positions without the advantage of higher education, suggesting that nonprofit activism places a value on "local knowledge" and the wisdom of those who have experienced firsthand the problems that the organizations address. Activism was not necessarily the intended career path for these individuals right off the boat or the plane or, in the case of Reyna, ascending from the mud of the Rio Grande. Rather, the impetus for their efforts emerged from what they observed after they arrived.

## Reflections and Policy Recommendations

The changes that these activists have been working to effect include local-level goals such as wage increases in local businesses, state-level interventions such as protection of the rights of domestic workers and immigrants and access to education for undocumented immigrant youth, and proposals for national-level policies such as a more comprehensive across-state DREAM Act. Although each of these women was reporting success in her work, these activists figuratively faced a wall that leaders such as Martin Luther King Jr. did not: for noncitizens, there is a more limited list of rights to which noncitizen immigrants can make claims. Whereas King's approach might be called "critical citizenship," for the women discussed in this chapter who are not citizens, we might deem it "critical extracitizenship." Coalitions with and support from the native-born, therefore, are important. There are many examples of such efforts that are already in place, such as the well-established organization the Hebrew Immigrant Aid Society (HIAS), formed by Jewish immigrants and continued by native-born individuals in coalition with more recent immigrants, to resettle and serve refugees and immigrants across ethnicities.

Despite a general media silence over immigrant women's contributions to activism (with notable exceptions, such as the reporting of Nina Bernstein for the *New York Times*), there is at least one signal that this trend might turn the corner. In November 2008, for example, the news channel CNN profiled ten heroes in the United States who created their own unique entrepreneurial social-change projects around the world. Among these ten, seven were women, and four of those seven women were foreign-born.[18]

Activists such as Marleine and Marga are working to make change in the sphere of culture: a very slow arena to change, particularly at the level of values and attitudes. Such work could be bolstered by increased mass-media portrayals of the contributions of immigrant cultures and the leadership of immigrant women activists. The work of reforming the immigration system at the governmental level must be accompanied by reforms at the deeper stratum of culture: this is where the collectively held "natural attitude" toward the immigrant as a singular, unidimensional type sits mired in a static, uncritical state.

# 10

# "Making History"

*Drawing Conclusions, Looking Forward*

We need to treasure our roots, our history. Immigrant women came here from different parts of the world, of different backgrounds, with different cultures. One hundred years from now, they will become history. Can you imagine? One hundred years from now, young girls will see movies, read books about them, and say, "One hundred years ago, this happened. They made history." It's amazing.

—Kieu Chinh

One of the final questions that we asked the women we interviewed was whether they consider themselves to be members of a community of immigrant women. We were struck by the number of women who said no or "I never thought about it." Several women did say yes—and said it quite adamantly and proudly. And yet those repeated hesitations that we noticed offer evidence for our assertion that the gendered face of immigration is not yet part of the public imagination. Those hesitations also offer further evidence of the multidimensionality of the locution "immigrant woman." Additionally, perhaps a question about community belonging invokes images of other subcommunities: ethnic or religious communities, for example, rather than a community across such groups. Further, some individuals hesitate because they do not self-identify as an immigrant. Hung Liu's self-naming in her self-portraits (figs. 10.1, 10.2, and 10.3) suggests an incarnation, or transmigration, as she drops the "immigrant" label once she becomes a "citizen"—mirroring the present state of legal terminology in immigration law. Her incarnation gives her a settled, confident, and more determined face, as well as one of age and wisdom.

The goal of this book—throughout the forays into specific topics of means of migration, work, culture, and activism—has been to use a gen-

Figure 10.1. *Proletarian*. Artwork by Hung Liu.

dered lens to understand immigration to the United States as we profile our present-day population of immigrant women. By examining this
intersection between the social locations of gender and nativity, we have
asked how these women express agency. What have the women in this
book taught us about this gendered side of immigration and about their
own agency as migrants and women? In this chapter, we summarize the
profile of today's immigrating women, synthesize the interpretations
from these women's "emic" perspectives regarding their own agency, and
glean from these interpretations some recommended directions for public
policy.

## Immigration and Women:
## At the Intersections of Nativity and Gender

There are a number of trends that we have identified across the demographic data and the interviews that help us pull together a portrait of this diverse, multidimensional community of immigrant women. First, we found evidence to support what researchers have termed a "feminization of migration" among adult migrants to the United States. Comparing U.S. Census data, there are more foreign-born women (who migrated as adults) than foreign-born men living in the country today. Each year, a growing proportion of new lawful permanent residents are women, outnumbering men. Further,

Figure 10.2. *Immigrant.* Artwork by Hung Liu.

Figure 10.3. *Citizen.* Artwork by Hung Liu.

although the estimated undocumented population continues to be majority male, there is also a growing female presence in this population. A high proportion of new lawful permanent resident women are in managerial and professional jobs. Although this trend reflects the tendency of available employment visas to favor managerial-level positions, it is nonetheless noteworthy that these visas are increasingly going to women as well as men.

On the basis of these data and our interviews, we learned that large numbers of women are migrating autonomously, suggesting a pattern rather than an exception. Although women tend to receive the larger proportion of family-reunification visas, thus illustrating that women are being sponsored by family members who have already settled, even within these numbers are women sponsored by other women, breaking the predominant historical pattern of men leading the chain migration, with wives trailing later.

In addition to our findings regarding a feminization of migration, we have learned that on average, immigrant women are more highly educated than in previous generations and are also more likely to be employed. Although a striking number are filling positions in the domestic employment sector— and, in fact, the country's pool of domestic workers is predominantly for-eign-born—many professional/middle-class sectors are seeing a rise in the presence of immigrant women. The foreign-born woman doctor, engineer, or lawyer is not a mere anomaly. Other research has documented that the majority of the foreign-born in the United States, in fact, are in white-collar jobs. Therefore, as we saw from the census data, immigrant women are filling positions at two ends of the labor continuum, which social scientists char-acterize as a "U" pattern statistically—that is, they are filling labor-market niches left by the inverse U pattern that more typically characterizes native-born workers today. Immigrant women, for example, were strongly clustered in household labor on one end of this U pattern and were also well repre-sented in the professions requiring advanced educational degrees.

We learned that the post-9/11 securitization culture is unquestionably affecting women's options as well as their feelings regarding inclusion in the United States. Women who have been in the country for longer periods of time reported a much easier process of regularizing their status or not fall-ing out of status prior to the stricter laws passed in the 1990s and the post-9/11 restrictions. Although the current state of laws and culture is placing constraints on many of these women, quite a number are fighting back and raising questions about the place of such governmental approaches given the social construction of the United States as a nation of immigrants and a bea-con for other countries regarding human rights.

Across these women's positions in U.S. society, we noticed a repeated theme of resilience, in the lives that the women endured in their previous home country and the experiences they—sometimes surprisingly—encoun-tered after they migrated. Although personal resources were important for this resilience, the women also lauded the social capital that they acquired through various networks that helped them navigate this new terrain. Those networks included established institutions such as religious communities and more informal activist organizations. The women often had to innovate to identify the needed networks, as they also reported feeling closed out of some opportunities: banks reluctant to lend, for example. Further, we heard mixed stories about the value of ethnic networks, but those women who did not cite these networks as useful to them may have had family demands that leave some women little time for regular outside meetings. We heard more stories about ethnic networks from domestic workers than from other groups. Across various employment categories, are there gender-specific networks that are replacing ethnic networks, such as women's business associations (including Asian or Latina women's associations, for example)?

As we listened to the voices of immigrant women through empirical research, the theme of gender identity seemed particularly salient, finding expression in several women's artworks, business approaches, and activist activities. In the interviews, the women seemed to hold a particular passion regarding how societies viewed their lot in life as women, as well as the strengths and resources that they offered *as women*. This leads us to conclude that there is a gendered "reading" to the immigrant experience that crosses social class, occupation, and geographic location. We leave as an open question whether an identification with a community of women shapes, reshapes, or partially replaces the immigrant woman's ethnic community as a master identity marker. Given that some of the interviewed women hesitated to use the term *immigrant* for whatever reason—preferring, for example, "citizen of the world," "American," "Black," or "Latina" or referring to their move here as a "relocation"—we can only conclude that identity markers, if used at all, are freely chosen and vary widely depending on the geographical and temporal context of exit and reception. Further, the growing prevalence of mixed ethnicity, and living in a mixed-ethnic or mixed-status family, necessitates the search for new labels or the abandonment of labels altogether.

### Listening to Interpretations

What are the meanings that the immigrant women we interviewed hold, or create, at the personal level, as they reinvent themselves in a new geographic place? We learned that there are a number of nuances and complexities in the answer to this question that are insightful, as these interpretations potentially unsettle the "natural attitude": the standard, accepted image of the immigrant in the popular imagination of the native-born. One scholar, Caroline Waldron Merithew, conducted an oral history with an immigrant woman and observed the following: "The construction of Katie over time comprised domains often imagined and experienced by many as contradictory or competing: the foreigner/the citizen, the personal/the political, the internationalist/the American, and the home/the community."[1] In our research, we also found instances in which the women were blurring or challenging some of these binaries, as well as others, such as legal/illegal, resistance/conciliation, autonomy/collaboration, temporary/permanent, and cosmopolitan/traditional. The women replaced them with other binaries, such as justice/injustice, humane/inhumane, and fair/unfair. Again, identity for these women is fluid and agentially chosen. We now explore several themes related to the meanings of immigration for these women and their relationships to the question of agency.

## Agency and the Construction of Self

Across many examples from our interviews, we heard of constraints countered and reimagined by acts of agency. The artist Lilian Fernandez was not selected in an art competition; but through her public ripping of her painting, she created her own exhibition. The moods of agency include the various styles of escape from home—from the desperate but strategic to the negotiated escape. There are many instances of invention of something from nothing—most evident in the stories of entrepreneurs and artists—and the reconstruction of self using tools such as one's familiar heritage, as Lilian Fernandez suggested. Memory of home cultures, in fact, was often woven into these women's entrepreneurial and artistic products, providing raw material for their reconstructed lives. Among those memories were individuals—men and women—whom these women looked to for inspiration. Risk taking was evident across many of the stories, from those in gender-atypical professions to domestic workers moving into the homes of strangers, to entrepreneurs pouring all of their hard-earned savings into a new venture.

Further, there are numerous examples of social constraints that these women looked in the face and ignored, disempowered, or deemed irrelevant. Constraint often dialectically inspired resistance or refusal. Some of this refusal was a response to societal expectations of gendered norms. The triumphant face of agency was represented by the woman who asked us to call her "*Victoria*" in this book because she had been victorious. The emotional awakenings of activists such as Reyna, who feared for her life after her illness from janitorial cleaning chemicals, were simultaneously reasoned decisions, clearly calculated with potential risks taken into account. Across women's stories, their agency resulted in an ongoing dynamism of shifting roles, identities, and positions in their new society. Agency proceeded from leaving home to redefining home and, in the process, often redefining self.

The challenge of the migration and settlement experience, including enduring tough conditions in places such as New York City, was often instrumental in this reconstruction of self. As Liliana, from Bulgaria, explained this process, after struggling through exploitative jobs, meeting people who tried to take advantage of her, and then pushing herself to go to college and find respectable employment, "I feel it's a test you have to go through. The way I walk on the street now is different. I was very submissive to my mother and brother. I found myself here pretty much. If I had gone back to Bulgaria, I wouldn't like myself now."

## Redefining "Home"

> There's a cemetery here in New York on the way to the airport, and supposedly you can hear the immigrants calling out from there, "I'm going home. I'm going home."
>
> —Liliana, Bulgaria

Will the women in this book remain temporary sojourners or become permanent transplants? Have they integrated themselves into any form of American collective identity? Do they want to return home? A substantial proportion of immigrants, in fact, do return to their native country. The economic decline of 2008 and 2009 and the unwelcome climate for many immigrants reportedly resulted in quite a number of individuals returning home, whether or not they had originally intended to do so. Many (although not all) of the women we interviewed whose children had grown up in the United States envisioned their futures here, in the United States, rather than back in their home country. Their grown children were establishing lives in the States, and if opportunity for children is one of the driving forces of immigration, it would make sense that parents assume that their children will remain in the States. When the children's father is absent for whatever reason, a woman may be even more likely to stay in the same country with her children. Thus, motherhood is a social location that carries with it particular opportunities and constraints that exemplify how the immigration experience—which includes this more existential question of "where is home?"—is a gendered process.

*Dama,* from India, is someone who has never had an intention of returning, but interestingly, that desire to stay in her new home has come from the similarities she sees between her home culture and that of the United States. She says that she always felt an affinity with the United States because India had drawn on the U.S. Constitution and looked to the American Revolution as a model. And when we asked the Romanian bed-and-breakfast owner *Elisabeta* if she sees herself as part of a community of immigrant women, she said no. Why not? "I feel like I belong everywhere." Would she go home? "No. I left so long ago. I've gotten spoiled. I see how people struggle there."

For several of the women in this book, the temporary is becoming more permanent, in contrast to their original intentions. The Irish-born Kelly twins, for example, insurance brokers, reflected, in a back-and-forth banter: "I had no intention of this being a permanent arrangement." "We weren't mad about that cold weather you get over there." "Or the city life." "Or the city life: New York and stuff like that." And the Nepalese domestic worker whom we met in chapter 5 mused that fate has unfortunately left her here. After the struggles of domestic work, she concluded that she must have sinned in her previous life to come here. Several women expressed an ambivalence about where their home is now but also a satisfaction that they are making a home; one of our respondents remarked, "I'm here now, and I'm doing what women do to make a life." Clearly, for those who escaped torture, abuse, natural disaster, or war, the question of return may not ever be articulated.

We have learned that an immigrant's intention to stay does not necessarily lead to the formation of a personal national identity as an American. As one woman said to us, "I think this is my children's home, not my home." *Lara* loves the United States and wants to stay—but wants to keep her distinction as a Brazilian. She complained, "There is no category for me on surveys: 'White'? No. 'Hispanic'? No, I don't speak Spanish. I'm Brazilian. I'm the proudest Brazilian. I don't want to lose my accent, because that's my personality. I am so proud of my accent."

The fluidity of the relationship to home—exemplifying those blurring binaries mentioned earlier—reflects the unfolding, negotiated, uncertain, and perpetually changing nature of the experience. It illustrates both the temporal and the spatial nature of agency—the multiple combinations of then-there, here-now, there-now (for transnational situations), and here-then that is characteristic of the experience of migration. Through these women's expressions of those temporal and spatial (or geographical) moods of agency, we can view the workings of those larger social structures that are the grounds for constraints and enablements of agency. A workplace raid that results in the deportation of an undocumented worker suddenly unsettles the subjective meaning of "home."

## Gender and *the* Cultural Icon of Immigration

Although we never intentionally solicited this theme directly in our interviews, it was striking to us how often women referred to the Statue of Liberty. What is the meaning of this, in an era when immigrants no longer sail into New York Harbor to be greeted by this figure? It appears that for many immigrants, she is still iconic, and it is important to note her gender in the context of the theme of this book. The Statue of Liberty theme was not only a function of geography—in other words, it arose in interviews that took place outside the East Coast. Among the East Coast dwellers who mentioned the Statue is *Anica,* who fled Romania during the Cold War. She actually watched the Statue of Liberty appear in her field of vision as she flew into New York. As she stated in her description that we quoted in chapter 3, it "is the symbol of hope for every soul that can breathe behind the Iron Curtain." The physical marker of the Statue represented a zenith that, once reached, signified a border crossing of a thick variety—for *Anica,* it conveyed a protective feeling amid the ominous uncertainty of the Cold War. As *Elisabeta,* also from Romania, passionately insisted, "Nobody has the right to step on your dreams and kill them, one by one by one. Nobody. You are the master of your dreams. I wish that when an immigrant woman looks at the Statue of Liberty, she imagines there is another torch that says 'freedom of the soul for the immigrant woman.'"

Implied in *Elisabeta's* vision is a reflection on the many cultures that women view as constraining their options, on her own past with a controlling partner, and on a sense that there is a gendered meaning to the word *freedom* that warrants a parallel torch. These are also references to two areas of American culture that intersect in the lived experience of immigration and womanhood: the place of the Statue of Liberty in public political culture as representing a particular dream of freedom for the foreign-born and of a culture of freedom that American women have begun to create for their gender—and are still attempting to create. For one woman who escaped violence and war in Iraq, the arrival in a place of peace, stability, and freedom was particularly significant. The Statue in the American mythical imagination is doubly gendered, if we consider that the frequently cited poem "The New Colossus"[2] inscribed on its base was penned by a woman, the young New York poet Emma Lazarus, who was not an immigrant herself but who, as a Jew, advocated on behalf of Jewish immigrants forced out of Europe during the pogroms and anti-Semitism of the late nineteenth century.

Chinese immigrant Hung Liu invokes a reference to the Statue through the title of her painting *Goddess of Love, Goddess of Liberty.* The painting was completed in 1989, the year that Chinese students protesting in Beijing saw their own construction that they called the "Goddess of Democracy" as well as the "Goddess of Liberty" ultimately destroyed by public authorities.

Hung's painting included a footbound woman, juxtaposing "liberty" with the strictures of her own cultural traditions. The title of Hung's painting both paid homage and indicted.[3]

The women we interviewed referenced the Statue in New York Harbor not only iconically but also ironically. They held her up as a mirror to our immigration attitudes and policies, noting when we have fallen short of, if not openly defied, her spirit. She is a transhistorical cultural reference point infused with more fixed historical meanings. The example of the woman from Iraq, where the violence is a direct result of U.S. intervention, calls forth one of those ironies. And as one immigrant woman said, "When I came, I looked at the Statue, but where is the freedom?" Marleine Bastien's poem publicly referenced the lived experiences of Haitian refugee women:

> The dream of being comforted
> By the sweet arms of mother liberty
> Kept us going, hoping
> Then reality sinks in
> Our dreams are shattered

The ironic and the iconic seem to fuse in a painting by a Pakistani immigrant to New Jersey, Ahmed Shikoh. In her painting *Self Portrait—1,* she has reimagined the Statue of Liberty in her own image: in a Pakistani wedding dress, as a pregnant immigrant, and as a regal mother, baby on hip. We did not interview Ahmed Shikoh, but her artwork offers an additional example to this discussion, since it intentionally intertwines themes of modernity and tradition as it plays with the complex meaning of womanhood, through the imagery of the Statue of Liberty. In all these examples, we see the continued resonance of the Statue's symbol, her gendered quality, her power as a female, and the specificity of marking her with an ethnic quality of new migration, perhaps reenlivening her. Like the living immigrants, the Statue's identity is constantly in flux, being redefined. It appears that today's immigrant women are agentially reconstructing her and imbuing her with a symbolic agency of her own. But is the iconic/ironic reading an indictment of the Statue? Is she guilty? Is she ultimately deceptive? Or is her agency one of a bewildered gaze toward the present-day reality of disappointing immigration policies? Significantly, she still stands, unharmed, in eyesight of Ground Zero, the place that also designates a temporal moment when our borders quickly tightened.

## On Gender, Assimilation, and Agency

Across our interviews, the question of whether women will return to their original homeland was often answered with reference to how their social location as women in the United States contrasts with those in their home culture. Repeatedly, women reported on the newly found autonomy that they enjoy as women in the United States and its relative unavailability in their home country. Once they tasted that autonomy, many decided not to return. The active decision *not* to move back home, something seemingly inactive, is an example of how the continuation of a particular life path nevertheless is agential. Like the foreign-born women interviewed by Erez, Adelman, and Gregory,[4] some women in our sample were able, through immigration to the United States, to support themselves economically and leave abusive partners, and thus they had reason to want to remain.

Although the social sciences have moved away from earlier research (and normative) agendas that gave central attention to whether immigrants were able or willing to assimilate—to move out of their home culture's habits and take on those of the United States—we find that an assimilation lens bears mention in the context of discussions of gender. The historian Donna Gabaccia has stated that assimilation means something different for immigrant women than for men. For the women, it is about becoming an American *woman*—and the meaning of that identity fluctuates from one era to another.[5] If perceptions abound that the United States offers better opportunities for women, we may be seeing more women immigrating for precisely those reasons. If they are mothers, they also foresee the same possibilities for their female children. In a study of Mexican women in California, Hondagneu-Sotelo learned that the experience of living in the United States resulted in changes away from the traditional gender roles that were more common in their regions of Mexico. These women often negotiated with husbands for more egalitarian relationships as they simultaneously became more independent and involved in economic and political activities.[6] Such a change might have more than one source: the cultural influence of the new environment or the movement to any new place where the women become more active workforce participants.

Mary Waters has reminded us that the category of assimilation needs to be disaggregated by, for example, ethnicity. Whereas assimilation for some ethnic groups (Europeans, for example) can carry certain social class benefits, such as climbing the American social hierarchy, for other groups, such as West Indians, assimilation may lead to absorption into African American worlds, which still suffer from racist exclusions and lower access to certain levels of income and power.[7] Alejandro Portes and Min Zhou have offered the theoretical model of "segmented assimilation" to denote how immigrants may assimilate into the habits and cultures of various social classes.[8] Both models offer potential parallels here, as immigrant women adapt to a segment of the population—that of their gender. Combining the insights of Waters and Portes and Zhou into a model that considers gender as a subculture into which immigrants enter, we begin to see a picture of how intersectionality works for immigrants, as they move into certain orders of ethnicity, social class, and gender, even as those orders are constantly in the process of redefinition. Diane Negra's research into the assimilation myths that early female, ethnically European Hollywood stars helped to fix in the public imaginary echoes how race becomes clarified as a marker for who is in and who is out. She demonstrates how "Hollywood models the domestication of white feminine ethnicity as a means of maintaining crucial cultural myths about American assimilative capacities."[9]

Despite certain potential gains from assimilating into American womanhood—if we can call it that—many of our respondents chose to keep a critical distance from some aspects of American culture. The women spoke of not wanting to lose certain values from their own culture that gave them meaning, such as the importance of community. Several had critiques of capitalist objectification, consumer "me-ism," and isolated individualism. This signals to us as social scientists that assimilation cannot be approached as an either-or proposition but must be seen as a process on a multilayered continuum. In fact, the cultural clash that results when women and girls assimilate into freer forms of womanhood when women are traditionally viewed as upholding and reproducing ethnic cultures can lead to family conflict. Yen Le Espiritu has documented this issue within Filipino families in the United States: parents hoped to control their teenage daughters' sexuality by accusing them of disloyalty to their ethnicity.[10]

We have located another, seemingly inverse, take on assimilation to American womanhood as a single path toward progress. Many women we interviewed, for example, were symbolically turning the Statue of Liberty's gaze on our country's practices and policies regarding *women*, in addition to its approach to *immigrants*. Around the world, for instance, countries mark International Women's Day on March 8. Although some women have felt cynical toward meanings that their government imposed on this holiday from the "top down," the day remains important as a grass-roots-level expression of the power of women's contributions to society and as a continued platform for claims making to expand women's rights and opportunities. Ironically, this holiday was invented in the United States in 1909, but it is not a broadly or officially practiced celebration here. Confused immigrant women ask why a country that is viewed as a "city on a hill" for women around the world seems ignorant about this holiday. Therefore, we take care not to portray migrating women's appreciation of newly found protections of women's rights as endorsing a new incarnation of modernization theory—a paradigm that characterized the West as representing the *telos* for the rest of the world.

To stretch the sociological categories of assimilation into new directions, we propose to imagine the incorporation of continuing flows of new immigrants as multicultured and multigendered contributions to the social-structural makeup of the society. The idea of assimilation assumes a static view of the culture into which immigrants are to insert themselves. A less static view, for example, is evident in the words of Iranian American writer and professor Azar Nafisi, who reflects on the meaning of *home* and insists, "I think that people who live in this country should feel that constantly: this country *survives* on the fact that strangers are constantly coming to this place, *stretching* it a little bit, *adding* to it, changing it, and making it their home."[11] The sentiment contained within this quotation moves out of the static vision of American society toward one that is never standing still, never ethnically owned by any one group. It is one in which there is a constant feedback loop between human agency and social structures, nurtured through cultural diversity. Further, it is a feedback loop that might be visualized as an upward spiral rather than a circle. To take the analogy to another level, ethnic, gender, and even social class cultures are never static either, and those feedback loops also catch such subcultural groups up in the process of change. All are historically contingent. And in a globalizing world where some national boundaries are being blurred, migrants are living transnationally, and cultural dissemination is a relatively uncontrolled process through the rapid means of new communications media, such feedback loops between agents and structures are not confined within one territory.

We hope that this volume has helped to amplify the voices of immigrant women and to underscore their contributions to the arts, domestic labor, the sciences, trades, activism, business development, nonprofit leadership, and charitable contributions. Many of these women are breaking glass ceilings, in addition to playing a leadership role in their family and community. This is not, however, to forget the myriad ways in which immigrants and women are victimized by continued exclusions and discrimination, as well as gaps in policy. It is to those gaps that we next turn.

## The Future of Policy

On a sweltering, sunny Sunday afternoon in June 2007, about forty Latino women, men, and children gather for an impromptu meeting in a one-room building near Miami, Florida. Once called to order, they listen attentively while a well-respected, trusted community organizer explains the current state of the national immigration debate. The organizer has lined the walls with large easel-board pages outlining a proposed new federal immigration bill. Across several hours, he explains the details of the bill in Spanish; the bill would increase fees for document processing, tighten regulations and time limits, create new family-reunification provisions, and make major revisions to guest-worker programs. As the meeting progresses, men and women become visibly anxious. The organizer concludes his presentation and asks for reactions—of which there are many. One woman stands and asks, "What will be next? Are they going to take our children?" The most vocal reactions to the reported information, in fact, come from women.

The proposed 2007 immigration reform bill died from unresolved congressional disputes, leaving a legislative status quo that immigrants view as far from ideal. As this vignette illustrates, immigrant women were highly involved in grass-roots efforts to reform the many gaps in the immigration system. If the utopian vision contained in Kieu Chinh's quotation that opened this chapter—that of a visible, integrated, and appreciated community of immigrant women—is to come to pass, what is the future of policy development to move that portrait forward? We have outlined specific suggestions within individual chapters, with attention to the need to recognize the intersection between nativity and gender in the availability of capital investments for new businesses, regulation of domestic labor, accessibility of opportunities to pursue gender-atypical professions, and expansion of the arts fields, among other areas. We have reviewed the work that many of these women are undertaking on their own to address policy gaps and discrimination: from Marleine's organization of Haitian women and Reyna's advocacy on behalf of immigrant cleaning staff to the calls for workers' rights by women in the domestic-labor field. In other writings, we have discussed policy gaps not covered in this book, such as the need to address the predicaments that immigrant women suffering from domestic abuse face in a criminal justice system that prioritizes street crime, uses punitive measures that women do not always prefer, deports batterers (leaving a family without a breadwinner), and misunderstands cultural differences.[12]

Although, as Saskia Sassen[13] and other scholars have observed, globalization is erasing borders and disempowering the nation-state and undermining its sovereignty, when it comes to immigration policy, the nation-state still reigns. Nation-states make immigration policy; when they make policy in tandem with other nations, this is negotiated *as nations,* not through the auspices of transnational organizations such as the United Nations. A noted exception to this is the European Union, built deliberately to unite people across borders, which has a set of immigration policies to be uniformly applied. Immigration activists have critiqued this set of policies, however, for using the "least common denominator" rule in writing the laws. This means that the country with the most restrictive border-control policies becomes the policy model, and it is applied across the board to all EU member states.[14] As a transnational body, the United Nations sets protocols for refugees, but it is left to individual nation-states to set quotas and admission standards and to hold court for asylum seekers. Therefore, for countries such as the United States that are not members of a unit like the EU, the target for reform efforts continues to be primarily directed domestically. This is not to ignore the ongoing work of advocates to press for reforms in those international bodies; in fact, the United Nations has been approached to consider how its refugee policies prioritize the needs of men over those of women, by giving central attention to individuals displaced because of public, political conflicts, rather than because of experiences such as private-life violence, to which women are more routinely exposed.[15]

Given that women are known for being faithful about sending remittances to their family in their home country, some states strongly encourage their female citizens to migrate to a richer country. Barbara Ehrenreich and Arlie Russell Hochschild report estimates that women send between half and almost all of their wages back home.[16] Those remittances are providing a major source of economic development for lower-income countries—as was the case for European countries in earlier eras of migration to the "New World." Numerous women whom we interviewed were also supporting charities, economic development, disaster relief, and activist causes in their home country. Thus, U.S. immigration policy does not exist in a vacuum isolated from other policy arenas. Both international relations and global economic development are tightly interwoven with immigration in a larger, globally interdependent tapestry. Sassen, for instance, has documented the relationship between the continued struggles of highly indebted countries in the global South and the process of immigration—particularly how it feeds irregular migration such as human trafficking.[17]

Significantly, therefore, women's agency as migrants is a central thread in this tapestry—as is women's vulnerability to the extreme forms of irregular migration as societal structures change. The globalization of the economy that has been leading to lower labor costs and loss of factories in many countries need not continue in this direction for the sake of stabilization of businesses. Angela Chan, owner of a wheel-manufacturing company, for example, offers advice based in her own experience:

Competitors are trying to underbid me. But we don't want to play the price war. We don't want to go too far down, which will sacrifice quality. We remain competitive not by lowering prices but by having excellent service, inventory, direct and open communications, and on-time delivery. Meeting these promises to our clients raises our firm's credibility. China doesn't understand American culture: they think that the cheap price is the most important. But it's not. Service, inventory, and on-time delivery are more important.

If the present-day direction toward a more borderless world continues, what are the implications for the continued location of policy setting and enforcement at the domestic level? Several women in this book referenced international norms and conventions such as human rights treaties. These may be most relevant for those who are technically "stateless." Should individuals be able to claim rights and protections by some transnational body if they lack them in one or more domestic or migration context? A number of scholars and activists are exploring the future potential of bodies of global governance with more teeth than current international bodies now have and are advocating for a global civil society with clear avenues for representation by those from the global South as well as the global North.[18] The complex issue of international migration belongs at the table in such discussions.

It is unlikely that such bodies will fully supplant the nation-state as overseer of the people residing within its borders; therefore, a level of national sovereignty is bound to continue. In response to how the United States could improve, the women whom we interviewed called for cultural as well as technical legal changes. One activist, Marta, for example, suggested that there is room for broad public education within the United States. At the individual level, she stated, people need to learn more about different cultures, immigrants, and the "broken law system." She said that she believes both immigrants and citizens need to do so, as she also encounters "legal" immigrants who stereotype newcomers, particularly those without authorization. She continued, "The nation is immersed with different cultures; the government needs to make sure all feel welcome. They are only patching things here and there."

What Marta called the "broken law system" is a repeated mantra of immigration reformers in the early part of the twenty-first century. Because of a series of legal changes, as well as an absence of changes to meet changing economic and social conditions, there are not enough legal visas to go around. In addition, there are long waits for status change and asylum decisions and numerous policy gaps where immigrant women and men fall between the cracks. Where gender is concerned, there are vestiges of the laws of coverture, in which the woman's legal status was once derived from that of her husband, resulting in a continued dependence that many immigrant women have on the immigration status held by their partner. In 2009, the U.S. government began to address several of these gender gaps, such as a decision to allow women to make a claim for asylum if they are escaping domestic violence in their home country (with some exceptions) and ending the widow's penalty, where individuals lost their legal immigration status on the death of the spouse from whom their status was derived.

Although targeted fixes are needed to attend to aspects of immigration policy that disadvantage one gender, these will be less effective without a fuller, more sweeping immigration policy reform. Such fixes might amount to, using Marta's language, "patching things here and there." As this book has chronicled, the immigration legal code is only one piece of the puzzle: the entanglement of this code with criminal law, labor law, and the ever-fluctuating separation between state and federal powers operates as a structural constraint over and above the constraints of these legal codes taken separately. Historical context is critical and complicates the issue of border management. Using the language of sociologist Anne Swidler, it appears that we live in a moment of social transformation characterized by "unsettled lives."[19] Is this unsettled moment anchored most centrally in the anxieties following the 9/11 events? And how is immigration interpreted as part and parcel, if not causal, in relation to this transformation? Swidler argues that in times like these, people hold competing ideologies and adhere to them very strongly; such a cultural context presents serious challenges to the possibility of agreements on immigration policy reform.

In 2010, the national research and advocacy organization the Immigration Policy Center offered an assessment of the progress and lack of progress made by the Department of Homeland Security on the seventh anniversary of its founding. The center concluded that despite progress on some fronts, including clearing some visa-processing backlogs, little progress had been made on improving due process, ending inconsistent decision-making, shifting enforcement priorities from noncriminal to criminal violations, and reversing its practice of "expedited removals" of asylum seekers. Further, it charged that

> DHS has continued to make use of Operation Streamline, a zero-tolerance policy along the southern border which requires mandatory criminal prosecution of non-violent border crossers, clogging federal courts and draining resources away from prosecuting more serious criminals involved in drugs, weapons, and organized crime. It remains unclear whether Operation Streamline has any deterrent effect on migrants crossing the border.[20]

We supplement this pessimistic diagnosis of cultural constraint with the optimism that was apparent in the activist stories of this book. For some of these activists, assimilation also involved learning the activist techniques of U.S. culture, such as petitions, which were new to them, and a surprised awareness that they could protest without fear of getting killed. For these activists, empowering aspects of their new culture were useful tools to counter the disempowering elements. Clearly, there continue to be regular reports of activist work in the United States with unsafe consequences, including immigration advocacy, even if such consequences might result in legal challenge. And if domestic workers are prohibited from unionizing by federal law, there are limits to the extent of advocacy that is possible for a key employment sector for foreign-born women.

### Policy and Today's Immigrating Woman

Between the stories of the women in this book and the broader statistical story of foreign-born women of the United States, we can read a narrative of change as well as continuity: as they move into more public roles, shifting their status within families, immigrating women's life paths are beginning to mirror those of immigrating men. At the same time, their continued social place within lower-status positions and their shouldering of greater responsibilities for home and child care narrate a second plotline with more historical continuity, of life experiences that are distinct from those of men. Policy reform needs to give attention to both of these narratives. Are visa categories, for example—including "dependent" visas for trailing family members—defined with this changing, while partly historically continuous, profile of women in mind? Should not a student spouse have the right to work legally, since her presence in the United States could potentially *hurt* her own career due to the employment gap on her résumé, reduce income opportunities for her family, and make her fully dependent on her spouse for both income and legal status?

As the census data profiles and our interviews have made clear, these women are forging their own changes in their lives within larger contexts that are constantly in flux as well: the social structures that define their contexts of exit are never static, nor are their contexts of reception—whether at the level of culture, policy, or economics. Both the contexts of exit and contexts of reception are characterized by the intersecting social locations of race, national origin, citizenship, immigration legal structures, ethnicity, religion, social class, and gender. Those social locations carry meanings through continuously changing cultural practices, affecting immigrant women's experiences and life chances at the multiple intersections between them. Although a woman with an undocumented legal status may subjectively define herself as a survivor with multiple strengths, she is nevertheless in one of the most vulnerable positions in our social structure, which is layered by culturally held attitudes that paint her as a thief or worse. Yet, as we observed in these interviews, the undocumented woman may have landed in this state against her will or, even if she risked moving into an undocumented status knowingly, may have worked to adjust her status and use her local knowledge to press for social change. This further illustrates how identities, and their social-structural references, are fluid. Immigrating women in the United States are not only a multidimensional group, but those dimensions are ever shifting.

We return here to the concept of "gender pioneers"—a term borrowed from Donna Gabaccia—as a reminder that many of the women profiled in this book are emerging as societal leaders. The recognition and integration of such leadership across the spheres of American society can offer an important entrée into the development of policy priorities regarding both international development and immigration policy reform—one that takes a gender lens. And based on the histories of the women we have met in this book, it is inevitable that many of those who reconfigure and reform the immigration policies that will shape the lives of future immigrating women will, themselves, be immigrating women, including some of those whose stories we have shared here.

# Appendix A

*Notes on Research Methods*

This was a mixed-method study, which means that we used both quantitative and qualitative methods, with the primary emphasis on the latter. The quantitative data were all from secondary sources: they were from available datasets such as the U.S. Census Bureau (provided through IPUMS from the University of Minnesota) and tables from the United States Citizenship and Immigration Services (USCIS). With the census data, we controlled for women who migrated as adults and produced simple tables (cross-tabulations) of the variables in question. The USCIS data were disaggregated by age, so our data summaries consisted of simple addition.

Regarding our qualitative research, we used both snowball and convenience sampling to recruit participants. Often, our recruiting was carried out through organizations such as professional associations and advocacy organizations. Personal contacts through colleagues, friends, students, family members, and other activists were also important sources of referrals. Several women volunteered to be interviewed when they learned of the project (people we met in our travels, such as at hotels or restaurants). Primarily, the goal was to locate women who were employed in the targeted arenas that the book covers (such as domestic workers, artists, and activists). Secondarily, without claiming to be fully representative of all nationalities, we attempted to stratify the sample when possible, seeking out women from ethnic groups that had particular concentrations in the locales where we traveled. For example, we made sure to interview Mexicans and an Iranian in Los Angeles, a Vietnamese in Houston, and Haitians and Cubans in Miami. Given the high number of Mexican women in the United States, we made sure that many in our sample were of Mexican descent; Mexican-born women constitute more than 10 percent of those interviewed. Although we indicate the country of birth in our list of those interviewed in appendix B, it is important to note that some do come from mixed ethnic/national backgrounds.

The majority of the interviews were conducted face to face, with a handful conducted by telephone due to scheduling conflicts. We collected consent forms from each respondent. Some women chose to have their real names used in the book; for others, we assigned pseudonyms. In some cases, we took care to disguise the identities even further than a pseudonym, such as when someone was critical of her former government or had to flee her country for some other reason, or if there was concern over immigration authorities in the United States. We are aware that the assurance of confidentiality seems to contradict the requirement of signing a consent form. We take further precautions to protect confidentiality by keeping any identifying records in a secure place.

We were encouraged and gratified to see how many women willingly shared their stories with us, even when we cold-called them. There were still, however, some women who declined, and those examples offer important insight into immigrant women's experiences as well. One woman, for example, came to the interview, but when she saw the consent form, declined the interview because she was concerned over signing a form. Another, a domestic worker, would not return telephone calls from her employer, who had passed on our request for the interview. Although neither woman shared with us her immigration status, it is possible that one or both were undocumented immigrants and therefore more distrusting of what ramifications their involvement in the project could have. While we do have undocumented immigrants in our sample, and we did all we could to reassure people that their identities would be disguised, we can understand their hesitance. We note these experiences to illustrate the impact that the securitized culture had on this research process. This was not the only reason that individuals declined the interview. A woman of French origin seemed to refuse because she did not want to talk about France—shaking her head and crossing her fingers as she backed away and spoke the word "France."

For those who consented to the interviews (the overwhelming majority of those whom we approached), each interview was recorded and transcribed, unless the woman requested not to be recorded. In such cases, the interviewer would write up notes about the interview as soon as possible after the interview. Our interview guide consisted of a list of questions that all respondents answered, as well as a set of questions tailored to the respondent's work, such as activism, atypical occupations, and entrepreneurship. At times, however, the woman simply told her story, and we did not follow the interview format strictly. Generally, in these cases, the women inadvertently covered issues that we would have asked and included other topics that we found valuable for the research. If they did not cover our intended topics, we probed to fill these gaps.

Where possible, we also walked through neighborhoods where these women worked or lived, visited meetings such as activist gatherings, and attended gallery events. Some of our descriptions arose from our own advocacy experiences; the three of us met through our engagement in immigration rights advocacy, rather than through academia. We were attentive to the issue of reciprocity out of gratitude for the respondents' time, from eating meals in their restaurants to agreeing to be interviewed for one of our contact's projects. More broadly, we interpret our contributions to potential policy change as a gesture of reciprocity.

As the writing was in process, there was an opportunity to bring together several of the women we interviewed. Staff at the National Archives contacted Susan Pearce as they were planning an event called "Citizens by Choice"—consisting of a panel of women entrepreneurs who had migrated to the United States. We quote from the lively discussions of that panel in the chapter on entrepreneurship.

# Appendix B

*List of Interviewed Women*

TABLE B.1

*Interviewed Women*

| Name | Country of Origin |
|------|-------------------|
| *Aileen* | Iran |
| *Ana* | El Salvador |
| Ana Martinez | Honduras |
| Angela Chan | China |
| *Anica* | Romania |
| Anne Kelly | Ireland |
| *Beatriz* | El Salvador |
| *Bettina* | Argentina |
| *Betty* | China |
| *Carmen* | Mexico |
| *Celia* | Panama |
| Christina Robinson | Mexico |
| *Dama* | India |
| *Deborah* | Zambia |
| Deirdre Kelly | Ireland |
| Denise Davies | Canada |
| *Elisabeta* | Romania |
| *Ella* | Guatemala |
| *Estella* | Mexico |
| *Estelle* | Gabon |
| Esther Armstrong | Ghana |
| Femi Agana | England |

| Name | Country of Origin |
|------|-------------------|
| Firoza Diddee | India |
| *Golnaz* | Iran |
| *Gracia* | Philippines |
| *Gwendolyn* | Trinidad |
| Hung Liu | China |
| *Ingrid* | Mexico |
| *Johanna* | Germany |
| *Josefina* | Paraguay |
| *Josselyn* | Ecuador |
| Judith Rodriguez | Mexico |
| Karen Walrond | Trinidad |
| *Khursheeda* | Bangladesh |
| Kieu Chinh | Vietnam |
| *Kiran* | Nepal |
| Lilian Fernandez | Cuba |
| Liliana Petrova | Bulgaria |
| Liliane Nérette Louis | Haiti |
| *Linda* | Guatemala |
| *Lucia* | Mexico |
| Luck Pongsamart | Thailand |
| *Luna* | Nepal |
| *Malathi* | India |
| Marga Fripp | Romania |
| Maria de Lourdes Sobrino | Mexico |
| Maria Xiquin | Guatemala |
| Marleine Bastien | Haiti |
| *Marta* | Mexico |
| Martine Divahe | Gabon |
| *Matilda* | England |
| *Meenu* | India |
| *Nadia* | Iran |
| *Natalia* | Columbia |
| *Nataly* | Peru |
| Natasha Duwin | Argentina |

| Name | Country of Origin |
| --- | --- |
| Neri Torres | Cuba |
| *Nina* | Ukraine |
| Ola Lissowska | Poland |
| Pari Sayeri | Iran |
| *Paula* | Columbia |
| Quincy Nguyen | Vietnam |
| *Rashmi* | India |
| Reyna Gómez | Honduras |
| Rita Kalwani | India |
| Rocio Rameriz | Mexico |
| *Rosalinda* | Columbia |
| *Rosita* | Mexico |
| Roya Pazooki | Iran |
| Rubina Chaudhary | India |
| *Sara* | Mexico |
| *Sarla* | Nepal |
| Shana Castro | Brazil |
| *Shanice* | Trinidad/Tobago |
| Sheela Murthy | India |
| *Shelly* | England |
| Shirley Nathan-Pulliam | Jamaica |
| *Sonya* | Jamaica |
| *Stella* | Mexico |
| Susie Thang | Vietnam |
| *Svetlana* | Russia |
| *Teresa* | Argentina |
| Trang Nguyen | Vietnam |
| *Valeria* | Mexico |
| *Victoria* | Argentina |
| *Xia-Hwa* | Taiwan |
| *Xui Li* | China |
| Yolanda Voss | Ecuador |
| *Yue* | Taiwan |
| *Zareen* | Iran |

# Appendix C

*Timeline: U.S. Immigration Policy
and Women, 1875–2009*

1875   **"Page Law":** Exclusions included felons, contract laborers, prostitutes, and Asian women thought to be brought over for "lewd and immoral purposes." In reality, it was used to exclude most Asian women attempting to immigrate.

1903   **Immigration Act:** Exclusions expanded to include all involved in the prostitution trade. Pregnancy was also listed as a ground for exclusion.

1907   **Gentlemen's Agreement:** Excluded further Japanese labor migration, but allowed wives of Japanese immigrants already in the United States. The practice of "picture brides" immigrating became an important way for Japanese women to enter legally.

1907   **Immigration Act:** Again expanded excluded groups, and expanded grounds for deportation. Women who entered into prostitution within three years of arrival were now subject to deportation.

1910   **Mann Act:** Enacted due to fears of "white slave trade." Furthered bans against women being imported for purposes of prostitution.

1920   **"Ladies Agreement":** The agreement between the United States and Japan ended immigration of "picture brides."

1921   **Quota Act:** Quotas were set on how many immigrants could enter from any given country, giving preference to immigrants from Northern and Western Europe. Within quotas, family members were given preference.

1922   **Cable Act:** Ended the practice of American women losing their citizenship upon marrying foreigners, provided the foreigners were themselves eligible for citizenship. Also ended the practice of foreign women automatically obtaining American citizenship upon marrying American citizens. Such women now had to go through the naturalization process.

1924   **National Origins Act:** Reduced quotas, particularly from Southern and Eastern Europe. Also made Asian exclusion more complete.

1945   **War Brides Act:** Allowed the foreign wives and fiancées of American servicemen to immigrate.

**1952** **McCarren-Walter Act:** Ended exclusion of Asians, but created very small quotas for immigrants from Asian countries. Also specified "subversives" and gays and lesbians as excludable and deportable categories.

**1965** **Hart-Celler Act (Immigration and Nationality Act):** Ended racially based national quotas. Placed a new emphasis on family reunification immigrants and workplace skills in high demand.

**1986** **Immigration Marriage Fraud Amendments:** Increased penalties for those involved in "sham marriages," and created a 2-year provisional green card for immigrant spouses of citizens and permanent residents.

**1986** **Immigration Reform and Control Act:** Allowed limited amnesties for undocumented immigrants. Also made it more difficult for undocumented immigrants to work in the United States, by requiring employers to check workers' documents.

**1994** **Violence Against Women Act (VAWA):** Allowed certain battered immigrants to file for immigration relief without assistance of or knowledge by their abuser, in order to seek safety and independence from the abuser.

**1996** **Illegal Immigration Reform and Immigrant Responsibility Act:** Limited public benefits available to immigrants, increased deportable crimes, and made it more difficult for poor immigrants to sponsor family members.

**1996** **Defense of Marriage Act:** Not specifically an immigration policy, but impacted efforts of same-sex couples in regards to immigration, by defining marriage as only between male-female couples.

**2000** **Victims of Trafficking and Violence Protection Act (TVPA):** Criminalized trafficking in persons, including sex trafficking. Created the T visa, to give interim relief for victims of trafficking, and the U visa, for foreign-born victims of certain crimes. Regulations for the U visa were not released, so applicants could not yet receive it.

**2005** **VAWA:** Reauthorized.

**2005** **International Marriage Broker Regulation Act (IMBRA):** Screens individuals who petition to bring a noncitizen to the United States for marriage, to prevent domestic violence and abuse. Contained within VAWA reauthorization.

**2007** **Regulations for the U Visa for Victims of Crime:** Released, giving applicants access to this visa.

**2008** **William Wilberforce Trafficking Victims Protection Reauthorization Act (TVPRA):** Strengthened the State Department's international role and further protected victims.

**2009** **Asylum:** Recommended for Rodi Alvarado, who escaped intimate partner violence.

**2009** **Widow's Penalty:** Abolished.

# Notes

NOTES TO CHAPTER 1

1. UNFPA, *State of World Population 2006: A Passage to Hope*, p. 3.

2. Suhl, *Ernestine L. Rose.*

3. Segura and Zavella, introduction to *Women and Migration in the U.S.-Mexico Borderlands*, ed. Segura and Zavella, p. 11. The authors make the same charge against the media.

4. Website introduction to UNFPA, *State of World Population 2006: A Passage to Hope*, http://www.unfpa.org/public/publications/pid/379.

5. DeLaet, "Introduction: The Invisibility of Women in Scholarship on International Migration."

6. U.S. Department of Homeland Security, "Table 8: Persons Obtaining Legal Permanent Resident Status by Gender, Age, Marital Status, and Occupation."

7. U.S. Census Bureau, American Community Survey 2008.

8. UNFPA, *State of World Population 2006: A Passage to Hope*, p. 21.

9. Ibid.

10. Geertz, *Local Knowledge.*

11. UNFPA, *State of World Population 2006: A Passage to Hope*, p. 2.

12. Parreñas, *The Force of Domesticity*, p. 2.

13. See Donato et al., "A Glass Half Full?"; Lipszyc, "The Feminization of Migration"; United Nations Commission on Population and Development, "Feminization of Migration, Remittances, Migrants' Rights"; and Yinger, "The Feminization of Migration."

14. This is not to ignore the fact that a growing scholarship base has been coming into existence on gender and migration across disciplines; a bibliography of this literature fills 339 pages in Donna R. Gabaccia's *Immigrant Women in the United States: A Selectively Annotated Multidisciplinary Bibliography* and 499 pages in Eleanore O. Hofstetter's book *Women in Global Migration, 1945–2000,* and such literature has expanded further since these books' publication. Much of this valuable literature consists of targeted case studies of particular ethnicities, topics, or localities, however, or comparisons between specific groups and locations, rather than fuller national portraits of current trends or analyses of immigrant women as active agents in history. Among the growing studies on this subject are Yen Le Espiritu's *Home Bound: Filipino American Lives across Cultures, Communities, and Countries,* Donna Gabaccia's *From the Other Side: Women, Gender, and Immigrant Life in the U.S., 1820–1990,* Miriam Ching Yoon Louie's *Sweatshop Warriors: Immigrant Women Workers Take on the Global Factory,* Denise A. Segura and Patricia Zavella's edited volume *Women and Migration in the U.S.-Mexico Borderlands,* Pierrette Hondagneu-Sotelo's

*Gendered Transitions: Mexican Experiences of Immigration,* and Evangelia Tastsoglou and Alexandra Dobrowolsky's *Women, Migration and Citizenship,* describing women's immigration to Canada. The anthology *Domestic Violence at the Margins: Readings on Race, Class, Gender, and Culture,* edited by Natalie J. Sokoloff with Christina Pratt, maps out how social locations such as nativity and race affect the experience of domestic violence. Martha Gardner has produced a rich, detailed history of immigrant women and immigration policy in the United States, entitled *The Qualities of a Citizen: Women, Immigration, and Citizenship, 1870–1965.* We are positioning *Immigration and Women* as a contribution to this expanding literature, with forays into topic areas that have not been fully explored to date, such as immigrant women in the arts, in atypical occupations for women, and in business ownership.

15. Morokvašic, "Birds of Passage Are Also Women," p. 886. See also Pedraza, "Women and Migration."

16. Following an October 2008 conference on immigration in Washington, DC, a scholar stood and observed to the crowd, "We have talked about immigration all day as if it isn't gendered. What about the women?"

17. United Nations, Department of Economic and Social Affairs, "2004 World Survey on the Role of Women in Development," p. 1.

18. Demos, "Marriage, Dowry, and Women's Early Twentieth-Century Migration from Greece."

19. Hess and Ferree, *Analyzing Gender.*

20. See, for example, Kimmel and Messner, *Men's Lives.*

21. The term "natural attitude" is taken from the phenomenological philosophy of Edward Husserl and Alfred Schutz. Schutz describes this as the "world-given-to-me-as-being-there." See Schutz, *The Phenomenology of the Social World.*

22. Names in italics are pseudonyms.

23. In 2008, native-born children on a Prince William County, Virginia, playground were repeating the following rhyme: "I don't want to go to Mexico no more. . . . There's a big, fat guy at the door. . . . If you open it up, he'll [urinate] on the floor." See Mack, "Pr. William's Mothers of Dissension," p. A01.

24. Lindsley, "Gendered Assaults."

25. Collins, *Black Feminist Thought,* p. 78.

26. Koser, *International Migration,* p. 10.

27. Sassen, "Global Cities and Survival Circuits," 256.

28. Crenshaw, "Mapping the Margins."

29. Erez, Adelman, and Gregory, "Intersections of Immigration and Domestic Violence," p. 33.

30. Collins, *Black Feminist Thought.*

31. Hulko, "The Time- and Context-Contingent Nature of Intersectionality and Interlocking Oppressions."

32. Touraine, *Return of the Actor.*

33. Weber, *The Theory of Social and Economic Organization.*

34. Wieviorka, "Sociology on the Move."

35. Segura and Zavella, introduction to *Women and Migration in the U.S.-Mexico Borderlands,* p. 3.

36. Ehrenreich and Hochschild, introduction to *Global Woman,* p. 13.

37. Emirbayer and Mische, "What Is Agency?"

38. Giddens, *The Constitution of Society*.

39. Habermas, *The Theory of Communicative Action*, vol. 2.

40. Marx, "The Eighteenth Brumaire of Louis Bonaparte," p. 112.

41. Bourdieu, *Outline of a Theory of Practice*.

42. There were varying numbers of interviews across these cities.

43. Glaser and Strauss, *The Discovery of Grounded Theory*.

44. Charmaz, "Grounded Theory."

45. Van Maanen, *Tales of the Field*, p. 101; Clough, *The End(s) of Ethnography*, p. 65.

46. Smith, *Institutional Ethnography*, p. 24.

47. Holliday, *Doing and Writing Qualitative Research*, p. 19.

48. There were a handful of exceptions. For example, due to a miscommunication, one interview was halfway through before it became clear that the interviewee had been younger than eighteen when she immigrated.

49. See Fuentes, *Eat First*.

50. Weber, *The Sociology of Religion*, p. 405.

51. Reed, "Justifying Sociological Knowledge," p. 118.

52. Prengaman, "Day-Laborer Study Finds Community Ties."

53. Donna Gabaccia, personal correspondence, 2005.

NOTES TO CHAPTER 2

1. Blackstone, *Commentaries on the Laws of England*, p. 442.

2. Campion, *Ann the Word*.

3. McCunn, *Thousand Pieces of Gold*; McCunn, "Reclaiming Polly Bemis."

4. Portes and Rumbaut, *Immigrant America*, pp. 92–96, 201–4.

5. Reitz, "Host Societies and the Reception of Immigrants," p. 1006.

6. Tilly, *Big Structures, Large Processes*.

7. International Organization for Migration, *World Migration Report 2005*, p. 110.

8. Parreñas, *The Force of Domesticity*, p. 2.

9. Ibid.

10. UNIFEM, "Who Answers to Women?" p. 55.

11. Appadurai, "Disjuncture and Difference in the Global Culture Economy."

12. Yinger, "The Feminization of Migration."

13. For a description of critical transnationalism, see Le Espiritu, *Home Bound*, pp. 3–6.

14. Scelfo, "Trickledown Downsizing."

15. UNIFEM, "Who Answers to Women?"

16. Gardner, *The Qualities of a Citizen*, p. 4.

17. Ibid., p. 15.

18. Ibid., p. 17.

19. "Suffrage from a Mother's Standpoint." Thank you to Julie Stocks for locating this information.

20. Gardner, *The Qualities of a Citizen*, p. 14.

21. Ibid., pp. 29–30.

22. Ibid., p. 139.

23. Ibid., p. 146.

24. U.S. Department of Agriculture, "Food Stamp Policy on Immigrants."

25. Daniels, *Guarding the Golden Door,* p. 236. See also A. Zolberg, *A Nation by Design,* on the changes in immigration law at local and state levels.

26. Hobbs and Stoops, "Demographic Trends in the 20th Century," p. 78.

27. Federal Interagency Forum on Child and Family Statistics, "America's Children."

28. Hirschkorn, "New York Reduces 9/11 Death Toll by 40"; Griswold, "Panel Discussion on Immigration and Border Security."

29. "Record-Breaking Number of Women Will Serve in the 111th Congress."

30. National Coalition against Domestic Violence, "Domestic Violence Facts."

31. Daniels, *Guarding the Golden Door,* p. 240.

32. Ibid., p. 63.

33. Gibson and Lennon, "Historical Census Statistics on the Foreign-Born Population of the United States."

34. U.S. Department of Homeland Security, "Table 8: Persons Obtaining Legal Permanent Resident Status by Gender, Age, Marital Status, and Occupation." Note that the data are aggregated into age categories, so we are using the numbers for ages twenty and above to indicate adults.

35. For comparative data from 1820 through 1979, see Gabaccia, *From the Other Side,* p. 28.

36. Jacoby, "Immigrant Women."

37. Eissa, "Diversity and Transformation."

38. U.S. Census Bureau, U.S. Decennial Census 1940–2000.

39. Choy, *Empire of Care.*

40. Ibid., pp. 61–93.

41. The data from 2008 in this section were taken from the Integrated Public Use Microdata Series, authored by Steven Ruggles et al. It was analyzed with the IPUMS Online Data Analysis System. In order to select the cases of women who immigrated as adults, we created a variable by subtracting the individuals' years in the United States from their age and took all values of eighteen and above.

42. U.S. Census Bureau, American Community Survey 2008.

43. Foner, *In a New Land,* pp. 158–59.

44. Ibid.

45. Passel, "Estimates of the Size and Characteristics of the Undocumented Population."

46. We have chosen not to do a full examination of the data at this level, however, for several reasons. One has to do with agency and intersections, in fact: in the 2000 decennial census many individuals of Latino descent chose their own approaches to answering census questions about their race. Some boycotted the question altogether; others refused to check the choice "Hispanic," because they do not identify with that label, for example, if they have strong roots in an indigenous group in Latin America.

47. UNESCO, "Global Education Digest 2009," p. 15.

48. Ibid., p. 43.

49. Safa, "The Differential Incorporation of Hispanic Women Migrants into the United States Labor Force," p. 240.

50. See Chambers, *A Woman Alone.*

51. See Zakrzewska and Victor, eds., *Woman's Quest.*

52. U.S.-born women saw a steeper rise—from 48 percent in 1960 to 79 percent in 1990. See Kritz and Gurak, "Immigration and a Changing America."

53. Foner, *In a New Land*, p. 95.

54. Gabaccia, "Immigrant Women."

55. Weatherford, *Foreign and Female*, p. 224.

56. Ibid., p. 223.


NOTES TO CHAPTER 3

1. Piper, "Gendering the Politics of Migration," p. 142.

2. U.S. Department of Homeland Security, "Table 9: Persons Obtaining Legal Permanent Resident Status by Broad Class of Admission and Selected Demographic Characteristics."

3. Ibid.

4. Morrison, "Attracting New Americans into Baltimore's Neighborhoods."

5. It is important to note that such a motivation has a class basis. Knowing English would likely be more useful in middle- and upper-class jobs in the home country, and the family's ability to financially afford sending a child to the United States to study is also related to class.

6. Countless numbers of individuals enter the United States from war-torn or politically repressive environments seeking to receive asylum based on their fear of persecution because of their race, religion, nationality, membership of a particular social group, or political opinion—the same categories for which refugee status is granted. The difference is that refugees have been approved to migrate after, for example, living in refugee camps, whereas asylum seekers arrive without prior approval, often because they had to make a hasty escape. And although international human rights treaties state that asylum seekers have the right to move to pursue their own safety, they must petition the courts in the receiving country for asylum status. The women we talked to generally came as refugees, although in a few cases they came under other types of visas and later gained asylum.

7. Beyani, "The Needs of Refugee Women," p. 29.

8. Lee, "A Theory of Migration," p. 51.

9. U.S. Department of Homeland Security, "Table 9: Persons Obtaining Legal Permanent Resident Status by Broad Class of Admission and Selected Demographic Characteristics."

10. Avci, "Immigrant Categories," p. 203.

11. Donato and Tyree, "Family Reunification, Health Professionals, and the Sex Composition of Immigrants to the United States," p. 226.

12. Donato, "Current Trends and Patterns in Female Migration," p. 751.

13. Fine, "Current Approaches to Understanding Family Diversity," p. 235.

14. United Nations, Department of Economic and Social Affairs, Population Division, *International Migration Policies*, p. 13.

15. Gillespie, "Beyond the Family Way."

16. Zlotnik, "Migration and the Family," p. 264.

17. Martin, "Family-Based U.S. Immigration," p. 4.

18. United Nations High Commission on Refugees, *Convention and Protocol Relating to the Status of Refugees*, p. 16.

19. Kumin, "Gender: Persecution in the Spotlight," p. 12.

20. Ibid.

21. Oswin, "Rights Spaces," p. 350.

22. Beyani, "The Needs of Refugee Women," p. 31.

23. Schaffer, "Domestic Violence and Asylum in the United States."

24. Preston, "U.S. May Be Open to Asylum for Spouse Abuse."

25. Oswin, "Rights Spaces," p. 351.

26. Ibid., p. 348.

27. Ibid., p. 352.

## NOTES TO CHAPTER 4

1. Passel and Cohn, "Unauthorized Immigration."

2. The research also includes ongoing discussions with these activists and engaged professionals; interviews with six professionals conducted specifically for this book; one courtroom observation; and attendance/participation in conferences, grassroots activist meetings, state assembly hearings, and other related meetings.

3. Passel and Cohn, "Trends in Unauthorized Immigration."

4. Passel, "The Size and Characteristics of the Unauthorized Migrant Population in the U.S.," p. 6.

5. Passel and Cohn, "Trends in Unauthorized Immigration."

6. Passel and Cohn, "A Portrait of Unauthorized Immigrants in the United States," p. i.

7. Ibid., pp. 13–14.

8. Passel, "The Size and Characteristics of the Unauthorized Migrant Population in the U.S.," p. 12.

9. Ibid., p. 13.

10. U.S. Department of State, "Distinctions between Human Trafficking and Human Smuggling."

11. "Women's Council Created." This news source reported, "In 2008, nearly 10 percent of women in Immigrations and Customs Enforcement facilities were pregnant, often as a result of rape, the Texas Observer reported Feb. 20. . . . But the women held in ICE facilities are not offered the option of obtaining an abortion because the agency insists on keeping them on standby status and ready to deport at any moment."

12. Southern Poverty Law Center, "Under Siege."

13. Maril, *The Fence.*

14. Gabaccia, "Send Me Your Rich and Talented."

15. Ensor, "Displaced Once Again," p. 294.

16. Massey, Durand, and Malone, *Beyond Smoke and Mirrors.*

17. Hondagneu-Sotelo, "Review Essay: *Beyond Smoke and Mirrors.*"

18. Hill, *The Guest Worker.*

19. Seelye, "U.S. Strikes at Smuggling Ring That Exploited Foreign Nurses."

20. Susan Pearce interviewed these individuals in their Los Angeles office, which has since closed, although the national organization, Polaris, continues to exist.

21. U.S. Department of State, "Victims of Trafficking and Violence Protection Act of 2000."

22. The same point goes for guns but in a different sense: once a gun is sold, the new owner can also sell it only once; in the case of prostitution, a pimp (the "new owner") can use the woman as a commodity multiple times and "sell" her to someone else when he deems her to be no longer as lucrative.

23. See U.S. Department of State, "Distinctions between Human Trafficking and Human Smuggling"; and Gozdziak and Collett, "Research on Human Trafficking in North America."

24. Protection Project, "The Protection Project's Review of the U.S. Department of State Office to Monitor and Protect Trafficking in Persons," p. 25.

25. Hughes, "The Natasha Trade."

26. Humantrafficking.org, "News and Updates."

27. Office of the Texas Attorney General, "The Texas Response to Human Trafficking."

28. Human Rights Center, "Hidden Slaves," p. 10.

29. McDonnell and White, "Sweatshop Workers to Get $2 Million."

30. May, "Diary of a Sex Slave," parts 1, 2, 3, and 4.

31. U.S. Department of Justice, Northern District of California, "San Francisco Brothel Owner Sentenced to One Year in Prison for Money Laundering."

32. O'Shaughnessy, "Long Island Case Turns Spotlight on Hundreds Trapped as Slaves"; Asian American Legal Defense and Education Fund, "Indonesian Domestic Workers Sue Convicted Traffickers in Long Island Slavery Case."

33. Coalition Against Trafficking in Women, "Sex Trafficking of Women in the United States," p. 8.

34. Scholes and Phataralacha, "Appendix A." These estimates, though a few years old now, are the ones that researchers and advocates continue to cite; we are not aware of an update.

35. U.S. Senate Committee on Foreign Relations, testimony of Michelle A. Clark.

36. Semple, "Senate Measure Gives Rights to Widows of Citizens."

37. "These Are Military Families, Too"; "Wife of Missing G.I. Gets Her Green Card"; "Remains of Jimenez, Fouty Buried Together." In 2009, the U.S. military began offering paths to citizenship for foreign-born individuals who were in the United States on temporary visas, as a recruiting strategy for the wars in Iraq and Afghanistan. See Preston, "U.S. Military Will Offer Path to Citizenship."

38. If a foreign-born individual marries a U.S. citizen, she or he is given conditional permanent resident status for two years to ensure that the marriage is not a fraudulent or "green card" marriage and, following this waiting period, can adjust to a green card. Rules vary depending on whether the marriage took place abroad or in the United States but not depending on whether it was a mail-order or other type of arrangement.

39. Women in Prison Project, "Immigration and the Criminal Justice System Fact Sheet."

40. In December 2006, the U.S. Supreme Court, in an eight-to-one decision, ruled that a noncitizen is *not required* to be deported for a drug crime that is a misdemeanor under federal law but is a felony in the state where the immigrant was tried. See L. Greenhouse, "Court Rejects Interpretation of Immigration Drug Law." This clarification still does not necessarily protect an immigrant from getting deported for such a crime.

41. Kolodner, "Private Prisons Expect a Boom"; GEO Group, "The GEO Group Announces the Opening of a 192-Bed Expansion"; "GEO Stock."

42. GEO Group, "The GEO Group Announces the Opening of a 192-Bed Expansion."

43. L. Greenhouse, "Court Rejects Interpretation of Immigration Drug Law." There are certainly foreign-born women within the criminal justice system who have violated criminal law. Women are often used as "drug mules," for example, to smuggle drugs

into the country for suppliers and dealers. Even if they succeed without getting caught, however, they do not profit at anywhere near the same scale—if they profit at all—as those who have "hired" their services.

44. Detention Watch Network, "About the U.S. Detention and Deportation System."

45. Ibid.

46. National Immigrant Justice Center, "The Situation of Immigrant Women Detained in the United States."

47. Palevsky, "Sheriff Joe Arpaio Separates Mother from Children, Immigrant Crack Down."

48. Dow, *American Gulag,* ix–xiii.

49. Siskind Susser Immigration Lawyers, "Allegations of Sexual Abuse at Krome Detention Center."

50. National Immigrant Justice Center, "The Situation of Immigrant Women Detained in the United States."

51. Lutheran Immigration and Refugee Service and the Women's Commission for Refugee Women and Children, "Locking Up Family Values," p. 2.

52. Southwest Institute for Research on Women, "Unseen Prisoners."

53. Thompson, "Some Immigrants Who Lose Freedom Face Loss of Custody."

54. Bernstein, "Rhode Island."

55. Moreno, "Immigrant Raids Often Mark Start of Years of Limbo."

56. Nizza, "Estimate for Deporting Illegal Immigrants."

57. Ibid.

58. Olivo, "Immigration Agency's Airline Flies Tens of Thousands of Deportees Out of U.S."

59. Falcone, "100,000 Parents of Citizens Were Deported over 10 Years."

60. Sontag, "Immigrants Facing Deportation by U.S. Hospitals."

61. Maza, "For Haitian Immigrants, Hurricanes Complicate Deportation Cases."

62. Those states are Alaska, Arizona, Arkansas, California, Colorado, Connecticut, Delaware, Florida, Georgia, Hawaii, Idaho, Illinois, Indiana, Iowa Kansas, Kentucky, Louisiana, Maryland, Michigan, Minnesota, Mississippi, Missouri, Montana, Nebraska, Nevada, New York, North Carolina, Oregon, Pennsylvania, Rhode Island, South Carolina, Texas, and Washington. See Center for Women Policy Studies, "U.S. Policy Advocacy to Combat Trafficking."

63. Break the Chain Campaign.

64. Polaris Project, "About Polaris Project."

65. Protection Project, "The Protection Project's Review of the U.S. Department of State Office to Monitor and Protect Trafficking in Persons," p. 25.

66. Parreñas, *The Force of Domesticity,* p. 159.

67. Ibid., pp. 136–37.

68. Cavalieri, "Between Victim and Agent," p. 17n. 71.

69. Dinnerstein, "The 'New' and Exciting U."

70. Orlandi. "Deported Mother Sends Her Child to U.S. Protests."

71. Pomareda, "Chicago Immigration Activist Marks Year in Church."

72. Foucault, *Power/Knowledge.*

73. Writing in the context of World War II, Arendt lamented the replacement of the term *stateless* with *displaced persons,* as the latter presumed that the displaced still had

a state/nation to which they belonged and could return. In reality, many (particularly Jews) lacked protection from any state. See Arendt, *The Origins of Totalitarianism*, p. 279.

NOTES TO CHAPTER 5

1. Human Rights Watch, "Swept under the Rug."
2. Elder and Schmidt, "Global Employment Trends for Women," p. 11.
3. Ehrenreich and Hochschild, in *Global Woman*, use the phrase "global care chains" to describe transnational migration of women to provide caregiving jobs.
4. U.S. Census Bureau, U.S. Decennial Census 1940–2000.
5. Gammage, "Women Immigrants in the U.S. Labor Market."
6. ACLU, "Trapped in the Home."
7. It is notable that data on migrant women domestic workers are not readily available and not a priority in data collection.
8. Piper, "Gendering the Politics of Migration," p. 144.
9. Hondagneu-Sotelo, *Doméstica*; Glenn, "From Servitude to Service Work." The term "social reproduction" has been used by feminist scholars to refer to an "array of activities and relationships involved in maintaining people both on a daily basis and intergenerationally" (Glenn, "From Servitude to Service Work," p. 1). Feminist scholars have used this concept to refer to "reproductive labor in the analysis of domestic service." Glenn notes simultaneous race and gender construction of reproductive labor in the United States and points to an aspect that has been ignored, that of the "racial division of reproductive labor." The discussion in this chapter contextualizes reproductive labor in domestic service on multiple nodes such as ethnicity, immigrant status, class, skills, and labor and immigration policies, in addition to race and gender, making for a more complex picture of intersectionality.
10. Katzman, *Seven Days a Week*, p. 53, table 2-2.
11. Ibid., pp. 64–65, and p. 71, table 2-10.
12. However, the decline of European immigration was just one of many reasons for this migration.
13. Katzman, *Seven Days a Week*, p. 72, table 2-7.
14. Clark-Lewis, "This Work Had an End," p. 198.
15. Katzman, *Seven Days a Week*, p. 7.
16. Ibid., p. 55. Chinese menservants also became a part of this workforce for a short period of time in California and Washington State.
17. Hondagneu-Sotelo, *Doméstica*, p. 83n. 65. In 1920, Mexican immigrants accounted for 75 percent of domestics in El Paso, and in 1930, Mexicans were 45 percent of all employed domestics in the Southwest.
18. Romero, *Maid in the USA*, p. 86n. 84.
19. Hondagneu-Sotelo, *Doméstica*, p. 16n. 35.
20. Domestic Workers United and DataCenter, "Home Is Where the Work Is."
21. Ibid.
22. Ibid., p. 4.
23. Capps et al., "A Profile of the Low-Wage Immigrant Workforce"; Sum et al., "New Immigrants in the Labor Force."

24. De la Luz Ibarra, "Mexican Immigrant Women and the New Domestic Labor," p. 456.

25. Hondagneu-Sotelo, *Doméstica*, p. x.

26. *Bettina, Stella, Rashmi, Malathi,* and *Meenu.*

27. *Majida, Khursheeda, Stella, Rosita,* and *Gracia.*

28. *Sarla, Kiran,* and *Nina.*

29. Ingrid. Reports indicate that domestic service is one of the common activities associated with trafficking of children and women. But primary or statistical data on this aspect are scant. See Human Rights Watch, "Hidden in the Home"; Human Rights Center, "Hidden Slaves."

30. A large body of literature talks about the informal sector and women's induction and participation in it as part of globalizing economies. See Sassen, "Global Cities and Survival Circuits."

31. Hondagneu-Sotelo, *Doméstica,* p. x.

32. These are special temporary visas for individuals, usually women, to work as live-in domestic workers: A-3 visas if hired by diplomats, G-5 visas for domestic workers/personal employees hired by officials of international organizations such as the World Bank and International Monetary Fund (U.S. Department of State, "Diplomats and Foreign Government Officials"), and B-1 visas if the employee works for people with nonimmigrant status in the United States or for U.S. citizens who are residing abroad but who are visiting the United States or for employers assigned to the United States for no more than four years. See Human Rights Watch, "Hidden in the Home."

33. "Agency" here implies the nongovernmental organization that provided support to her and of which she is a member.

34. The student spouse visa category (F2) does not allow the visa holder to be legally employed in the country; domestic service, as *Kiran* reported, is one the accessible ways for female spouses of international students to sustain the family.

35. The later sections of this chapter provide details.

36. The personalistic or informal aspects have contradictory effects, as some aspects may be beneficial for women workers, for instance, no requirement of any specific training or skills, flexibility around personal needs or schedules, and personal relations with the employing family. However, this informality is more advantageous to the employer than to the domestics.

37. Regarding the different aspects of the relationship between a female employer and employee, see especially Rollins, *Between Women,* and her concept of "maternalism."

38. For example, see Hondagneu-Sotelo, *Doméstica*; Rollins, *Between Women*; and Human Rights Watch, "Hidden in the Home."

39. Human Rights Watch, "Hidden in the Home."

40. Domestic Workers United and DataCenter, "Home Is Where the Work Is," pp. 2, 6.

41. DataCenter, "Behind Closed Doors," p. 4. This report is based on a survey in the San Francisco Bay Area, administered by thirty trained immigrant women from 240 surveys from their peers.

42. National Employment Law Project, "Immigrant Status and Your Rights as a Worker."

43. Center for Humane Immigrant Rights of Los Angeles.

44. "Didi" is a kin term in the Hindi language for an older sister.

45. Domestic Workers United and DataCenter, "Home Is Where the Work Is."

46. See Childress, *Like One of the Family*; Romero, *Maid in the USA*; and Rollins, *Between Women,* among other literature on domestic service, especially ethnographic works focusing on live-in work.

47. Other conditions of such employment include various forms of emotional, physical, or psychological abuse, sexual abuse, and lack of privacy, such as employers' monitoring of the worker's mail and phone conversations and accessing the worker's personal belongings. Employers also place limits on the personal and social life of workers, which adds to the confinement and isolation that the workers encounter as a result of living in the employers' household. Some employers are known to withhold passports, to limit the workers' right to communicate with others or to leave the confines of the employer's home, and to deny food and health care or treatment. See Human Rights Watch, "Hidden in the Home."

48. Ibid.

49. Zarembka, "America's Dirty Work."

50. Romero, *Maid in the USA*, p. 161.

51. Hondagneu-Sotelo, *Doméstica*, p. 24.

52. For instance, Andolan, Domestic Workers United, and Damayan in New York and CHIRLA in Los Angeles.

53. The women interviewed belonged to organizations such as Andolan, Domestic Workers United, and Adhikar in New York and New Jersey and CHIRLA and Pilipino Workers' Centre in Los Angeles.

54. *Priscilla*; also see Gonzales and Smith, "Celebrate Human Rights Day by Honoring the Human Rights of Domestic Workers."

55. Sum et al., "New Immigrants in the Labor Force."

56. As mentioned earlier, A-3, G-5, and B-1 visas; a description of these can be found in Human Rights Watch, "Hidden in the Home."

57. The underreporting of this work by both employers and employees has been widely reported in the United States. See Pisani and Yoskowitz, "The Maid Trade"; Ehrenreich, *Nickel and Dimed.*

58. Major dailies cover these stories regularly now; for example, see Sun, "'Modern-Day Slavery' Prompts Rescue Efforts"; Vitello, "From Stand in Long Island Slavery Case."

59. See Feminist Majority Foundation, "Government Accountability Office Releases Domestic Worker Abuse Report." This report recommends that "records on alleged abuse be maintained by the Secretary of State, that consular officers seek guidance before issuing A-3 or G-5 visas to those applying to work with diplomats that are suspected of abusing workers, and that compliance with the terms of A-3 or G-5 visas be spot-checked."

60. However, as Hondagneu-Sotelo remarks, "we must distinguish between regulation of labor and regulation of foreign domestic workers." *Doméstica*, p. 21.

61. AFL-CIO, "National Alliance of Domestic Workers Formed at Social Forum."

62. Global Rights, "Global Rights Urges UN Human Rights Committee."

63. Chang, *Disposable Domestics*; Bakan and Stasiulis, "Foreign Domestic Workers Policy in Canada."

64. Chang, *Disposable Domestics.*

65. Bridget Anderson, *Doing the Dirty Work?*

66. Hondagneu-Sotelo, *Doméstica*, pp. xiii, 22.

1. Carnegie Endowment for International Peace, "Immigrant Entrepreneurs."

2. Fairlie, "Self-Employment Rates by Immigrant Status."

3. Aguilar, "Women's Participation in Microfinance."

4. Apitzsch and Kontos, "Self-Employment, Gender and Migration," p. 68.

5. Coughlin and Thomas, *The Rise of Women Entrepreneurs.*

6. Howe, "Immigration as a Factor in Nineteenth-Century Women's Employment in West Virginia Cities," p. 18.

7. According to the 2008 American Community Survey, the top states where foreign-born entrepreneurial women work are, in order starting with the highest number, California, New York, Florida, Texas, Illinois, New Jersey, Virginia, Georgia, Arizona, and Washington. The top-ten metropolitan areas are Los Angeles, New York, Washington, DC, Chicago, Houston, San Francisco, Orange County, CA, San Diego, Atlanta, and Dallas.

8. The national profile of immigrant women business owners is based on data from the U.S. Census Bureau and other sources. The data in the U.S. Census Bureau report are confined to business owners who are employed at least fifteen hours per week and fourteen weeks per year, which eliminates entrepreneurs in the most informal and least steady businesses. Horticultural and veterinary services are included as nonagricultural industries. This selection of categories for immigrant self-employment follows the methodology of Robert W. Fairlie, associate professor of economics at University of California, Santa Cruz, with one difference: Fairlie limited the data to those who work at least twenty weeks per year. Due to the dataset used here, which placed the number of weeks worked into intervals in which twenty weeks was within an interval, rather than at its lower limit, we are using fourteen weeks as the lower limit. "Native-born" refers to U.S. citizens by birth, whether born in the United States, abroad, or at sea, and includes those born in Puerto Rico. "Immigrant" refers to both naturalized U.S. citizens and noncitizens. Immigrants are one of the most undercounted populations by the Census Bureau; therefore, actual figures may be as much as 5–10 percent higher (conversation with undercount specialist, U.S. Census Bureau, December 2004).

9. For additional statistics, see Pearce, "Today's Immigrant Woman Entrepreneur." The rates in that report vary from those presented here to some extent, due to the use of different sample sizes (1 percent was used for that report, and 5 percent for this book); that report also limited the sample to those who worked twenty weeks per year, as opposed to fourteen weeks in the current study (see note 8). Further, we confined the population in this current study to those who immigrated as adults.

10. The data from 2008 in this section were taken from Ruggles et al., "Integrated Public Use Microdata Series." It was analyzed with the IPUMS Online Data Analysis System. In order to select the cases of women who immigrated as adults, we created a variable by subtracting the individuals' years in the United States from their age and then took all values of eighteen and above. In order to calculate the rate of business ownership, we used the total number of employed individuals eighteen and older, regardless of number of hours worked per week and weeks per year. Some researchers calculate self-employment rates more narrowly, confining it to the standard working-age population, eliminating the retirement-age population. We included all cases that were age eighteen and above, given the fluidity of retirement age.

11. Center for Women's Business Research, "Minority Reports."

12. American Community Survey 2008, taken from the PUMS 5 percent sample.

13. Griffith, Contreras, and Kissam, "*Calidad y Confianza.*"

14. Parreñas, *The Force of Domesticity.*

15. Aguilar, "Women's Participation in Microfinance."

16. Bourdieu, *Distinction.*

17. See Galuszka, "Are Women Still 'Disadvantaged'?" The number of women receiving SBA assistance may be overrepresented here in relation to the national average, since it was an SBA representative who provided the contacts for those interviews. This representative, Don Mitchell, has passed away since these interviews were conducted, and we honor his spirit and contribution.

18. Min and Bozorgmehr, "USA: The Entrepreneurial Cutting Edge," p. 34.

19. Carnegie Endowment for International Peace, "Immigrant Entrepreneurs," p. 6.

20. Giddens, *The Constitution of Society*, p. 41.

21. Excerpted from National Archives, "Citizens by Choice."

22. Ibid.

23. Min and Bozorgmehr, "USA: The Entrepreneurial Cutting Edge."

24. Abrams, "Women in Venture Capital."

25. Portes and Jensen, "The Enclave and the Entrants."

26. For a summary of these theories, see Zhou, "The Role of the Enclave Economy in Immigrant Adaptation and Community Building"; see also Aldrich and Waldinger, "Ethnicity and Entrepreneurship"; and Portes and Zhou, "Self-Employment and the Earnings of Immigrants."

27. For an analysis of the economic contributions, including homeownership, see Pearce, "Today's Immigrant Woman Entrepreneur," p. 11. Homeownership has a domino effect on consumption, as the homeowner purchases furnishings, renovations, repairs, cleaning services, landscaping, and other amenities.

28. Center for Women's Business Research, "Minority Reports."

29. A reference to the report "Today's Immigrant Woman Entrepreneur," by Susan C. Pearce.


NOTES TO CHAPTER 7

1. Kahling, "U.S. Women Workers," p. 1.

2. Ibid., p. 2.

3. Ibid., p. 4.

4. Toren, "Women and Immigrants," p. 86.

5. Reskin and Padavic, "Sex, Race, and Ethnic Inequality in United States Workplaces."

6. Kahling, "U.S. Women Workers," p. 11.

7. Toren, "Women and Immigrants," p. 77.

8. Ibid.

9. U.S. Department of Labor, "Facts on Executive Order 11246."

10. Kahling, "U.S. Women Workers," p. 11.

11. Ibid., p. 13. While there are many benefits inherent in working in a gender-atypical field, the physical nature of the work brings some danger as well, to both men and women. For example, Marion Brown notes that over four thousand Latinos died from fatal workplace injuries between 1995 and 2000, with construction leading the way as the

most dangerous. In keeping with the gendered nature of such work, 94 percent of those killed were male. Brown, "Immigrant Workers," pp. 228–58.

12. Kahling, "U.S. Women Workers," p. 13.

13. Researchers have found that, for immigrants, it is not just *what* education one has that matters but also *where* that education was received. On average, those immigrants who receive their education in the host country outearn those whose education was attained in their home country. Akresh, "Occupational Trajectories of Legal U.S. Immigrants."

14. She seemed to think he was speaking quite literally, referring to artists executed during China's Cultural Revolution.

15. *Dama* is in a gender-atypical position within a gender-atypical field. That is, engineering is a male-dominated field, and a woman's being an engineering department head is even more unusual, with one study showing 90 percent of engineering department heads being male (Niemeier and González, "Breaking into the Guildmasters' Club," p. 161).

16. Toren, "Women and Immigrants," p. 80.

17. Ibid., p. 82.

18. Ibid., p. 90.

19. It is also possible that the women's emphasis on gender could be to some extent an effect of the interviewers in these cases being native women: perhaps the interviewees focused on the shared bond of gender, rather than the difference of nativity, in these discussions.

20. Erlich and Grabelsky, "Standing at a Crossroads."

21. This is not to say that such solidarity *cannot* exist. Immigrant activism has increasingly drawn on alliances among various Latino, Asian, and other groups of immigrants, and nativist groups can bring together Americans who are diverse racially. What we are arguing here instead is that we cannot *assume* that either immigrants or natives would feel solidarity among themselves solely on the basis of immigrant or native status.

22. Although unions lament the increasing tendency of employers to use nonunion— often immigrant— labor, Nissen and Grenier argue that construction-trades unions have historically been very exclusionary, to women, people of color, and immigrants (Nissen and Grenier, "Local Union Relations with Immigrants").

23. Bix, "From 'Engineeresses' to 'Girl Engineers' to 'Good Engineers.'"

24. Toren, "Women and Immigrants," p. 93.

NOTES TO CHAPTER 8

1. De Jesus, "Hands, Hickeys, and Hurly-Burly."

2. Billson, *Keepers of the Culture.*

3. Although men have also contributed profoundly to textile work, along with the other cultural arenas mentioned here, women have been particularly prominent in this arena; immigrant women's sewing skills provided an economic base for a family, for example, during the early American settlements. The history of the textile industry in the United States is simultaneously the history of immigration and the history of immigrant women's work. See Louie, *Sweatshop Warriors.*

4. Beattie, "Immigrant Art Exhibitions."

5. Miazgowicz, introduction to "In Your Face" exhibit.

6. See, for example, Bowler, "Methodological Dilemmas in the Sociology of Art"; Becker, "Art as Collective Action"; and V. Zolberg, *Constructing a Sociology of the Arts.*

7. "Hung Liu, Internationally-Acclaimed Chinese Mural Artist."

8. Said, *Orientalism.*

9. Liu, "Artist's Statement."

10. Miazgowicz, introduction to "In Your Face" exhibit.

11. McCunn, *Thousand Pieces of Gold.*

12. Giddens, *The Consequences of Modernity.*

13. Le Espiritu, *Home Bound,* p. 2.

14. Ibid., p. 10.

15. Nafisi, "Literature and History."

16. Hansberry, *A Raisin in the Sun,* p. 146.

17. Emirbayer and Mische, "What Is Agency?" p. 1012.

18. Ibid.

NOTES TO CHAPTER 9

1. This is the title of a 2007 book by Laurel Thatcher Ulrich: *Well-Behaved Women Seldom Make History.*

2. Crawford, Rouse, and Woods, *Women in the Civil Rights Movement.*

3. Penn, *Solidarity's Secret.*

4. Asher, "Dorothy Jacobs Bellanca."

5. Felder, *The 100 Most Influential Women of All Time,* p. 49.

6. Ibid., p. 48.

7. Gerth and Mills, *From Max Weber,* pp. 249–50.

8. In declaring the camp unconstitutional, U.S. District Court Judge Sterling Johnson Jr. wrote, "The Haitians' plight is a tragedy of immense proportion, and their continued detainment is totally unacceptable to this court." Quoted in Ratner, "The Legacy of Guantánamo."

9. Dow, *American Gulag.*

10. SEIU, "SEIU History."

11. Daleiden, "Suzanne Lacy's Stories of Work and Survival."

12. Empowered Women International, "Our Model: Why Art?"

13. Speaker in the artist-activist event "Suzanne Lacy's Stories of Work and Survival," June 2007, Los Angeles Museum of Contemporary Art.

14. Portes, "Bridging the Gap."

15. Irizarry, "Merging Public and Personal Histories."

16. Touraine, "The Subject Is Coming Back."

17. Cooper, "Women Raise Heat on Immigration Debate."

18. CNN.com, "2008 CNN Heroes Archive."

NOTES TO CHAPTER 10

1. Merithew, "Sister Katie," p. 84.

2. The original Colossus, in fact, was male. It was a statue of the god Helius, which also stood in a harbor and signified freedom, built around 300 BC on the island of Rhodes.

3. Tsing-yuan, "The Birth of the Goddess of Democracy." Other communities across the United States have also collectively memorialized this former Chinese effigy, a woman also holding a torch, but with Asian facial features, by reconstructing her and erecting her in public places in San Francisco, Washington, DC, and Arlington, Virginia, among others. Many people have noted the resemblance to the Statue of Liberty, although the original designers denied that it was their intended model and wanted to distance themselves from a pro-American cultural reference. They stated that the model was a sculpture by Russian socialist-realist sculptor Vera Mukhina.

4. Erez, Adelman, and Gregory, "Intersections of Immigration and Domestic Violence."

5. Gabaccia, "Immigrant Women."

6. Hondagneu-Sotelo, *Gendered Transitions.*

7. Waters, *Black Identities.*

8. Portes and Zhou, "The New Second Generation."

9. Negra, *Off-White Hollywood,* p. 4.

10. Le Espiritu, *Home Bound.*

11. Nafisi, "Literature and History."

12. See Clifford and Pearce, *Women and Current Immigration Policies*; and Sokoloff and Pearce, "Locking Up Hope."

13. Sassen, *Cities in a World Economy.*

14. Baldaccini, "Refugee Protection in Europe."

15. For an excellent overview of this question, see Boyd, "Gender, Refugee Status, and Permanent Settlement."

16. Ehrenreich and Hochschild, introduction to *Global Woman,* p. 7.

17. Sassen, "The U.S. at a Time of Global Conflict."

18. "Global Democracy: Civil Society Visions and Strategies (GO5)."

19. Swidler, "Culture in Action."

20. Murray and Giovagnoli, "DHS Progress Report," pp. 5–6.

# Bibliography

Abrams, Erin. 2008. "Women in Venture Capital." *The Glass Hammer,* April 14. Retrieved September 17, 2009, from http://www.theglasshammer.com/news/2008/08/14/women-in-venture-capital/.

ACLU. 2007a. "Modern Enslavement of Migrant Domestic Workers by Foreign Diplomats in the United States." Retrieved October 29, 2009, from http://www.aclu.org/womensrights/employ/domesticworkers.html.

———. 2007b. "Statement to the House Foreign Affairs Committee Hearing on 'International Trafficking in Persons: Taking Action to Eliminate Modern-Day Slavery.'" Retrieved June 7, 2009, from http://www.aclu.org/womensrights/employ/32786leg20071018.html.

———. 2007c. "Trafficking and Exploitation of Migrant Domestic Workers by Diplomats and Staff of International Organizations in the United States." Retrieved June 7, 2009, from http://www.aclu.org/womensrights/humanrights/28034res20070117.html.

———. 2007d. "Trapped in the Home: Global Trafficking and Exploitation of Migrant Domestic Workers." Retrieved June 7, 2009, from http://www.aclu.org/womensrights/humanrights/28031res20070117.html.

AFL-CIO. 2007. "National Alliance of Domestic Workers Formed at Social Forum." Retrieved June 7, 2009, from http://blog.aflcio.org/2007/07/09/national-alliance-of-domestic-workers-formed-at-social-forum/.

Aguilar, Verónica González. 1999. "Women's Participation in Microfinance." Retrieved September 7, 2010, from http://www.globenet.org/archives/web/2006/www.globenet.org/horizon-local/ada/9905women.html.

Akresh, Ilana Redstone. 2008. "Occupational Trajectories of Legal U.S. Immigrants: Downgrading and Recovery." *Population and Development Review* 34:435–56.

Aldrich, Howard, and Roger Waldinger. 1990. "Ethnicity and Entrepreneurship." *Annual Review of Sociology* 16:111–35.

Andersen, Margaret L. 2005. "Thinking about Women: A Quarter Century's View." *Gender and Society* 19:437–55.

Anderson, Benedict. 1983. *Imagined Communities: Reflections on the Origin and Spread of Nationalism.* New York: Verso.

Anderson, Bridget. 2000. *Doing the Dirty Work? Global Politics of Domestic Labour.* London: Zed Books.

Apitzsch, Ursula, and Maria Kontos. 2003. "Self-Employment, Gender and Migration." *International Review of Sociology/Revue Internationale de Sociologie* 13:67–76.

Appadurai, Arjun. 1990. "Disjuncture and Difference in the Global Culture Economy." *Theory, Culture, and Society* 7:295–310.

Arendt, Hannah. 1951. *The Origins of Totalitarianism.* New York: Harcourt, Brace.

Asher, Nina. 1984. "Dorothy Jacobs Bellanca: Women Clothing Workers and Runaway Shops." Pp. 195–226 in *A Needle, a Bobbin, a Strike,* edited by Joan M. Jensen and Sue Davidson. Philadelphia: Temple University Press.

Asian American Legal Defense and Education Fund. 2008. "Indonesian Domestic Workers Sue Convicted Traffickers in Long Island Slavery Case." Press release, July 22. Retrieved February 3, 2009, from http://www.aaldef.org/article.php?article_id=373.

Avci, Gamze. 1999. "Immigrant Categories: The Many Sides of One Coin?" *European Journal of Migration and Law* 1 (2): 199–213.

Bakan, Abigail, and Daiva Stasiulis. 1997. "Foreign Domestic Worker Policy in Canada and the Social Boundaries of Modern Citizenship." Pp. 29–52 in *Not One of the Family: Foreign Domestic Workers in Canada,* edited by Abigail Bakan and Daiva Stasiulis. Toronto: University of Toronto Press.

Baldaccini, Anneliese. 2004. "Refugee Protection in Europe—Reconciling Asylum with Human Rights." *JUSTICE Journal* 1:117–28.

Beattie, Rich. 2006. "Immigrant Art Exhibitions: Insights of Passage," *New York Times,* May 19.

Becker, Howard S. 1974. "Art as Collective Action." *American Sociological Review* 39:767–76.

Bernstein, Nina. 2009. "Rhode Island: Suit over Detainee Death." *New York Times,* February 9. Retrieved February 10, 2009, from http://www.nytimes.com/2009/02/10/us/10brfs-SUITOVERDETA_BRF.html?scp=1&sq=chinese%20immigrant%20Rhode%20Island%20detention&st=cse.

Beyani, Chaloka. 1995. "The Needs of Refugee Women: A Human-Rights Perspective." *Gender and Development* 3:29–35.

Billson, Janet Mancini. 1995. *Keepers of the Culture: The Power of Tradition in Women's Lives.* New York: Lexington Books.

Bix, Amy Sue. 2004. "From 'Engineeresses' to 'Girl Engineers' to 'Good Engineers': A History of Women's U.S. Engineering Education." *NWSA Journal* 16:27–49.

Blackstone, William. 1765. *Commentaries on the Laws of England.* Vol. 1. Oxford, UK: Clarendon.

Bloemraad, Irene. 2006. *Becoming a Citizen: Incorporating Immigrants and Refugees in the United States and Canada.* Berkeley: University of California Press.

Bourdieu, Pierre. 1987. *Distinction: A Social Critique of the Judgement of Taste.* Translated by Richard Nice. Cambridge, MA: Harvard University Press.

———. 1977. *Outline of a Theory of Practice.* Translated by Richard Nice. Cambridge: Cambridge University Press.

Bowler, Anne. 1994. "Methodological Dilemmas in the Sociology of Art." Pp. 247–66 in *The Sociology of Culture,* edited by Diana Crane. Oxford, UK: Blackwell.

Boyd, Monica. 2001. "Gender, Refugee Status, and Permanent Settlement." Pp. 103–23 in *Immigrant Women,* edited by Rita James Simon. New Brunswick, NJ: Transaction.

Break the Chain Campaign. n.d. Retrieved September 7, 2010, from http://www.breakthe-chaincampaigndc.org/.

Brown, Marianne P. 2006. "Immigrant Workers: Do They Fear Workplace Injuries More Than They Fear Their Employers?" Pp. 228–58 in *Gender, Race, Class, and Health: Intersectional Approaches,* edited by Amy Schulz and Leith Mullings. San Francisco: Jossey-Bass.

Campion, Nardi R. 1976. *Ann the Word: The Life of Mother Ann Lee, Founder of the Shakers.* Boston: Little, Brown.

Capps, Randy, Michael Fix, Jeffery S. Passel, and Jason Ost. 2003. "A Profile of the Low-Wage Immigrant Workforce." Washington DC: Urban Institute. Retrieved August 20, 2009, from http://www.urban.org/UploadedPDF/310880_lowwage_immig_wkfc.pdf.

Carnegie Endowment for International Peace, International Migration Policy Program. 1997. "Immigrant Entrepreneurs." *Research Perspectives on Migration* 1:1–15. Retrieved February 22, 2009, from http://www.migrationpolicy.org/files/RPMVol1-No2.pdf.

Casa de Maryland. 2008. "Montgomery County Executive Signs Historic Domestic Workers Rights Bill Providing Protection to Housekeepers and Nannies." Press release, July 22. Retrieved June 7, 2009, from http://www.casademaryland.org/index.php?option=com_content&task=view&id=383.

Cavalieri, Shelley. 2011. "Between Victim and Agent: A Third-Way Feminist Account of Trafficking for Sex Work." *Indiana Law Journal* 86:1–53.

Center for Women Policy Studies. 2008. "U.S. Policy Advocacy to Combat Trafficking." Retrieved July 27, 2008, from http://www.centerwomenpolicy.org/programs/trafficking/default.asp.

Center for Women's Business Research. "Minority Reports." Retrieved September 17, 2009, from http://www.womensbusinessresearch.org/minorityreports.html.

Chambers, Peggy. 1958. *A Woman Alone: A Biography of Elizabeth Blackwell.* Glasgow, Scotland: Abelard-Schuman.

Chang, Grace. 2000. *Disposable Domestics: Immigrant Women Workers in the Global Economy.* Cambridge, MA: South End.

Charmaz, Kathy. 2000. "Grounded Theory: Objectivist and Constructivist Methods." Pp. 509–536 in *Handbook of Qualitative Research,* 2nd ed., edited by Norman K. Denzen and Yvonna S. Lincoln. Thousand Oaks, CA: Sage.

Childress, Alice. 1986. *Like One of the Family: Conversations from a Domestic's Life.* Boston: Beacon.

Chon, Katherine. 2009. "*The Washington Post*: A Paper Pimp? Parts I and II." *The North Star: The Polaris Project Blog.* Retrieved April 10, 2009, from http://www.polarisproject.org/component/option,com_wrapper/Itemid,108/.

Choy, Catherine Ceniza. 2003. *Empire of Care: Nursing and Migration in Filipino Nursing History.* Durham, NC: Duke University Press.

Clark-Lewis, Elizabeth. "'This Work Had an End': African-American Domestic Workers in Washington, D.C., 1910–1940." Pp. 196–212 in *"To Toil the Livelong Day": America's Women at Work, 1780–1980,* edited by Carol Groneman and Mary Beth Norton. Ithaca, NY: Cornell University Press.

Clifford, Elizabeth J., and Susan C. Pearce. 2004. *Women and Current Immigration Policies.* Fact sheet published by Sociologists for Women in Society. Fall. Retrieved November 15, 2009, from http://www.socwomen.org/socactivism/womenimm.pdf.

Clifford, Elizabeth J., Susan C. Pearce, and Reena Tandon. 2006. "Two Steps Forward? Reinventing U.S. Immigration Policy for Women." In *Proceedings for the Annual Conference of the Institute for Women's Policy Research,* Washington, DC, June 19–21, 2005.

Clough, Patricia T. 1992. *The End(s) of Ethnography: From Realism to Social Criticism.* Newbury Park, CA: Sage.

CNN.com. 2008. "2008 CNN Heroes Archive." Retrieved May 16, 2009, from http://www.cnn.com/SPECIALS/cnn.heroes/archive/.

Coalition Against Trafficking in Women. 2001. "Sex Trafficking of Women in the United States: International and Domestic Trends." New York: Coalition Against Trafficking in Women.

Colen, Shellee. 1990. "Housekeeping for the Green Card: West Indian Household Workers, the State, Stratified Reproduction in New York." Pp. 89–118 in *At Work in Homes: Household Workers in World Perspective,* edited by Roger Sanjek and Shellee Colen. Washington, DC: American Ethnological Society.

Collins, Patricia Hill. 1990. *Black Feminist Thought: Knowledge, Consciousness, and the Politics of Empowerment.* New York: Routledge.

Cooper, Cynthia L. 2007. "Women Raise Heat on Immigration Debate." *Women's eNews,* May 18. Retrieved May 16, 2009, from http://www.womensenews.org/article.cfm/dyn/aid/3172.

Coughlin, Jeanne Hallady, and Andrew R. Thomas. 2000. *The Rise of Women Entrepreneurs: People, Processes, and Global Trends.* Westport, CT: Quorum Books.

Crawford, Vicki L., Jacqueline Anne Rouse, and Barbara Woods, eds. 1993. *Women in the Civil Rights Movement: Trailblazers and Torch-Bearers, 1941–1965.* Bloomington and Indianapolis: Indiana University Press.

Crenshaw, Kimberlé. 1996. "Mapping the Margins: Intersectionality, Identity Politics, and Violence against Women of Color." Pp. 357–83 in *Critical Race Theory: The Key Writings That Formed the Movement,* edited by Kimberlé Crenshaw, Neil Gotanda, Garry Peller, and Kendall Thomas. New York: New Press.

Daleiden, Sara. 2007. "Suzanne Lacy's Stories of Work and Survival: Sharing a Meal with Public Intimacy." Los Angeles Museum of Contemporary Art, July 6. Retrieved May 16, 2009, from http://www.moca.org/wack/?p=307.

Daniels, Roger. 2004. *Guarding the Golden Door.* New York: Hill and Wang.

DataCenter. 2007. "Behind Closed Doors: Working Conditions of California Household Workers." A report by DataCenter, Mujeres Unidas y Activas and Day Labor Program Women's Collective of La Raza Centro Legal. Retrieved July 4, 2009, from http://www.datacenter.org/reports/behindcloseddoors.pdf.

De Jesus, Carlos Suarez. 2006. "Hands, Hickeys, and Hurly-Burly: Art Basel Leaves Its Mark on Wynwood." *Miami New Times,* December 14. Retrieved February 22, 2009, from http://www.miaminewtimes.com/2006-12-14/culture/hands-hickeys-and-hurly-burly/.

DeLaet, Debra L. 1999. "Introduction: The Invisibility of Women in Scholarship on International Migration." Pp. 1–20 in *Gender and Immigration,* edited by Gregory A. Kelson and Debra L. DeLaet. New York: New York University Press.

de la Luz Ibarra, Maria. 2000. "Mexican Immigrant Women and the New Domestic Labor." *Human Organization* 59:452–64.

Demos, Vasilikie. 2008. "Marriage, Dowry, and Women's Early Twentieth-Century Migration from Greece." Paper presented at the annual meeting of the American Sociological Society, Boston, August 1.

Detention Watch Network. n.d. "About the U.S. Detention and Deportation System." Retrieved February 8, 2009, from http://detentionwatchnetwork.org/aboutdetention.

Dinnerstein, Julie E. 2007. "The 'New' and Exciting U: No Longer Just My Imaginary Friend." Pp. 451–72 in *Tenth Annual AILA New York Chapter Immigration Law Symposium Handbook.* New York: American Immigration Lawyers Association.

Domestic Workers United. 2008. "Domestic Workers Gather for National Congress." Retrieved August 24, 2009, from http://www.domesticworkersunited.org/shownews/14.

Domestic Workers United and DataCenter. 2006. "Home Is Where the Work Is: Inside New York's Domestic Work Industry." Retrieved June 7, 2009, from http://www.domesticworkersunited.org/media.php?show=9.

Donato, Katharine. 1993. "Current Trends and Patterns in Female Migration: Evidence from Mexico." *International Migration Review* 27:748–71.

Donato, Katharine, Donna Gabaccia, Jennifer Holdaway, Martin Manalansan IV, and Patricia R. Pessar. 2006. "A Glass Half Full? Gender in Migration Studies." *International Migration Review* 40:3–26.

Donato, Katharine M., and Andrea Tyree. 1986. "Family Reunification, Health Professionals, and the Sex Composition of Immigrants to the United States." *Sociology and Social Research* 70:226–30.

Dow, Mark. 2004. *American Gulag: Inside U.S. Immigration Prisons.* Berkeley: University of California Press.

Ehrenreich, Barbara. 2002. *Nickel and Dimed.* New York: First Owl Books.

Ehrenreich, Barbara, and Arlie Russell Hochschild, eds. 2004. *Global Woman: Nannies, Maids, and Sex Workers in the New Economy.* New York: Metropolitan Books.

Eissa, Salih Omar. 2005. "Diversity and Transformation: African Americans and African Immigration to the United States." Washington, DC: Immigration Policy Center. March. Retrieved February 22, 2009, from http://www.immigrationpolicy.org/index.php?content=pr0503b.

Elder, Sara, and Dorothea Schmidt. 2004. "Global Employment Trends for Women: Employment Strategy Papers, Employment Trends Unit Employment Strategy Department, ILO." Retrieved June 7, 2009, www.ilo.org/public/english/employment/strat/download/esp8.pdf.

Emirbayer, Mustafa, and Ann Mische. 1998. "What Is Agency?" *American Journal of Sociology* 104:962–1023.

Empowered Women International. n.d. "Our Model: Why Art?" Retrieved August 26, 2010, from http://www.ewint.org/.

Ensor, Marisa O. 2008. "Displaced Once Again: Honduran Migrant Children in the Path of Katrina." *Children, Youth and Environments* 18:280–302.

Erez, Edna, Madelaine Adelman, and Carol Gregory. 2009. "Intersections of Immigration and Domestic Violence: Voices of Battered Immigrant Women." *Feminist Criminology* 4:32–56.

Erlich, Mark, and Jeff Grabelsky. 2005. "Standing at a Crossroads: The Building Trades in the Twenty-First Century." *Labor History* 46:421–45.

Fairlie, Robert. 2005. "Self-Employment Rates by Immigrant Status." Retrieved February 22, 2009, from http://people.ucsc.edu/~rfairlie/serates/seimmig7903.pdf.

Falcone, Michael. 2009. "100,000 Parents of Citizens Were Deported over 10 Years." *New York Times,* February 13. Retrieved May 10, 2009, from http://www.nytimes.com/2009/02/14/us/14immig.html.

Federal Interagency Forum on Child and Family Statistics. 2007. "America's Children: Key National Indicators of Well-Being: Children of at Least One Foreign-Born Parent." Retrieved January 6, 2009, from http://www.childstats.gov/americaschildren07/famsoc4.asp.

Felder, Deborah G. 2001. *The 100 Most Influential Women of All Time*. New York: Citadel.

Feminist Majority Foundation. 2008. "Government Accountability Office Releases Domestic Worker Abuse Report." *Feminist Daily News Wire*. Retrieved August 24, 2009, from http://feminist.org/news/newsbyte/uswirestory.asp?id=11188.

Fine, Mark A. 1993. "Current Approaches to Understanding Family Diversity." *Family Relations* 42:235–37.

Foner, Nancy. 2005. *In a New Land: A Comparative View of Immigration*. New York: New York University Press.

Foucault, Michel. 1980. *Power/Knowledge: Selected Interviews and Other Writings, 1972–1977*. Edited by C. Gordon. New York: Pantheon.

Fuentes, Sonia Pressman. 1999. *Eat First—You Don't Know What They'll Give You: The Adventures of an Immigrant Family and Their Feminist Daughter*. Philadelphia: Xlibris.

Gabaccia, Donna R. 2007. "Send Me Your Rich and Talented." *Contemporary Perspectives on Immigration*, June 22. Retrieved February 10, 2009, from http://blog.lib.umn.edu/ihrc/immigration/2007/06/.

———. 1999. "Immigrant Women: A Talk with Historian Donna Gabaccia." Radio interview on *Talking History*, March 8. Retrieved January 21, 2010, from http://talking-history.oah.org/arch1999.html#Anchor-Immigran-4421.

———. 1994. *From the Other Side: Women, Gender, and Immigrant Life in the U.S., 1820–1990*. Bloomington: Indiana University Press.

———. 1989. *Immigrant Women in the United States: A Selectively Annotated Multidisciplinary Bibliography*. Westport, CT: Greenwood.

Galuszka, Peter. 2008. "Are Women Still 'Disadvantaged'? The SBA Says Yes, but Only in Four Industries—Including Kitchen-Cabinet Making." CNNMoney.com, March 14. Retrieved September 19, 2009, from http://money.cnn.com/2008/03/10/smbusiness/sba_set_asides.fsb/index.htm.

Gammage, Sarah. 2002. "Women Immigrants in the U.S. Labor Market: Second-Rate Jobs in The First World." Pp. 75–94 in *Women Immigrants in the United States,* edited by Philippa Strum and Danielle Tarantolo. Washington, DC: Woodrow Wilson International Center for Scholars. Retrieved August 20, 2009, from http://www.wilsoncenter.org/topics/pubs/womenimm_rpt.pdf.

Gardner, Martha, 2005. *The Qualities of a Citizen: Women, Immigration, and Citizenship, 1870–1965*. Princeton, NJ: Princeton University Press.

Geertz, Clifford. 1983. *Local Knowledge: Further Essays in Interpretive Anthropology*. New York: Basic Books.

GEO Group. 2009. "The GEO Group Announces the Opening of a 192-Bed Expansion of 576-Bed Robert A. Deyton Detention Facility in Georgia." Press release, January 14. Retrieved February 7, 2009, from http://www.marketwatch.com/news/story/geo-group-announces-opening-192bed/story.aspx?guid=%7BFEC9050C%2DC80F%2D4099%2D8044%2D2E3E09AD5C33%7D&dist=TQP_Mod_pressN.

"GEO Stock." 2007. *Wall Street Journal*. Marketwatch, February 12. Retrieved February 22, 2009, from http://www.marketwatch.com/quotes/geo.

Gerth, Hans Heinrich, and C. Wright Mills. 1958. *From Max Weber: Essays in Sociology*. New York: Oxford University Press.

Gibson, Campbell J., and Kay Jung. 2006. "Historical Census Statistics on the Foreign-Born Population of the United States: 1850–2000." Population Division Working Paper

No. 81. Washington, DC: U.S. Census Bureau of the Census Population Division. Retrieved January 21, 2010, from http://www.census.gov/population/www/documentation/twps0081/twps0081.html.

Gibson, Campbell J., and Emily Lennon. 1999. "Historical Census Statistics on the Foreign-Born Population of the United States: 1850–1990." Population Division Working Paper No. 29. Washington, DC: U.S. Bureau of the Census Population Division. Retrieved January 21, 2010, from http://www.census.gov/population/www/documentation/twps0029/twps0029.html#intro.

Giddens, Anthony. 1990. *The Consequences of Modernity.* Cambridge, UK: Polity.

———. 1986. *The Constitution of Society: Outline of the Theory of Structuration.* Berkeley: University of California Press.

Gillespie, Nick. 1994. "Beyond the Family Way—Immigration." *Reason* 26:44–46.

Glaser, Barney G., and Anselm L. Strauss. 1967. *The Discovery of Grounded Theory.* Chicago: Aldine.

Glenn, Evelyn Nakano. 1992. "From Servitude to Service Work: Historical Continuities in the Racial Division of Paid Reproductive Labor." *Signs: Journal of Women in Culture and Society* 18:1–42.

———. 1986. *Issei, Nisei, War Bride: Three Generations of Japanese American Women in Domestic Service.* Philadelphia: Temple University Press.

"Global Democracy: Civil Society Visions and Strategies (GO5)." 2005. Montreál International Forum. Conference report. Montreál, Quebec, Canada, May 29–June 1. Retrieved April 9, 2010, from http://www.world-governance.org/IMG/pdf_G05_Report.pdf.

Global Rights. 2006a. "Domestic Workers' Rights in the United States: A Report Prepared for the U.N. Human Rights Committee, in Response to the Second and Third Periodic Report of the United States." Retrieved June 7, 2009, from http://www.globalrights.org/site/DocServer/Domestic_Workers_report-_FINAL.pdf?docID=5503.

———. 2006b. "Global Rights Urges UN Human Rights Committee to Hold the United States Accountable for Its Human Rights Violations." Retrieved August 15, 2009, from http://www.globalrights.org/site/DocServer/FinalfinalUNreleaseWEB_7.14.06.pdf?docID=5523.

Gonzalez, Priscilla, and Rebecca Smith. 2008. "Celebrate Human Rights Day by Honoring the Human Rights of Domestic Workers." *Huffington Post,* December 9. Retrieved January, 10 2009, from http://www.huffingtonpost.com/priscilla-gonzalez-and-rebecca-smith/celebrate-human-rights-da_b_149619.html?view=print.

Gozdziak, Elzbieta M., and Elizabeth A. Collett. 2005. "Research on Human Trafficking in North America: A Review of the Literature." Pp. 100–128 in *Data and Research on Human Trafficking: A Global Survey,* edited by Frank Laczko and Elzbieta Gozdziak. Geneva: International Organization for Migration.

Greenhouse, Linda. 2006. "Court Rejects Interpretation of Immigration Drug Law." *New York Times,* December 6. Retrieved November 15, 2009, from http://www.nytimes.com/2006/12/06/washington/06scotus.html?scp=1&sq=Court%20Rejects%20Interpretation%20Of%20Immigration%20Drug%20Law&st=cse.

Greenhouse, Steven. 2007. "Legislation Pushed to Require Minimum Wage for Domestic Workers." *New York Times,* June 1. Retrieved June 7, 2009, from http://www.nytimes.com/2007/06/01/nyregion/01nanny.html.

Griffith, David, Ricardo Contreras, and Ed Kissam. 2009. "*Calidad y Confianza* (Quality and Trust): Latino Entrepreneurship in North Carolina and Beyond." Keynote speaker presentation at the Second Latino Leadership Summit, June 5, Greenville, North Carolina.

Griswold, Daniel T. 2002. "Panel Discussion on Immigration and Border Security." National Immigration Forum Annual Conference, February 1. Retrieved January 7, 2009, from http://www.freetrade.org/node/364.

Habermas, Jürgen. 1987. *The Theory of Communicative Action*, vol. 2, *Lifeworld and System: A Critique of Functionalist Reason*. Boston: Beacon.

Hansberry, Lorraine. 1959. *A Raisin in the Sun*. New York: Samuel French.

Heisler, Barbara Schmitter. 2008. "The Sociology of Immigration." Pp. 83–111 in *Migration Theory: Talking across Disciplines*, edited by Caroline B. Brettell and James F. Hollifield. New York and London: Routledge.

Hess, Beth B., and Myra Marx Ferree. 1987. *Analyzing Gender: A Handbook of Social Science Research*. London: Sage.

Hill, Cynthia, dir. 2006. *The Guest Worker*. Documentary film. Durham, NC: Southern Documentary Fund.

Hirschkorn, Phil. 2003. "New York Reduces 9/11 Death Toll by 40." CNN.com, October 29. Retrieved January 7, 2009 from http://www.cnn.com/2003/US/Northeast/10/29/wtc.deaths/.

Hobbs, Frank, and Nicole Stoops. 2002. "Demographic Trends in the 20th Century." U.S. Census Bureau, Census 2000 Special Reports, Series CENSR-4, U.S. Washington, DC: U.S. Government Printing Office.

Hofstetter, Eleanore O. 2001. *Women in Global Migration, 1945–2000*. Westport, CT: Greenwood.

Holliday, Adrian. 2007. *Doing and Writing Qualitative Research*. London: Sage.

Hondagneu-Sotelo, Pierrette, ed. 2003a. *Gender and U.S. Immigration: Contemporary Trends*. Berkeley and Los Angeles: University of California Press.

———. 2003b. "Review Essay: *Beyond Smoke and Mirrors*: Mexican Immigration in an Era of Economic Integration." *Contemporary Sociology* 32:677–78.

———. 2001. *Doméstica: Immigrant Workers Cleaning and Caring in the Shadows of Affluence*. Berkeley and Los Angeles: University of California Press.

———. 1994. *Gendered Transitions: Mexican Experiences of Immigration*. Berkeley and Los Angeles: University of California Press.

Howe, Barbara. 2003. "Immigration as a Factor in Nineteenth-Century Women's Employment in West Virginia Cities." In *Conference Proceedings for V Taller Científico Internacional "Mujeres en el Siglo XXI."* Havana: University of Havana. 35 pages on CD-ROM.

Hughes, Donna. 2001. "The Natasha Trade: Transnational Sex Trafficking." *National Institute of Justice Journal*, January, pp. 8–15.

Hulko, Wendy. 2009. "The Time- and Context-Contingent Nature of Intersectionality and Interlocking Oppressions." *Affilia* 24:44–55.

Human Rights Center. 2004. "Hidden Slaves: Forced Labor in the United States." University of California and Free the Slaves. Retrieved June 8, 2009, from http://www.freetheslaves.net//Document.Doc?id=17.

Human Rights Watch. 2006. "Swept under the Rug: Abuses against Domestic Workers around the World." Retrieved June 8, 2009, from http://www.hrw.org/en/reports/2006/07/27/swept-under-rug-0.

————. 2001. "Hidden in the Home: Abuse of Domestic Workers with Special Visas in the United States." Retrieved June 7, 2009, from http://www.hrw.org/reports/2001/usadom/usadom0501.pdf.

Humantrafficking.org. 2006. "News and Updates: Part I: San Francisco Is Hub for Trafficking for Sexual Exploitation." November. Retrieved January 29, 2009, from http://www.humantrafficking.org/updates/466.

"Hung Liu, Internationally-Acclaimed Chinese Mural Artist." Platetectonic Music website. Retrieved February 28, 2010, from http://www.platetectonicmusic.com/id205.html.

International Organization for Migration. 2005. *World Migration Report 2005*. Geneva, Switzerland.

Irizarry, Ylce. 2008. "Merging Public and Personal Histories: Creating National Memory in Contemporary Latina Fiction." East Carolina University Women's Studies Research Series, Greenville, North Carolina, January 14.

Jacoby, Susan. 1974. "Immigrant Women." *APF Newsletter*. Washington, DC: Alicia Patterson Foundation. Retrieved January 21, 2010, from http://www.aliciapatterson.org/APF001974/Jacoby/Jacoby07/Jacoby07.html.

Kahling, Elizabeth. 2002. "U.S. Women Workers: Trends and Trade." Center of Concern website. Retrieved April 8, 2010, from http://www.coc.org/system/files/WomenWorkers.pdf.

Kahn, Ric. 2007. "Bound for Misery: On the Fast-Moving Circuit of International Sex Trafficking, Say Police, Women Regularly Shuttle In and Out of Boston." *Boston Globe,* January 7. Retrieved February 9, 2009, from http://www.boston.com/news/local/articles/2007/01/07/bound_for_misery/.

Kasinitz Philip, John H. Mollenkopf, Mary C. Waters, and Jennifer Holdaway. 2008. *Inheriting the City: The Children of Immigrants Come of Age*. Cambridge, MA: Harvard University Press.

Katzman, David. 1978. *Seven Days a Week: Women and Domestic Service in Industrializing America*. Urbana: University of Illinois Press.

Kimmel, Michael S., and Michael A. Messner, eds. 2009. *Men's Lives*, 8th ed. Boston: Allyn and Bacon.

Knörr, Jacqueline, and Barbara Meier, eds. 2000. *Women and Migration: Anthropological Perspectives*. New York: St. Martin's.

Kolodner, Meredith. 2006. "Private Prisons Expect a Boom: Immigration Enforcement to Benefit Detention." *New York Times,* July 19.

Koser, Khalid. 2007. *International Migration: A Very Short Introduction*. Oxford: Oxford University Press.

Kritz, Mary M., and Douglas T. Gurak. 2004. "Immigration and a Changing America." New York: Russell Sage Foundation, and Washington, DC: Population Reference Bureau.

Kumin, Judith. 2001. "Gender: Persecution in the Spotlight." *Refugees* 2:12–13. Retrieved November 1, 2009, from http://www.unhcr.se/se/Protect_refugees/pdf/magazine.pdf.

Lee, Everett S. 1966. "A Theory of Migration." *Demography* 3:47–57.

Le Espiritu, Yen. 2003. *Home Bound: Filipino American Lives across Cultures, Communities, and Countries*. Los Angeles and Berkeley: University of California Press.

Lipszyc, Cecilia. 2004. "The Feminization of Migration: Dreams and Realities of Immigrant Women in Four Latin American Countries." Paper presented at the conference "Reclaiming the Streets," Montevideo, Uruguay, April. Retrieved February 22, 2009, from http://www.diba.es/urbal12/PDFS/CeciliaLipszyc_en.pdf.

Lindsley, Syd. 2000. "Gendered Assaults: The Attack on Immigrant Women." *Differen-Takes* (a publication of the Population and Development Program at Hampshire College), Fall. Retrieved August 17, 2009, from http://popdev.hampshire.edu/sites/popdev/files/uploads/dt/DifferenTakes_06.pdf.

Liu, Hung. 2008. "Artist's Statement." For exhibit by Art Scene China. Retrieved February 22, 2009, from http://www.artscenechina.com/chineseart/artists/statements/hungliu.htm.

Louie, Miriam Ching Yoon. 2001. *Sweatshop Warriors: Immigrant Women Workers Take on the Global Factory.* Cambridge, MA: South End.

Louis, Liliane Nérette. 1999. *When Night Falls, Kric! Krac!* Santa Barbara, CA: Libraries Unlimited.

Lutheran Immigration and Refugee Service and the Women's Commission for Refugee Women and Children. 2007. "Locking Up Family Values: The Detention of Immigrant Families." February. Retrieved September 7, 2010, from http://www.womensrefugeecommission.org/docs/famdeten.pdf.

Mack, Kristen. 2009. "Pr. William's Mothers of Dissension: Stay-at-Home Moms Add Politics to Duties." *Washington Post,* January 2, p. A01.

Malone, Tara. 2008. "Chicago Church Offers Sanctuary to 2nd Illegal Immigrant: Friend of Previous Refugee, Elvira Arellano, Considers Defying Law, Taking Refuge There." *Chicago Tribune,* January 28. Retrieved April 9, 2009, from http://articles.chicagotribune.com/2008-01-28/news/0801270187_1_elvira-arellano-illegal-immigrant-adalberto-united-methodist-church.

Maril, Robert Lee. 2011. *The Fence: Immigration, Drugs, National Security, and Safety along the U.S.-Mexico Border.* Lubbock: Texas Tech University Press.

———. 2006. *Patrolling Chaos: The U.S. Border Patrol in Deep South Texas.* Lubbock: Texas Tech University Press.

Martin, Philip. 1999. "Family-Based U.S. Immigration: Patterns and Issues." Talk given at the Center for International and European Law on Immigration and Asylum, University of Kostanz Faculty of Law, Konstanz, Germany, June 29.

Marx, Karl. [1852] 2007. "The Eighteenth Brumaire of Louis Bonaparte." Pp. 112–21 in *Classical Sociological Theory,* edited by Craig J. Calhoun et al. Malden, MA: Blackwell.

Massey, Douglas S., Jorge Durand, and Nolan J. Malone. 2002. *Beyond Smoke and Mirrors: Mexican Immigration in an Era of Economic Integration.* New York: Russell Sage Foundation.

May, Meredith. 2006a. "Diary of a Sex Slave, Part 1: San Francisco Is a Major Center for International Crime Networks That Smuggle and Enslave." *San Francisco Chronicle,* October 6.

———. 2006b. "Diary of a Sex Slave, Part 2: A Youthful Mistake." *San Francisco Chronicle,* October 8.

———. 2006c. "Diary of a Sex Slave, Part 3: Bought and Sold." *San Francisco Chronicle,* October 9.

———. 2006d. "Diary of a Sex Slave, Part 4: Sex Slave Freed, Trapped." *San Francisco Chronicle,* October 10.

Maza, Erik. 2009. "For Haitian Immigrants, Hurricanes Complicate Deportation Cases." *New York Times,* January 9. Retrieved April 9, 2009, from http://www.nytimesinstitute.com/miami09/2009/01/09/for-haitianimmigrants-hurricanes-complicate-deportation-cases/.

McCunn, Ruthanne Lum. 2004. *Thousand Pieces of Gold: A Biographical Novel.* Boston: Beacon.

———. 2003. "Reclaiming Polly Bemis: China's Daughter, Idaho's Legendary Pioneer." *Frontiers: A Journal of Women Studies* 24:76–100.

McDonnell, Patrick, and George White. 1997. "Sweatshop Workers to Get $2 Million." *Los Angeles Times,* October 24, p. D1. Retrieved April 14, 2009, from http://articles.latimes.com/p/1997/oct/24/business/fi-46054.

Merithew, Caroline Waldron. 2009. "Sister Katie: The Memory and Making of a 1.5 Generation Working-Class Transnational." *Journal of Women's History* 21:84–110.

Miazgowicz, Britt. 2007. Introduction to "In Your Face" exhibit at the Bernice Steinbaum Gallery, Miami, Florida.

Min, Pyong Gap, and Mehdi Bozorgmehr. 2003. "USA: The Entrepreneurial Cutting Edge." Pp. 17–38 in *Immigrant Entrepreneurs: Venturing Abroad in the Age of Globalization,* edited by Robert Koosterman and Jan Rath. Oxford, UK, and New York: Berg.

Moreno, Ivan. 2009. "Immigrant Raids Often Mark Start of Years of Limbo." Associated Press. Retrieved August 30, 2010, from http://iaco.us/news/index.php?mod=article&cat=Immigration&article=480.

Morokvašic, Mirjana. 1984. "Birds of Passage Are Also Women." *International Migration Review* 18:886–907.

Morrison, Bruce A. 2002. "Attracting New Americans into Baltimore's Neighborhoods: Immigration Is the Key to Reversing Baltimore's Population Decline." Report prepared for the Abell Foundation. Retrieved November 1, 2009, from http://www.abell.org/pubsitems/cd_attracting_new_1202.pdf.

Murray, Royce Bernstein, and Mary Giovagnoli. 2010. "DHS Progress Report: An Analysis of Immigration Policy in the First Year of the Obama Administration." Washington, DC: Immigration Policy Center. Retrieved April 8, 2010, from http://www.immigrationpolicy.org/sites/default/files/docs/DHS_Progress_Report_-_030210.pdf.

Nafisi, Azar. 2005. "Literature and History." Recorded lecture for "Facing History and Ourselves" series, facinghistory.org. Retrieved February 22, 2009, from http://video.google.com/videoplay?docid=-4602009390796832062.

———. 2003. *Reading Lolita in Tehran: A Memoir in Books.* New York: Random House.

National Archives. 2008. "Citizens by Choice: Women in Business Leadership." Panel discussion, June 11.

National Coalition Against Domestic Violence. 2009. "Domestic Violence Facts." Retrieved January 6, 2009, from http://www.ncadv.org/files/DomesticViolenceFactShe et(National).pdf.

National Employment Law Project. 2002. "Immigration Status and Your Rights as a Worker." Retrieved August 20, 2009, from http://nelp.3cdn.net/fbfe668d1b2bde7e06_aem6b91zk.pdf.

National Immigrant Justice Center. 2007. "The Situation of Immigrant Women Detained in the United States." Briefing paper. April 16. Retrieved November 15, 2009, from http://www.immigrantwomennetwork.org/Resources/Briefing%20Paper_Women%20in%20Detention_UN%20Special%20Rapporteur%202007%2004%2017%20FINAL.pdf.

Negra, Diane. 2001. *Off-White Hollywood: American Culture and Ethnic Female Stardom.* London and New York: Routledge.

Niemeier, Debbie, and Cristina González. 2004. "Breaking into the Guildmasters' Club: What We Know about Women Science and Engineering Department Chairs at AAU Universities." *NWSA Journal* 16:157–71.

Nissen, Bruce, and Guillermo Grenier, 2001. "Local Union Relations with Immigrants: The Case of South Florida." *Labor Studies Journal* 26:76–97.

Nizza, Mike. 2007. "Estimate for Deporting Illegal Immigrants: $94 Billion." *New York Times,* September 13. Retrieved February 10, 2009, from http://thelede.blogs.nytimes.com/2007/09/13/estimate-for-deporting-illegal-immigrants-94-billion/.

Office of the Texas Attorney General. 2008. "The Texas Response to Human Trafficking." Report to the 81st Legislature. Retrieved January 29, 2009, from http://www.oag.state.tx.us/AG_Publications/pdfs/human_trafficking.pdf.

Olivo, Antonio. 2009. "Immigration Agency's Airline Flies Tens of Thousands of Deportees Out of U.S.: ICE Air Flew 367,000 Illegal Immigrants Home Last Year." *Chicago Tribune,* February 9. Retrieved February 9, 2009, from http://www.chicagotribune.com/news/nationworld/chi-deportees-09-feb09,0,5333975.story?track=rss.

Olsen, Tillie. 1978. *Silences.* New York: Delacorte/Seymour Lawrence.

Orlandi, Lorraine. 2007. "Deported Mother Sends Her Child to U.S. Protests." *Women's eNews,* September 14. Retrieved November 15, 2009, from http://www.womensenews.org/story/the-courts/070914/deported-mother-sends-her-child-us-protests.

O'Shaughnessy, Patrice. 2008. "Long Island Case Turns Spotlight on Hundreds Trapped as Slaves." *New York Daily News,* June 28. Retrieved February 3, 2009, from http://www.nydailynews.com/news/ny_crime/2008/06/28/2008-06-28_long_island_case_turns_spotlight_on_hund.html.

Oswin, Natalie. 2001. "Rights Spaces: An Exploration of Feminist Approaches to Refugee Law." *International Feminist Journal of Politics* 3:347–64.

Palevsky, Matt. 2009. "Sheriff Joe Arpaio Separates Mother from Children, Immigrant Crack Down." *Huffington Post,* January 16. Retrieved April 10, 2009, from http://www.huffingtonpost.com/2009/01/16/sheriff-joe-arpaio-separa_n_158660.html.

Palmer, Phyllis. 1989. *Domesticity and Dirt: Housewives and Domestic Servants in the United States, 1920–1945.* Philadelphia: Temple University Press.

Parreñas, Rhacel Salazar. 2008. *The Force of Domesticity: Filipina Migrants and Globalization.* New York: New York University Press.

———. 2001. *Servants of Globalization: Women, Migration, and Domestic Work.* Stanford, CA: Stanford University Press.

———. 2000. "Migrant Filipina Domestic Workers and the International Division of Reproductive Labor." *Gender and Society* 14:560–80.

Passel, Jeffrey S. 2006. "The Size and Characteristics of the Unauthorized Migrant Population in the U.S." Washington, DC: Pew Hispanic Center. March 7. Retrieved February 10, 2009, from http://pewhispanic.org/files/reports/61.pdf.

———. 2005. "Estimates of the Size and Characteristics of the Undocumented Population." Washington, DC: Pew Hispanic Center. March 21. Retrieved April 9, 2010, from http://pewhispanic.org/files/reports/44.pdf.

Passel, Jeffrey S., and D'Vera Cohn. 2009. "A Portrait of Unauthorized Immigrants in the United States." Washington, DC: Pew Hispanic Center. April 14. Retrieved January 1, 2010, from http://pewhispanic.org/files/reports/107.pdf.

———. 2008a. "Trends in Unauthorized Immigration: Undocumented Inflow Now Trails Legal Inflow." Washington, DC: Pew Hispanic Center. October 2. Retrieved December 31, 2008, from http://pewhispanic.org/reports/report.php?ReportID=94.

———. 2008b. "Unauthorized Immigration: Measurement, Methods, and Data Sources." Paper presented at the Immigration Data Users' Seminar, Migration Policy Institute and Population Reference Bureau, Washington, DC, October 16. Retrieved December 31, 2008, from http://74.125.45.132/search?q=cache:705XIwRuS1AJ:www.prb.org/presentations/passel.ppt+visa+overstays+40+percent&hl=en&ct=clnk&cd=21&gl=us.

Pearce, Susan C. 2005. "Today's Immigrant Woman Entrepreneur." *Immigration Policy in Focus* (Washington, DC: Immigration Policy Center), January. Retrieved February 22, 2009, from http://www.immigrationpolicy.org/images/File/infocus/Immigrant%20Women%20Entrepreneurs.pdf.

Pedraza, Silvia. 1991. "Women and Migration: The Social Consequences of Gender." *Annual Review of Sociology* 17:303–25.

Penn, Shauna. 2008. *Solidarity's Secret: The Women Who Defeated Communism in Poland.* Ann Arbor: University of Michigan Press.

Piper, Nicola. 2006. "Gendering the Politics of Migration." *International Migration Review* 40:133–64.

Pisani, M. J., and D. W. Yoskowitz. 2002. "The Maid Trade: Cross-Border Work in South Texas." *Social Science Quarterly* 83: 568–79.

Polaris Project. n.d. "About Polaris Project." Retrieved February 7, 2009, from http://www.polarisproject.org/content/view/13/42/.

Pomareda, Fabiola. 2009. "Chicago Immigration Activist Marks Year in Church." Translated by Elena Shore. *La Raza News Report,* February 1. Retrieved August 21, 2010, from http://news.newamericamedia.org/news/view_article.html?article_id=a638607540d8157d443448d3a90e332e.

Portes, Alejandro. 2007. "Bridging the Gap: Immigrant Organizations and the Political Incorporation of Migrants in America." Paper presented at the American Sociological Association meeting, New York, August 12.

Portes, Alejandro, and Leif Jensen. 1989. "The Enclave and the Entrants: Patterns of Ethnic Enterprise in Miami before and after Mariel." *American Sociological Review* 54:929–49.

Portes, Alejandro, and Rubén G. Rumbaut. 2006. *Immigrant America: A Portrait,* 3rd ed. Los Angeles and Berkeley: University of California Press.

Portes, Alejandro, and Min Zhou. 1996. "Self-Employment and the Earnings of Immigrants." *American Sociological Review* 61:219–30.

———. 1993. "The New Second Generation: Segmented Assimilation and Its Variants." *Annals of the American Academy of Political and Social Science* 530:74–96.

Prengaman, Peter. 2006. "Day-Laborer Study Finds Community Ties: Immigrants Often Have Families, Attend Church and Are Hired by Homeowners." *Washington Post,* January 23.

Preston, Julia. 2009a. "U.S. May Be Open to Asylum for Spouse Abuse." *New York Times,* October 29, p. A14. Retrieved November 15, 2009, from http://www.nytimes.com/2009/10/30/us/30asylum.html?scp=2&sq=Rody&st=cse.

———. 2009b. "U.S. Military Will Offer Path to Citizenship." *New York Times,* February 14. Retrieved April 8, 2010, from http://www.nytimes.com/2009/02/15/us/15immig.html.

Protection Project of the Foreign Policy Institute at the Johns Hopkins University School of Advanced International Studies. 2006. "The Protection Project's Review of the U.S. Department of State Office to Monitor and Protect Trafficking in Persons: 2006 Trafficking in Persons Report." Retrieved February 7, 2009, from http://www.protectionproject.org/sites/default/files/Final_collection.pdf.

Putnam, Robert. 2000. *Bowling Alone*. New York: Simon and Schuster.

Ratner, Lizzy. 2003. "The Legacy of Guantánamo." *Nation*, July 14. Retrieved August 21, 2010, from http://www.thenation.com/article/legacy-guantánamo.

"Record-Breaking Number of Women Will Serve in the 111th Congress." 2008. *Women in Government Relations Newsletter*, November. Retrieved January 6, 2009, from http://www.wgr.org/news_events/index.cfm?fa=whatarticle&id=244.

Reed, Isaac. 2008. "Justifying Sociological Knowledge: From Realism to Interpretation." *Sociological Theory* 26:101–29. Retrieved January 7, 2009, from http://www.asanet.org/galleries/default-file/Jun08STFeature.pdf.

Reitz, Jeffrey G. 2002. "Host Societies and the Reception of Immigrants: Research Themes, Emerging Theories and Methodological Issues." *International Migration Review* 36:1005–19.

"Remains of Jimenez, Fouty Buried Together." 2009. Associated Press, February 17. Retrieved May 10, 2009, from http://www.pownetwork.org/gulfII/jimenez.htm.

Reskin, Barbara F., and Irene Padavic. 1999. "Sex, Race, and Ethnic Inequality in United States Workplaces." *Handbook of the Sociology of Gender* 1:343–74.

Rollins, Judith. 1995. *Between Women: Domestics and Their Employers*. Philadelphia: Temple University Press.

Romero, Mary. 1992. *Maid in the USA*. New York: Routledge.

Ruggles, Steven, Matthew Sobek, Trent Alexander, Catherine A. Fitch, Ronald Goeken, Patricia Kelly Hall, Miriam King, and Chad Ronnander. 2008. "Integrated Public Use Microdata Series: Version 4.0." Machine-readable database. Minneapolis: Minnesota Population Center (producer and distributor).

Safa, Helen I. 1981. "The Differential Incorporation of Hispanic Women Migrants into the United States Labor Force." Pp. 235–66 in *Female Immigrants to the United States: Caribbean, Latin American, and African Experiences*, edited by Delores M. Mortimer and Roy S. Bryce-Laporte. Washington, DC: Research Institute on Immigration and Ethnic Studies, Smithsonian Institution.

Said, Edward W. 1979. *Orientalism*. New York: Vintage Books.

Sassen, Saskia. 2006. *Cities in a World Economy*. Thousand Oaks, CA: Pine Forge.

———. 2004. "Global Cities and Survival Circuits." Pp. 254–74 in *Global Woman: Nannies, Maids, and Sex Workers in the New Economy*, edited by Barbara Ehrenreich and Arlie Russell Hochschild. New York: Metropolitan Books.

———. 2005. "The U.S. at a Time of Global Conflict: Challenges We Face beyond War." *Contexts* 4:29–31.

Scelfo, Julie. 2008. "Trickledown Downsizing." *New York Times*, December 10. Retrieved December 19, 2008, from http://www.nytimes.com/2008/12/11/garden/11domestics.html?pagewanted=all.

Schaffer, Haley. 2001. "Domestic Violence and Asylum in the United States: In Re: R—A—." *Northwestern University Law Review* 95:779.

Scholes, Robert J., and Anchalee Phataralacha. 1999. "Appendix A: The 'Mail-Order Bride' Industry and Its Impact on U.S. Immigration." Pp. 22–35 in *International Matchmaking Organizations: A Report to Congress*. Retrieved September 10, 2010, from http://www.uscis.gov/files/article/Mobrept_full.pdf.

Schutz, Alfred. 1967. *The Phenomenology of the Social World*. Evanston, IL: Northwestern University Press.

Seelye, Katherine Q. 1998. "U.S. Strikes at Smuggling Ring That Exploited Foreign Nurses." *New York Times,* January 14.

Segura, Denise A., and Patricia Zavella, eds. 2007. *Women and Migration in the U.S.-Mexico Borderlands: A Reader*. Durham, NC: Duke University Press.

SEIU. n.d. "SEIU History." Retrieved February 22, 2009, from http://www.seiu.org/a/ourunion/seiu-history.php.

Seller, Maxine Schwartz, ed. 1981. *Immigrant Women*. Philadelphia: Temple University Press.

Semple, Kirk. 2009. "Senate Measure Gives Rights to Widows of Citizens." *New York Times,* October 20. Retrieved November 15, 2009, from http://www.nytimes.com/2009/10/21/us/21widows.html?scp=1&sq=widow%20penalty&st=cse.

"Shackling Immigrants in Arpaio's America." 2009. *International Herald Tribune,* February 6. Retrieved February 8, 2009, from http://www.iht.com/articles/2009/02/06/opinion/edarpaio.1-424179.php.

Siskind Susser Immigration Lawyers. 2000. "Allegations of Sexual Abuse at Krome Detention Center." June. Retrieved November 15, 2009, from http://www.visalaw.com/00jun1/13jun100.html.

Smith, Dorothy E. 2005. *Institutional Ethnography*. Lanham, MD: AltaMira.

Sokoloff, Natalie J., with Christina Pratt, eds. 2005. *Domestic Violence at the Margins: Readings on Race, Class, Gender, and Culture*. New Brunswick, N.J.: Rutgers University.

Sokoloff, Natalie J., and Susan C. Pearce. 2008. "Locking Up Hope: Immigration, Gender, and the Prison System." *S&F Online* 6 (Summer). Retrieved February 22, 2009, from http://www.barnard.edu/sfonline/immigration/sokoloff_pearce_04.htm.

Sontag, Deborah. 2008. "Immigrants Facing Deportation by U.S. Hospitals." *New York Times,* August 3. Retrieved June 7, 2009, from http://www.nytimes.com/2008/08/03/us/03deport.html?_r=1&scp=110&sq=citizen%20man%20deported%20Germany&st=cse.

Southern Poverty Law Center. 2009. "Under Siege: Life for Low-Income Latinos in the South." Montgomery, Alabama. Retrieved May 10, 2009, from http://www.splcenter.org/legal/undersiege/index.jsp.

Southwest Institute for Research on Women, University of Arizona. 2009. "Unseen Prisoners: A Report on Women in Immigration Detention Centers in Arizona." January. Retrieved April 8, 2009, from http://sirow.arizona.edu/files/UnseenPrisoners.pdf.

Spivak, Gayatri Chakravorty. 1988. "Can the Subaltern Speak?" Pp. 271–313 in *Marxism and the Interpretation of Culture,* edited by Cary Nelson and Lawrence Grossberg. Urbana-Champaigne: University of Illinois Press.

Strum, Philippa, and Danielle Tarantolo, eds. 2003. *Women Immigrants in the United States*. Washington, DC: Woodrow Wilson International Center for Scholars.

"Suffrage from a Mother's Standpoint." 1920. *News and Observer* (Raleigh, NC), August 8.

Suhl, Yuri. 1990. *Ernestine L. Rose: Women's Rights Pioneer.* New York: Biblio.

Sum, Andrew, Ishwar Khatiwada, Paul Harrington, and Shiela Palma. 2003. "New Immigrants in the Labor Force and the Number of Employed New Immigrants in the U.S. from 2000 through 2003: Continued Growth amidst Declining Employment among the Native-Born Population." Boston: Center for Labor Market Studies, Northeastern University. Retrieved August 20, 2009, http://www.mygreencard.com/downloads.php?file=ImmigrantsInLaborForce.pdf.

Sun, Lena H. 2004. "'Modern-Day Slavery' Prompts Rescue Efforts: Groups Target Abuse of Foreign Maids, Nannies." *Washington Post,* May 3. Retrieved June 7, 2009, from http://www.washingtonpost.com/ac2/wp-dyn?pagename=article&contentId=A61457-2004May2&notFound=true.

Sweetman, Caroline, ed. 1998. *Gender and Migration.* Oxfam Focus on Gender. Oxford, UK: Stylus.

Swidler, Anne. 1986. "Culture in Action: Symbols and Strategies." *American Sociological Review* 51:273–86.

"Targets of Suspicion: The Impact of Post-9/11 Policies on Muslims, Arabs and South Asians in the United States." 2004. *Immigration Policy Center in Focus* 3 (2) (May). Retrieved April 6, 2009, from http://immigration.server263.com/images/File/infocus/Targets%20of%20Suspicion.pdf.

Tastsoglou, Evangelia, and Alexandra Dobrowolsky. 2006. *Women, Migration and Citizenship.* Hampshire, UK, and Burlington, VT: Ashgate.

"These Are Military Families, Too." 2007. *Boston Globe,* June 24. Retrieved May 10, 2009, from http://www.boston.com/news/globe/editorial_opinion/editorials/articles/2007/06/24/these_are_military_families_too/.

Thompson, Ginger. 2009. "Some Immigrants Who Lose Freedom Face Loss of Custody." *New York Times,* April 23. Retrieved April 23, 2009, from http://www.nytimes.com/2009/04/23/us/23children.html?_r=1&scp=1&sq=Some%20Immigrants%20Who%20Lose%20Freedom%20Face%20Loss%20of%20Custody%20&st=cse.

Tilly, Charles. 1989. *Big Structures, Large Processes, Huge Comparisons.* New York: Russell Sage Foundation.

Toren, Nina. 1999. "Women and Immigrants: Strangers in a Strange Land." *Gender Issues* 17:76–96.

Touraine, Alain. 2005. "The Subject Is Coming Back." *International Journal of Politics, Culture, and Society* 18:199–209.

———. 1988. *Return of the Actor: Social Theory in Postindustrial Society.* Minneapolis: University of Minnesota Press.

Trucios-Haynes, Enid. 1997. "'Family Values' 1990's Style: U.S. Immigration Reform Proposals and the Abandonment of the Family." *Brandeis Journal of Family Law* 36:241–50.

Tsing-yuan, Tsao. 1994. "The Birth of the Goddess of Democracy." Pp. 140–47 in *Popular Protest and Political Culture in Modern China,* edited by Jeffrey N. Wasserstrom and Elizabeth J. Perry. Boulder, CO: Westview.

Ulrich, Laurel Thatcher. 2007. *Well-Behaved Women Seldom Make History.* New York: Knopf.

UNESCO. 2009. "Global Education Digest 2009: Comparing Educational Statistics across the World." Montreal: UNESCO Institute for Statistics. Retrieved September 7, 2010, from http://www.uis.unesco.org/template/pdf/ged/2009/GED_2009_EN.pdf.

UNFPA. 2006. *State of World Population 2006: A Passage to Hope: Women and International Migration.* Retrieved July 20, 2008, from http://www.unfpa.org/swp/2006/english/introduction.html.

UNIFEM. 2008/2009. "Who Answers to Women? Gender and Accountability." New York: United Nations Development Fund for Women. Retrieved February 22, 2009, from http://www.unifem.org/progress/2008/media/POWW08_Report_Full_Text.pdf.

United Nations Commission on Population and Development. 2006. "Feminization of Migration, Remittances, Migrants' Rights, Brain Drain among Issues, as Population Commission Concludes Debate." New York: Department of Public Information. April 5. Retrieved January 6, 2009, from http://www.un.org/News/Press/docs/2006/pop945.doc.htm.

United Nations, Department of Economic and Social Affairs. 2006. "2004 World Survey on the Role of Women in Development: Women and International Migration." New York: United Nations Publishing Section. Retrieved December 20, 2008, from http://www.un.org/womenwatch/daw/Review/documents/press-releases/WorldSurvey-Women&Migration.pdf.

United Nations, Department of Economic and Social Affairs, Population Division. 1998. *International Migration Policies.* New York: United Nations.

United Nations High Commission on Refugees. 2007. *Convention and Protocol Relating to the Status of Refugees.* Geneva: UNHCR Media Relations and Public Information Service. Retrieved November 1, 2009, from http://www.unhcr.org/protect/PROTECTION/3b66c2aa10.pdf.

U.S. Department of Agriculture. 2002. "Food Stamp Policy on Immigrants." Retrieved April 8, 2010, from http://www.fns.usda.gov/snap/rules/Memo/2002/POLIMGRT.HTM.

U.S. Department of Homeland Security. 2008a. "Table 8: Persons Obtaining Legal Permanent Resident Status by Gender, Age, Marital Status, and Occupation: Fiscal Year 2008." In *Yearbook of Immigration Statistics: 2008.* Washington, DC: Department of Homeland Security, Office of Immigration Statistics. Retrieved April 8, 2010, from http://www.dhs.gov/files/statistics/publications/LPR08.shtm.

————. 2008b. "Table 9: Persons Obtaining Legal Permanent Resident Status by Broad Class of Admission and Selected Demographic Characteristics: Fiscal Year 2008." In *Yearbook of Immigration Statistics: 2008.* Washington, DC: Department of Homeland Security, Office of Immigration Statistics. Retrieved April 8, 2010, from http://www.dhs.gov/files/statistics/publications/LPR08.shtm.

U.S. Department of Justice, Northern District of California. 2007. "San Francisco Brothel Owner Sentenced to One Year in Prison for Money Laundering." Press release, March 7. Retrieved February 3, 2009, from http://sanfrancisco.fbi.gov/dojpressrel/2007/sfo30707a.htm.

U.S. Department of Labor, Office of Federal Contract Compliance Programs. 2002. "Facts on Executive Order 11246." Washington, DC. Retrieved April 2, 2010, from http://www.dol.gov/ofccp/regs/compliance/aa.htm.

U.S. Department of State. 2006. "Distinctions between Human Trafficking and Human Smuggling." April 1. Retrieved April 8, 2010, from http://www.state.gov/m/ds/hstcenter/90434.htm.

————. 2000. "Victims of Trafficking and Violence Protection Act of 2000." Washington, DC. 114 Stat. 1464, Public Law 106-386. Retrieved July 25, 2008, from http://www.state.gov/documents/organization/10492.pdf.

———. n.d. "Diplomats and Foreign Government Officials." Retrieved September 5, 2010, from http://travel.state.gov/visa/temp/types/types_2637.html.

U.S. Senate Committee on Foreign Relations. 2004. Testimony of Michelle A. Clark, codirector, Protection Project, Johns Hopkins University School of International Studies. July 13. Retrieved May 10, 2009, from http://www.protectionproject.org/commentary/brides.htm.

Van Maanen, John. 1988. *Tales of the Field: On Writing Ethnography*. Chicago: University of Chicago Press.

Vitello, Paul. 2007. "From Stand in Long Island Slavery Case, a Snapshot of a Hidden U.S. Problem." *New York Times,* December 3. Retrieved June 7, 2009, from http://www.nytimes.com/2007/12/03/nyregion/03slavery.html?_r=3&oref=slogin&adxnnlx=1196784478sMBD0MDuD0j63%20lljy4O6w&pagewanted=print.

Waters, Mary C. 2000. *Black Identities: West Indian Immigrant Dreams and American Realities*. Cambridge, MA: Harvard University Press.

———. 1990. *Ethnic Options: Choosing Identities in America*. Berkeley: University of California Press.

Waters, Mary C., and Reed Ueda, with Helen B. Marrow. 2007. *The New Americans: A Guide to Immigration since 1965*. Cambridge, MA: Harvard University Press.

Weatherford, Doris. 1986. *Foreign and Female: Immigrant Women in America, 1840–1930*. New York: Schocken Books.

Weber, Max. [1922] 1963. *The Sociology of Religion*. Translated by Ephraim Fischoff. Boston: Beacon.

———. 1947. *The Theory of Social and Economic Organization*. Translated by A. M. Henderson and Talcott Parsons. New York: Free Press.

Wieviorka, Michel. 2009. "Sociology on the Move." Announcement of July 2010 conference of the International Sociological Association World Congress of Sociology. Retrieved January 6, 2009, from http://www.isa-sociology.org/congress2010/.

"Wife of Missing G.I. Gets Her Green Card." 2007. *New York Daily News,* July 2. Retrieved May 10, 2009, from http://www.nydailynews.com/news/2007/07/02/2007-07 02_wife_of_missing_gi_gets_her_green_card-1.html#ixzzoF8ZnUBNJ&B.

Wilson, Colwick, and Leon Wilson. 1999. "Domestic Work in the United States: Past Perspectives and Future Directions." *African American Research Perspectives* 6:51–59.

Women in Prison Project. 2006. "Immigration and Criminal Justice Fact Sheet." Correctional Association of New York. August. Retrieved February 22, 2009, from http://www.correctionalassociation.org/publications/download/wipp/factsheets/Immigration_Fact_Sheet_2006.pdf.

"Women's Council Created; Abortion Harassment Rises." 2009. *Women's eNews,* March 14. Retrieved June 7, 2009, from http://www.womensenews.org/article.cfm?aid=3950.

Yinger, Nancy V. 2007. "The Feminization of Migration: Limits of the Data." Population Reference Bureau. February. Retrieved January 6, 2009, from http://www.prb.org/Articles/2007/FeminizationofMigrationLimitsofData.aspx.

Zakrzewska, Marie E., and Agnes C. Victor, eds. [1924] 1972. *Woman's Quest: The Life of Marie E. Zakrzewska M.D.* Manchester, NH: Ayer.

Zarembka, Joy M. 2003. "America's Dirty Work: Migrant Maids and Modern-Day Slavery." Pp.142–45 in *Global Woman: Nannies, Maids, and Sex Workers in the New Economy,* edited by Barbara Ehrenreich and Arlie Russell Hochschild. New York: Metropolitan Books.

Zhou, Min. 2004. "The Role of the Enclave Economy in Immigrant Adaptation and Community Building: The Case of New York's Chinatown." Pp. 37–60 in *Immigrant and Minority Entrepreneurship: Building American Communities,* edited by John Sibley Butler and George Kozmetsky. Westport, CT: Praeger.

Zlotnik, Hania. 1995a. "Migration and the Family: The Female Perspective." *Asian Pacific Migration Journal* 4 (2–3): 253–71.

———. 1995b. "The South-to-North Migration of Women." *International Migration Review* 29 (1): 229–54.

Zolberg, Aristede. 2008. *A Nation by Design: Immigration Policy in the Fashioning of America.* Cambridge, MA: Harvard University Press.

Zolberg, Vera L. 1990. *Constructing a Sociology of the Arts.* Cambridge: University of Cambridge Press.

# Index

activism: anti-trafficking, 221; and the arts, 197, 226–227, 234; becoming an activist, 230–232; domestic violence, 221–226; domestic workers, 219 – 221; feminist activism, 13, 163, 210; history of women activists, 208, 210; in home country, 54, 198, 211; labor unions, 210, 214–218; political activism, 54; immigrant rights activism, 152, 207–208, 211–214, 227–230

African Americans: attitudes towards immigrants, 229; black-empowerment, 156; comparison with immigrant history, 30; heritage, 143–144; and immigration policy, 30, 31; numbers, 26; women, 8, 42, 107–108

Agana, Femi, 159–174, *161*

agency: as activists, 230–232; construction of self, 241; contexts of exit, 23, 30, 63, 78; culture and symbols, 200, 226, 245; derided by male partners, 223; elasticity, 152; family reunification, 50, 57; and globalization, 251; and intersectionality theory, 9; irregular status, 100–101; multidimensionality of, 10, 243; and refugee/asylum claims, 73; resistance, 210; smuggling, 81, 83; structure-agency dance, 9, 149, 248; surmounting obstacles, 75; trafficking, 89; and voice in research, 11–12; women as lead pioneers, 6

"anchor baby," 6

Anderson, Benedict, 7. See also *Imagined Communities*

*Anica*: arrival in the U.S., 47, 244; escape from Romania, 53–54, 74

Appadurai, Arjun, 23

Armstrong, Esther, 138–139, 142, 143–144

arts, 177–203; and activism, 189–191, 197–200, 207, 226–227; careers in, 168; context of exit, 181; entertainment arts, 96; memory and vision, 185; sociology of the arts, 276n6; suppression of, 165

assimilation, 246–248, 253

asylum: gender-based, 71–73, 252; political, 211–212; seekers, deportation of, 95; seekers, detention of, 91, 93, 94, 201–211; seeking, 61–62, 79, 80, 92, 180

Bastien, Marleine, 211–214; changing perceptions of Haitian culture, 232; Fanm Ayisen Nan Miyami (FANM), 207, 213–214; picture of, 209; poetry, 207–208, 245

*Beatriz*, 56

Becker, Howard, 11

Bemis, Polly, 19–20, 30, 193

*Betty*: artwork, 200; changing status, 50, 58; decision to immigrate, 48; education, 165, 166; engineering, 165, 174; reaction to U.S., 189

Birds of Passage, 5

Blackstone, William, 19, 20

Bourdieu, Pierre, 10, 139, 154

Bracero Program, 35

Bush, George W., 72, 91, 96

Cable Act, 25

*Celia*, 53, 55, 57

Chan, Angela: becoming an entrepreneur, 136–137, 138; business success, 155, 251; philanthropy, 156

social class: and domestic service, 106; hierarchies, 12, 224, 231 - 232, 246; and intersectionality, 8, 254; and marriage, 98; segmented assimilation, 247

social movements, 21, 210, 233: civil rights movement, 30, 31, 107, 279n2

social structures, 9, 10, 248, 254; constraining and enabling, 26, 100, 243; resistance to, 210

social work, 9, 39, 213

Spivak, Gayatri Chakravorty, 12

Statue of Liberty, 47, 243–245, 247, 279

status dislocation, 63, 64–65, 136

*Stella*, 119, 120; activism, 122, 123, 124; gaining employment, 121; reasons for domestic work, 116–117

stereotypes, 72, 150, 151, 154, 170

Strauss, Anselm, 11, 262, 289

suffrage, 24

Supplemental Security Income, 25

*Svetlana*, 6, 61, 62

Temporary Assistance to Needy Families, 25

*Teresa*, 52, 57, 64

Thang, Susie, 13, 184, 187, 198

Tilly, Charles, 21

Torres, Neri, 181, 184, 189, 195, 197

Tourraine, Alaine, 9

Triangle Shirtwaist Factory fire, 41

T Visa. *See* visas

undocumented immigration: activism, 98; American complaints, 47; demographic estimates, 79–80, 238; deportations, 95, 254; falling out of status, 111, 159; fear of unionizing, 215; feminization of undocumented, 78; fluidity between statuses, 50, 109; hesitations to be interviewed, 256; leaving an abusive spouse, 90; legal changes, 39; local police enforcement, 92; prejudices of legal immigrants, 229; regularization process, 57; regularizing status through marriage, 56; responding to labor needs, 80, 82, 172; vulnerability for immigrant women, 110, 122; youth

access to higher education, 13, 202, 227, 228, 234

unions, labor: immigrants used as non-union labor, 171–172; janitors, 215–218, 232; Service Employees International Union, 217; weakening of, 171

United Nations, 4, 23, 69, 250: U.N. Declaration of Human Rights, 211, 230; U.N. Department of Economic and Social Affairs, 5; U.N. Human Rights Committee, 126; U.N. Population Fund, 1, 2

U.S. Census: American Community Survey, 32, 132; contradictions in government data, 27; definitions of foreign-born, 13; measuring entrepreneurship (self-employment), 132; as research data source, 11, 28, 237, 255

U.S. Citizenship and Immigration Services, 27, 89, 90, 111

U.S. Congress: ARTS Act, 201; Cable Act, 25; DREAM Act, 228; gender makeup of, 27; IMBRA, 98; immigration legislation, 26, 249; set asides, 142; Trafficking Victims Protection Act, 85–86; widow penalty, 89

*Valeria*, 227–230

Van Maanen, John, 11, 262, 304

VAWA. *See* Violence Against Women Act

*Victoria*: culture, 187–188; decision to immigrate, 53; discrimination against, 63; novel, 187, 192–193; pseudonym, 11, 241

Vietnam War, 22, 34, 197

Violence Against Women Act (VAWA), 90, 97–98

visas: employment, 14, 31, 34, 48, 51, 52, 53, 57, 58, 59, 71, 73, 82, 89, 97, 98, 104, 106, 109, 110, 111, 119, 125, 126; family-related, 14, 31, 48, 57, 70, 110, 112, 238, 253; non-immigrant, 55, 89; overstaying a visa, 79, 80, 94, 100, 111, 159; P Visa, 201, 202; student, 52, 57, 58, 59, 69, 89, 272; tourist, 52, 110, 111; T Visa, 80, 86, 222; U Visa, 97–98

Voss, Yolanda, 147, 15

# About the Authors

SUSAN C. PEARCE is Assistant Professor of Sociology at East Carolina University and coeditor of *Reformulations: Markets, Policy, and Identities in Central and Eastern Europe* and *Mosaics of Change: The First Decade of Life in the New Eastern Europe.*

ELIZABETH J. CLIFFORD is Associate Professor of Sociology and Director of American Studies at Towson University, where she is also the coordinator of the Baltimore Immigration Summit.

REENA TANDON is Sessional Lecturer in South Asian Studies at the University of Toronto and Coordinator of Service Learning at Ryerson University, Toronto, and the author of *Contemporary Hindi in Australia.*